D1474124

AFTER REASON

Also by Arianna Stassinopoulos

The Female Woman

AFTER REASON

ARIANNA
STASSINOPOULOS

"If you wanted to put the world to rights, who should you begin with: yourself or others? . . ."

—*Alexander Solzhenitsyn,*
"The First Circle"

STEIN AND DAY/*Publishers*/New York

First published in 1978

Designed by Karen Bernath
Printed in the United States of America
Stein and Day/*Publishers*/Scarborough House,
Briarcliff Manor, N.Y. 10510

Library of Congress Cataloging in Publication Data

Stassinopoulos, Arianna, 1950–
After reason.

1. Civilization, Modern—20th century.
2. Civilization, Occidental. I. Title.
CB425.S642 909'.09'821 77-92719
ISBN 0-8128-2465-2

For

AGAPI,

my sister

CONTENTS

ACKNOWLEDGEMENTS

The people who made this book possible fall into two categories: those who gave unconditional support, love and encouragement, and those who criticized, argued, edited, and improved. Halina Szpiro, Nicholas Brown, Natalie Franks, and my mother, who kept not only the support but the kitchens going through the long nights, are in the first category. I am grateful to them all.

In the second category are Professor David Martin, Christopher Booker, and Michael Sissons who made many valuable criticisms, suggestions, and corrections, and Frank Johnson who descended vigorously on all punctuation sins—however venal. The penultimate, and much longer version of the book was read by my two editors, Patricia Day in New York and Alan Brooke in London. I am deeply grateful to both of them for all the cuts and changes they suggested. All the various drafts of the book were deciphered and typed by Gwen Margrie. I want to thank her not only for remaining calm in the face of all pressures, but for remaining interested even though she must by now know certain passages by heart.

Spanning both categories is Bernard Levin who read every version of the book, from the slim first outline to the monstrous first draft, and whose help and support through the long period of writing and research were unceasing and invaluable. I still have at home a large part of his library together with an equally large part of Peter Bower's library, and I would like to thank them both for very greatly reducing the amount of time I had to spend in public libraries—suffering the ultimate deprivation of working without music. Most of the book was written to Haydn's 104 symphonies, and I am deeply indebted to him for providing the perfect musical accompaniment and a better stimulus than any amount of black coffee. I am equally indebted to my neighbors for putting up through all hours of the night not only with Haydn's symphonies but even with some of the more clamorous passages of Verdi.

INTRODUCTION

Our lives in the past decade have been increasingly dominated by political unrest, too much government, the concentration of power in fewer and fewer hands, and seemingly unending revelations of executive and legislative misrule. The takeover of life by politics is the single most important social development of the postwar period, and the threat that it poses to freedom and democracy is the most significant topic of public debate. But at the same time the individual, increasingly dominated by impersonal and seemingly irresistible forces, has been searching, more and more urgently, for a spiritual path out of the closing trap. This book makes the connection between this territory of the spirit and our Western political predicament.

Since the war we have had the Social Revolution, the Sexual Revolution, the Black Revolution, the Youth Revolution, and the Drug

Revolution. They all failed to fulfill what they promised. But they prepared the ground for the Spiritual Revolution, the only revolution that can transform our lives and the world because it is the only one based on inner realities. The "pursuit of happiness" has been reduced today to the pursuit of comfort. But so long as economic prosperity remains the supreme aim of Western societies, grown men will continue to be treated like children, with the state in the role of the Father and the "system" in the role of the Wicked Stepmother. And political servitude will be accepted as a fair price to pay for the continuation of material properity.

Today, despite the complete failure of collectivism, collectivist solutions continue to be advocated.

The bankruptcy of Western political leadership has meant that our destiny is in the hands of reactive politicians, eagerly practicing the art of the possible, and bowing to what they regard as inevitable. And it is unlikely that the great men who will help to change the environment of opinion and lessen the stronghold of politics on the individual will emerge from inside politics. For their greatness will not be in providing the age with political remedies, but in bearing witness in their lives to the integration of the rational with the long-neglected spiritual element in man.

It is obvious that the trivial preoccupations of our daily life can no longer satisfy our deepest needs. And the wounds grow deeper every day. Mental illness is the Western world's biggest health problem, and its casualties are magnifications of the suffering in ourselves, pleading for recognition in the crucial battle of our age—the battle of the individual for the meaning of his life.

The yearning for a new philosophy of life, for new symbols and new *individual* answers, has never been so strong. And it is only a spiritual awakening based on the eternal but forgotten truths about man that can save individual freedom, the single most important principle on which Western democracies are based.

1

THE UNWITTING ACCOMPLICES

"It is a terrible thing," said Franklin Roosevelt in 1937, "to look over your shoulder when you are trying to lead—and to find no one there." [1] This calamity is extremely unlikely to befall Western political leaders today. Leadership has been reduced to a masterly exercise in looking over your shoulder at opinion polls and newspaper editorials.

"I am their leader; I must follow them" is the one principle to which postwar Western political leaders are pledged. Yet there was a time when all political life was seen as the direct result of the conscious choices and activities of individuals. If the Spartans spurned material wealth, this was assumed to be entirely the achievement of Lycurgus who "descended, so to speak, into the depths of the hearts of his fellow citizens and there crushed the germ of the love of wealth." [2] And when they strayed from this Lycurgean path, it was supposed to be solely because another leader, Lysander, persuaded them that "new ties and new conditions called for new rules and a new policy." [3] The reaction to this extreme view of unconstrained leadership, led by the French historians of the Restoration, was just as extreme—and remains the source of the modern political leader's view of his role.

Of course political leaders, even the most autocratic, cannot change general trends. The Iron Chancellor himself admitted as much in 1869: "My influence on the events I took advantage of is usually exaggerated . . . we cannot make history: we must wait while it is being made. We will not make fruit ripen more quickly by subjecting it to the heat of a lamp. We must limit ourselves to seeing what is already ripe." [4] Bismarck called the constraints within which he had to operate history and "the natural course of things." Western democratic leaders today would call them public opinion, votes and elections.

Politics as the art of the possible—in practice the lowest possible, the course of least resistance—springs directly from the fatalistic view of political events as consequences of irresistible necessity. The irresistible necessity can take the form of an immutable law either hidden in nature or revealed by Marxist dialectics. In the West today it is most commonly enshrined in Dr. Gallup's polls and recorded in the level of noise emitted by aroused minorities.

Democratic political leaders, of course, have always been reactive—living and feeding on their immediate surroundings. They have always been instruments played on by the electorate and by strong, or simply noisy, organized special interests. But until recently they had been players too—not simply played on but playing, and by their special qualities influencing the fate of society and introducing into the course of events a new and unexpected force. Political leaders are not merely reacting to day-to-day polls, reports and resolutions. They are reacting to a cluster of beliefs and assumptions, both those stated and defended and even more importantly those never stated and never defended—because they reflect ideas, prejudices and aspirations so ingrained that they are never precisely understood or even recognized. They are, in other words, reacting to that elusive and easily misapplied concept, the "spirit of the age." But however vague and difficult to apply it may be, there is no doubt that after all some peoples do show a common will and some ages, a common spirit. The predicament of Western democracies today is that the spirit of the age is based on a bankrupt ideology and that our leaders remain ignorant not only of its bankruptcy but of the extent to which it shapes all their reactions and pronouncements.

For as long as the prevailing ideology remains unexamined and unexplained, modern leaders will remain committed to its assumptions, their pronouncements increasingly cut off from reality and their reactions bound to failure. Their disastrous performance and their meaningless statements are not incidental results of blemishes which can be "refined" away, through electoral reform, a Bill of Rights, federal funding of the parties, broadcasting of Parliament, or whatever is the panacea in vogue. It is not that leaders lack intellect and institutions need reforming—although a good case could undoubtedly be made for both these claims. It is rather that technocratic assumptions about the nature of man and society have warped their experience at the source.

The first step is to drag the tacit assumptions into the open and expose their implicit absurdities. It would be naïve to expect that the exposure of logical fallacies will do away with the emotional capital invested in the ideology, especially by those proud pragmatists who would laugh at the idea that there is an ideology at all, who have convinced themselves that they deal only in rationality, efficiency and progress and that they speak only the mental language of statistics uncontaminated by anything as mystical as a "world view." But of course we all hold a world view. We do not learn it in any conscious way—we catch it from the spirit of the times. We are converted to it by unaccountable experiences. And the more unaccountable and emotional the experiences, the less likely we are to be swayed by argument—emotions are much less nimble, more inert and more persistent than thoughts, and for those emotionally committed to a bankrupt ideology, nothing short of an authentic revelation will do. Until the fundamental lie of the world view behind all pragmatic solutions is recognized, explained and overcome, it will go on dictating the nature of political reality and imposing political constraints by determining what, within that reality, is to be held sacred.

So what are the deeper falsehoods behind the palpable political ones, the root assumptions so ingrained in the Western world view that they have become commonplaces automatically accepted?

The belief that permeates the political pronouncements, actions and manifestos of Socialists, Tories, Republicans, Communists and Christian Democrats alike is a profound political and social utopianism: the illusion of salvation through technological materialism and the conviction that through politics and government action, through the right policies of regulation, control, allocation and provision, society will be made rational and just. So widespread dissatisfaction with the present state of affairs goes hand in hand with a conviction that all that is unsatisfactory is curable, and that redemption can and must be achieved through government action. The notion that human society can be totally comprehended and manipulated by conscious human reason persists and dominates the structure of modern politics. The methods of the natural scientists, magnificent as they have been in producing results in their own field, are extolled and illegitimately expanded to society as a whole. What is more, methods become mentalities. And methods which work for circumscribed problems are diluted into something penetrating and all-pervasive, a philosophy with universal claims; they harden into a closed system unwilling or unable to assimilate any evidence, however overwhelming, that contradicts it.

Democratic leaders and democratic led go on drawing epicycles on the wall of Plato's cave, their backs firmly turned to the daylight of reality, while the collectivist onslaught continues unabated. As the multiplication of dollars, pounds, welfare programs, statutory instruments, commissions and bills fails to produce the promised merger between heaven and earth, we are assured that all that is needed is more public spending, more welfare programs, and more state control. And this at a time when in Britain the state is in control of nearly 60 percent of the national income and in the United States between the early sixties and the early seventies federal social spending has soared from $30 billion to $110 billion. As the traditional liberal medicine of more doses of public funds for all social ills fails to produce a cure, disillusionment spreads. But all panaceas, however discredited, will go on being advocated until it is realized that the underlying shortage has not been money but knowledge.

If we wanted, for purposes of official mourning, one symbolic date when the seed of the utopian scientific politics that has long dominated Western societies was sown, it would have to be the night of November 10, 1619, the night of the "Pentecost of Reason"; it was then that the twenty-three-year-old Descartes woke up from a dream and laid the foundations for the philosophical system that today underlies all political belief on both sides of the Iron Curtain. If it were reduced to the words of a debating motion, it would take the form of "This modern world believes that all truth will eventually be attained by scientific exploration." When Descartes began he was still sufficiently steeped in the ancient tradition in which he had been raised not to doubt that there was another form of knowledge—poetic, spiritual knowledge—that was of the same level of veracity as the scientific, although not applicable to the same questions and with different ways of demonstrating truths.

But in our time the split between the scientific and the spiritual is complete; when something today is described as "unscientific" it is automatically assumed to be untrue. In Descartes' ideal of the "mathematization" of all knowledge and then in the sunny, placid illusions of eternal progress that followed, in the eighteenth-century Enlightenment, in the absolutism of Hegel and Rousseau and the all-inclusive materialism of Marx, lay the germs of twentieth-century madness: the naïve belief in an absolute manageability through the state; the unconditional belief in all scientific and many pseudo-scientific solutions; and the hysterical optimism that has led to the dangerous belief in the political solubility of all problems and the willingness to countenance unlimited extensions of state power to bring about the ever-receding solutions.

This wave of the Cartesian tide has left its stain everywhere. "I hope you do not marvel," says the Devil in *Doctor Faustus,* "that 'the Great Adversary' speaks to you of religion. Gog's nails! Who else, I should like to know, is to speak of it today? Surely not the liberal theologian! After all, I am by now its sole custodian!" [5] Even the religious tinge of humanism has disappeared; there is nothing childlike left in man's gaze, and modern man, the unhistorical, uprooted self-reliant victor, has become a haunted fugitive. The march of conquest has become a flight, with grandiose political utopianism as the only haven. And yet despite the mounting evidence of its destructiveness—the horror of the Gulag Archipelago, the carnivorous bureaucracy, the moonscapes of the New Towns—our political leaders, our scientific experts and our media high priests cling to the remnants of the bankrupt ideology. The alternative is to jettison our collectivist illusions and rediscover the only values that ultimately matter and that today lie concealed under the dross of modern life—the values of the spirit, that are supremely individual and if invested in the state can only end in collective decay and systematic oppression.

The unique feature of the present crisis is the total exhaustion of the spiritual substance of Western society. One thing is certain—unless the vacuum is refilled from new spiritual sources, it will be filled, with an inevitability that would greatly have appealed to their prophet, by the modern Marxist totalitarians who have the theology ready for salvation through political action.

Yet the unsuspected revival of Marxism still baffles worldly, civilized social democrats—a category that includes socialists who believe in Parliament and conservatives as soon as they get office. The battle-cry for the 1975 Tory Party Conference was "The Crisis of Socialism." In fact, if we apply any of the tests by which socialism can be measured—the level of public expenditure, the proportion of the working population employed by public authorities, the size and privileges of the bureaucracy, the degree of intervention by the government in economic and other matters, the incidence of taxation—we find that the most recent Conservative governments have in practice been just as "socialist" as Labour governments.

Across the Atlantic, the story is in essence identical. When Nixon came to power in 1969, American Conservatives rejoiced that they had "made it." "Conservatism has come of age," [6] announced Stephen Tonsor, while John Chamberlain celebrated "the great story of our age . . . the Conservative counterculture's success in making a new climate for itself." [7] And then came Nixon's huge budget deficits, Nixon's wage and price controls, Nixon's expanding bureaucracy and Nixon's massive Family Assistance. Nixon was continuing in the great tradition of liberal activist Presidents, of "creeping socialism," and the "service state," increasingly all-powerful, increasingly anonymous and relentlessly reducing the individual states to colorful divisions on the map. Back in Europe, President Giscard, the leader of the Independent Republicans, is acting in a way that the leader of the Socialists should surely find unexceptionable. In the meantime, across the border in Italy, Signor Berlinguer, everybody's favourite Communist, is marching on.

The American Conservative Union is still blaming Nixon's opportunism, the French Gaullists go on castigating Giscard's leftward drift and Italian Christian Democrats are running for cover. But the bewilderment, and the disenchantment with non-socialist political leaders, will persist until it is realized that their constant lurches into statism and their betrayal of election promises and nominal ideology do not spring from exceptional feebleness or unique blemishes, but from the assumptions that their secular humanism shares with Marxism and that are in fact the dominant illusions of the age: man is seen as an exclusively rational being, and social ills as brought about by wrong choices, wrong leaders or wrong political systems. As soon as evils are explained by ideologies and systems, and not by reference to man himself, all skepticism about secular redemption through social engineering disappears. The clamor for political action becomes irresistible, and political leaders—whether Social Democrats or Conservatives, Christian Democrats or independent Republicans—become entirely reactive, bowing to the entrenched expectations of political utopianism.

And unless we reintroduce a spiritual dimension and an awareness of human fallibility into the debate of political issues, it is the impatient leaders of an all-consuming state who will go on setting the political pace. Democrats will be everywhere on the defensive as long as opposition to the increasing government control of society remains a *pragmatic* concern, uninformed by a new, or rather a very old but forgotten, view of man: not as the object of ideological concepts and theories, not as a random manifestation of general laws of human behavior, but as a unique being whose spiritual essence cannot be reduced to matter and economics nor to impersonal scientific laws interpreted by impersonal ideologies for the sake of a miserable and impersonal happiness.

It is precisely this kind of reductionism that is the second most important and most constant feature of our world view—and the most dangerous one. Alexander Solzhenitsyn has revealed it as the real source of the evil which in our contemporary world has found its most frightening expression in the archipelago of prisons and camps. Most of the facts of Gulag were known before publication. What Solzhenitsyn recreated for us is not the daily experience of prison life but the reality which is behind it, and which gives it its universal and not merely Russian or Communist significance—the radical reduction of man in the name of abstract ideas and ideology. "The imagination and the spiritual strength of Shakespeare's evildoers," he writes, "stopped short at a dozen corpses. Because they had no ideology. Ideology—that is what gives evildoing its long-sought justification and gives the evildoer the necessary steadfastness and determination. That is the social theory which helps to make his acts seem good instead of bad in his own and others' eyes, so that he won't hear reproaches and curses but will receive praise and honors. This was how the agents of the Inquisition fortified their wills: by invoking Christianity; the conquerors of foreign lands, by extolling the grandeur of their Motherlands; the colonizers, by civilization; the Nazis, by race; and the Jacobins (early and late), by equality, brotherhood, and the happiness of future generations." [8]

We in the West pride ourselves in having outgrown dogmatism and superstition; we go on blindly celebrating Western pragmatism at the same time as Barbara Castle cries out from the heart that "intrinsically, the National Health Service is a Church, and the nearest thing to the embodiment of the Good Samaritan we have in our public policy." [9] The same old atavistic urges—greed, envy, unrestrained passion and power mania—pick up respectable pseudonyms such as social justice, brotherhood or trade union struggle, and they become sacrosanct. Such is the emotional magnetism of the commanding ideology, that sanctity by association is automatically extended to anyone and anything doing battle in its name. And freedom is dying by hands guided by the best intentions: "They sow rye and grow weeds."

The Reign of the Sinners was bad, but, as Cromwell discovered, the Reign of the Saints was quite impossible. The Prohibition movement in the United States sprang from the most honorable intentions and ended in the reign of gangsterdom. The best intentions do not rule out either momentous errors or failures of judgment. Tragedy, in fact, whether in the theater or in life, rarely springs from vice or depravity and much more often from just such fatal misjudgments, from a lack of understanding of timeless human nature.

> In tragic life, God wot,
> No villain need be; passions spin the plot;
> We are betrayed by what is false within.[10]

Yet so totally caught up are we in the symbolism of our times, so emotionally attached to the fashionable ideology of social change, that put forward any measure, program or idea in the name of reform, equality or social justice and who could possibly be against it? But this is nothing more than the fetish of names and the ideological worship of idols, and the political implications are unmistakable.

Governments become entitled to bend the right of every man to the will of the rest. Alexis de Tocqueville called that particular form of tyranny Democratic Despotism: ". . . this confused mass being recognized as the only legitimate Sovereign, but carefully deprived of all faculties which would enable it either to divest or even to superintend its own Government. Above this mass a single officer charged to do everything in its name without consulting it. To control this officer, public opinion deprived of its organs; to arrest him, revolutions but no laws. In principle a subordinate agent; in fact a master." [11] Today, the master, the state Leviathan, has not just ideology but scientific expertise on its side. Armed with such mechanistic terms as *parameters, variables, structures, inputs* and *outputs, maximization* and *cost benefits,* our machine politician can totally mystify the popular mind by creating illusions of omnipotence and omniscience—just as the Pharaohs of ancient Egypt used their monopoly of the calendar to command the awed docility of ignorant subjects. At the same time they gain the authority of certified realists; they thoroughly mask the ideology that underlies all their policies and solutions; and they perpetuate the myth that they are dealing exclusively in political and economic necessities.

All moral and spiritual values that do not support the new kind of rationally reconstructed society are reduced to interests—indeed, dismissed as nothing but expressions of disguised self-interest. So there is in our pallid world a retreat from the enunciation of values other than in terms of political ends. Freedom, truth and justice are reduced to ornamental preliminaries of political speeches before our leaders begin to snarl about the "real" problems. What is worse, shorn of ultimate purpose, life loses its value and our activities are bereft of meaning; we are seized by a sense of futility, by restlessness, or by listless boredom.

Once we reject the existence of the Absolute, value judgments inevitably become expressions of subjective preference rather than objective truth; and once we accept that politics has to be approached with a "scientific" detachment divorced from all ethical considerations, then judgments about right and wrong, good and evil, justice and injustice, become outmoded and are reduced to discussions about utility and expediency. "I readily confess to a serious failure of judgment," boomed Mr. Haldeman. "Watergate," the patois void of all ethical content which Haldeman and his ex-boss both speak, has no words for guilt and no words for evil either. At one time the individual human eye knew what was evil, what constituted honesty and what deceit. But not any longer: "This twentieth century of ours," writes Solzhenitsyn, "devoid of a single scale of values, has proved to be more cruel than its predecessors . . . it is a world which upon seeing a slimy bog, exclaims: 'What a charming meadow!' " [12]

With the denial of objective truth there is no escape from the relativism of "Man is the measure of all things." Once notions of the rationality of man and the easy eradicability of social ills have taken over, the state is treated as the only possible instrument for the solution of all problems and the attainment of all reforms dreamt up in sociology departments, international foundations and research institutes.

The reduction of natural law as an objective moral order, to subjective natural rights, and of natural rights to economic rights, is another dominant perversion of the age. "I am bound to start with our economic prospects," was Mr. Callaghan's stirring opening in his first address to the nation as prime minister. In fact, political leaders throughout the West are very convincing reincarnations of that character from Fielding who "had conversed so entirely with money that it may be almost doubted whether he imagined there was any other thing really existing in the world." They launch their political speeches straight into the seas of gross national product, the purchasing power of the currency, the balance of payments or the cost of living. *Production* was Harold Wilson's sacred word. The stamp of economic monomania, of the reduction of politics to business, was put on postwar British politics by an earlier Harold, the patrician who invented the brashest and most vulgar of all political slogans: "You've never had it so good." Macmillan's attempts to invest budgets with poetry have produced some of the greatest masterpieces of metaphorical nonsense in the English language: "The Budget was to be a milestone to Conservative victory and the tombstone in the Socialist graveyard. Now at last the tide or our fortunes was to turn and flow in our favour." Harold Macmillan, the man who believed that "the luxuries of the rich have become the necessities of the poor" and was blind to the consequences that would follow once government was reduced to the satisfaction of arbitrarily defined and unlimited needs, is in fact the quintessential reactive postwar political leader. Such deficient understanding was not merely an error of judgment. It was an approach to politics designed not to solve problems, but with nods and winks, Edwardian geniality and relentless self-satisfaction, to refuse to recognize that problems exist—until the air finally began to escape from the balloon.

By then the reduction of political life to the outer fringes of economic significance was so entrenched that when the plump chickens came home not so much to roost as to have their necks wrung, his successors went on spasmodically reacting to every meticulously recorded decline in the value of the pound—failing and yet persisting in the belief that somehow that was where the solutions to all the problems of a noisy, mechanical, unimaginative, standardized society were to be found. And the chorus of newspaper editorials, from *The Daily Mail* ("Britain is a declining nation. With every week that passes the international purchasing power of the pound—*the measure of that decline*—has diminished" [13]), to *The Times* ("... the reality of the constant or gently rising money supply ... one of the great issues of economic and political controversy of our period of history; *on which the future of our society depends*" [14]) [both italics mine], reinforces the retreat of the political leaders from first principles, universal values and true knowledge, and intensifies the unreflective and hysterically reactive exercise of political leadership.

But the annihilation of spiritual being precedes the destruction of the temple walls. And that great spectacle of babyish naïveté, the economic theory of history, notwithstanding, *real* history is not economic history, *real* rights are not economic rights, and *real* politics, let alone real life, is not economics. There are undoubtedly economic laws that cannot be ignored and that if ignored will not go away. Two and two will not make five, however much irritation may be shown at this brute arithmetic fact. Where right-wing economists and politicians (Ludwig von Mises, Friedrich Hayek, Franz Josef Strauss, Keith Joseph and their acolytes) are wrong is in investing economic principles with a primary value they simply do not possess. "The essential teaching of liberalism," wrote Mises in his classic statement against "Omnipotent Government," "is that social cooperation and the division of labor can be achieved only in a system of private ownership of the means of production, i.e., within a market society or capitalism. All the other purposes of liberalism—democracy, personal freedom of the individual, freedom of speech and of the press, religious tolerance, peace among the nations—are consequences of this basic postulate. They can be realized only within a society based on private property." [15] Can there be a greater manifestation of the greatest modern human heresy—that the trees move the wind? And nothing will be reformed, and nothing saved, unless we abandon the heresy that the material circumstances create the spiritual ones and realize again that the spiritual fact comes first.

The economic Right may have economic truth on its side, but economic truth will never prevail unless it takes its proper subordinate place and allows spiritual truth, now labeled illusory and excluded from consideration, to be reinstated. Rationalist humanism has merely affirmed man's individual rights as something to be taken for granted. Devoid of any feeling for the transcendent mystery of man, it defined the human personality *conditionally* and so arbitrarily. We must now build again the link between the individual and the *absolute* source of his rights. Otherwise our sense of reality will remain truncated, and the demand for messianic political action will persist. In *The Rebel,* Albert Camus exposed the moral and intellectual anarchy created by the lack of limits at the personal level. What we have to discover today, individually and collectively, is the tyranny that follows the lack of limits at the political level. But the development of political limits will be impossible unless there is a restoration of the sense of reality which will put an end to illusions of temporal perfection through economic and social action. Man will stop seeking the meaning of his life in economic utopia only when he has rediscovered the meaning that went out of Western life at the time that the force of man's spiritual experience slowly ebbed away.

When the ultimate truths have taken their proper place over and above the economic truths, let alone the economic lies that have dominated the century, man's desire for salvation will be transferred from the economic and the political to the spiritual. Until this is done, our political masters will remain the unwitting accomplices of the destruction of Western democracy. They will go on reacting to the spirit of the age that demands secular salvation through the suspension of economic laws, and to electorates that have been led by the cosmic irresponsibility of electioneering politicians to assume that the luxuries of the rich have become not merely the necessities but the inalienable rights of the not-so-rich. "When the rules of economics and finance dictate policies which are nonsensical and destructive, then the rules must be questioned," threatens Mr. Benn, the infantile Left's prime representative in the British Cabinet. "The answer lies in replacing destructive market forces by planning . . . by the expansion of our public service, public investment, public accountability and public ownership."[16] In other words, the answer lies in paving the way for the totalitarian state. The same cavalier attitude to economic reality was displayed by the United Nations' Universal Declaration of Human Rights, which declares, among many other things in the same vein: "Everyone has the right to a standard of living adequate for the health and well-being of himself and of his family, including food, clothing, housing and medical care and necessary social services. . . ." By a sleight of hand, desirable conditions in life are elevated to inalienable rights, clamoring for government gratification.

Appeals to non-economic values are dismissed by all sound and practical men, in J. K. Galbraith's sage pronouncement, as an attempt "to fix people's eyes on noneconomic goals and to divert them from domestic difficulty."[17] On the other side of crackpot realism, the free-marketeers assure us that once the free market is reestablished, all else will follow. But of course it won't. First, because unless all professional experts at postponing the essential give up postponing, reaction to government and bureaucracy will remain at the transitional stage of disillusionment. And second, because even if the free market were established, what it would provide is not moral justice or truth or beauty, but economic efficiency—and justice and truth are neither entailed by economic efficiency nor reducible to it.

Another element of the spirit of the age is the amputation of the time dimension from Western culture—a progressive anti-traditional tradition that looks at the past as a series of errors to be discarded and replaced by a new utopia built afresh, untrammeled and self-generated. In the eighteenth century the prophets of progress with their grand dreams of an endless unfolding toward secular perfection took over. Voltaire was the first to come up with a universal secular history and a progressive social evolution; he was followed by the English utilitarians, Comte, Marx, Nietzsche and the bloody attempts in our century to turn various apocalyptic visions into substance.

It is the dream of these prophets, the dream of creating the Superman, the man-made being that will succeed the sorry creature of God's making, unhampered by historical realities, that twentieth-century totalitarians have tried to put into practice. And the connection of abstruse philosophical problems and "evil totalitarians" with our present-day political masters is not as remote as it might seem. All political leaders, however angelic their motives, who believe that recalcitrant reality can be as easily manipulated as the "reality" of their reasonable, disembodied plans, are potential totalitarian material. The road from unrestrained pride to totalitarianism is disconcertingly straight.

It should have been obvious by now, even to the most fanatical believers in the "locomotive of history," that something has gone badly astray and the suspicion that the engineer is a homicidal maniac can no longer be ruled out. Instead, the belief persists that the locomotive is somehow chugging on in the direction of progress.

Traditions, it is true, can be limiting, imprisoning, oppressive. But they are also roots in reality that guard man against the snares of utopians and the actions of crackpot realists who in fact know as much about the real as the man who describes the nature of a tortoise from the measurement of its shell. G. K. Chesterton called tradition democracy extended through time. Yet today appeals to tradition, history or fable are dismissed as conservative rationalizations of the defense of the indefensible. "Tradition," Chesterton wrote, "may be defined as an extension of the franchise. Tradition means giving votes to the most obscure of all classes, our ancestors. Democracy tells us not to neglect a good man's opinion, even if he is our groom; tradition asks us not to neglect a good man's opinion even if he is our father. . . . I would always trust the old wives' fables against the old maids' facts." [18] Can there be a greater heresy against the modern belief in government by data, statistics, experts and think tanks? Yet today, what Dostoevsky called "subservience to progressive little notions" is complete. And those who should know better fawn and retreat.

The amputation of a time dimension from Western culture extends to the future as well as the past, in two different ways. One is the product of the Left; the other of the Right. On the side of the Left—and the fellow-traveling Right—life becomes a series of longings to be satisfied, of problems to be solved *now*. Dissatisfaction with the world is of course as old as politics itself. What is new today is that all the myriad potential causes for dissatisfaction have been reduced to one—the fact that the world contains suffering. What is more, the sufferings of any class of individuals have become a *political* problem to be solved through political action and to be solved immediately. Government has been converted from a threat to individual freedom to an agent of individual happiness. But when a week is a long time in politics, impatience with the oblique and tortuous character of politics turns to exasperation; men of overdeveloped sensibility and underdeveloped sense of reality grow impatient and begin to advocate ways of short-circuiting the cumbersome democratic processes in the name, of course, of all the good things—like employment and health and education. The point about that kind of political liberal is that he sees political life as a complex of groups each struggling for its own interests, with victims who are by definition the product of their environment, noble and uncorrupted, and oppressors who are naturally not the product of their environment, but simply too evil to mend their ways. As for himself he is only a disinterested force for good, seeking to correct what all sensible men should recognize as evil. But this approach to politics, which regards it as merely a technical activity for the achievement of unanimously agreed ends, ignores the fact that in real life the ends are rarely reached and therefore the means are of crucial importance. In America, the state-induced residential Arcady has failed to materialize: the cities are not flowing with milk and honey but the urban-improvement programs are very effectively and at vast expense hastening their deterioration. In Britain, such ingenious legislative measures as the land-development proposals might well have been deliberately designed to augment the housing problem while providing jobs for a seemingly limitless number of public officials.

How many hells on earth have been unwittingly created by impatient visionaries with their gaze stubbornly fixed on their favorite brand of utopia? Obsessed with urgent political necessities, they remain oblivious of the fact that as even Machiavelli, that supreme technologist of political success, recognized, beyond the controllable half of man's life lies another half over which the future presides. But can we really go on regarding intention and motive, however unexceptionable, as the basis of moral judgment for what follows—whether it is the stranglehold of coercive bureaucracy in pursuit of welfare politics, or the Reign of Terror in pursuit of Jacobin salvation?

On the Right, the loss of a future dimension takes a different form. Hayek summed it up in "Why I am not a Conservative": "The admiration of the conservatives for free growth generally applies only to the past. They typically lack the courage to welcome the same undesigned change from which new tools of human endeavour will emerge . . . to let change run its course even if we cannot predict where it will lead." [19] So the issue is not, as it is so often put, for or against change, but for freedom against both coerced traditionalism and coerced utopianism. The traditionalist Right with its insistence on the need for closed systems and orthodoxies fails to see that power wielded in the name of traditions that have withered is no less arbitrary and oppressive than power wielded in the name of some technocratic utopia. Traditions reconcile reason and experience in a lived history, they are guarantees of needed continuity—but they are neither static nor independent of new realities. And those on the Right who plunge themselves into despair, parade their resignation to their coming extinction and withdraw into their hermitage, are guilty of a self-fulfilling abdication.

"On the Right," wrote Gustave Thibon in the early fifties, "there are far too many asleep: on the Left there are far too many who are dreaming. Our own task is to remain awake." [20] But it is becoming increasingly difficult to remain awake. What is exceptional about our times is that the central assumption of our "life spirit" finds expression not just in the dominant culture but in the dissent from it. Never has dissent been more vigorous and widespread—the adversary culture, the counterculture, the limitless discontent of the *enragês,* the cult of negation, the great Refusal—and yet never has it been more conformist and more steeped in the spirit of the age. The root premises of those protesting are identical with the root premises of those they are protesting against: a vague commitment to collectivism, obsession with economic goals, relativism and ignorance or dismissal of man's spirituality. The demands and solutions of the "adversary culture" are only an extension, the logical conclusion of these prevailing beliefs. This is why however powerful the jeremiads, mordant the criticism, and thoroughgoing the repudiation, they leave the fundamental fallacies of Western culture undisturbed, and so are received as a kind of diversion rather than a challenge, and automatically absorbed.

There are certain distinctive features of the times that explain the unprecedented porousness and conformity of both our established and our protesting cultures. The underlying belief that progress is good even when, indeed especially when, it hurts, means that dissenters, whether of the artistic avant-garde or the politics of protest, are immediately institutionalized, *"Il faut être absolument moderne,"* cried Rimbaud. "One must be of one's own time," insisted Hermann Hesse's Demian. So yesterday's avant-garde experiment in art is today's chic and tomorrow's cliché. And in politics, "dissenters," as long as they pass the supreme test of novelty, are instantly taken up by color supplements, talk shows and "sociologists of protest." The myth of a progressive, open, continuously renewed culture is perpetuated while the underlying orthodoxy goes unchallenged. As usual the progressives and the revolutionaries themselves are the last people to realize that they have turned into reactionaries—that all their ideas date not from *now* but from then, and are in fact part of an ossified consensus. And fashion has not taken over only in the externals of our lives; it has become a substitute for perennial truths. In the all-questions-are-open-questions society, truth is expected to emerge through a cacophony of facts; in practice Gresham's Law operates with a vengeance, and pseudoevents, counterfeit happenings, slogans and catchwords drive out the elusive hussy altogether.

In every age, the pull in man to repeat received ideas and rehash second-hand opinions is enormous. What is different today is that the noise and the surface hyperactivity disguise the stagnation and the growing estrangement from reality—and so fortify the phalanxes of inertia that preserve the orthodoxy intact. For the first time in history an opinion on everything has become an indispensable accessory of modern living, and everybody goes about in the cast-off clothing of the latest media gurus. As early as the middle of the last century, Kierkegaard saw what was happening: "In the world of opinion, newspapers demoralize men, by disaccustoming them from having an opinion of their own, and from developing themselves by carrying it in the face of opposition to the opinion of others, and by accustoming them, on the other hand, to have the guarantee for any opinion they may have that a significant number of men have the same opinion." [21]

The world is reduced into flat, surveyable, two-dimensional world events; and we can all enjoy the illusion that we know exactly what has happened in the last twenty-four hours and what precisely to think about what has happened. Except that the meaning and significance that even the least spiritual and most averse to thought among us need, remain lost. The news and opinions, the perishable, ephemeral and valueless facts with which alone we are bombarded is as much of a substitute for the truths we long for, as a telephone number is for its subscriber. So it is not so much that we know more and more about less and less but that we know more and more about the less and less important; and the more the precision of our knowledge increases, the more trivial the questions we seek to answer.

How likely is it that those most visibly tackling the crisis, our political leaders at the center of the stage or waiting in the wings, will shift their attention from the latest rise in the price of potatoes and the latest fall in the export of turbines, and instead focus their collective squint on the crisis of ideas that underlies all other crises? Miracles do of course happen, but political leaders have traditionally been absorbers of ideas; they have very rarely initiated new visions. And in a culture as porous and fundamentally conformist as our own, political leaders have developed an uncontrollable penchant for the obsolete; they are frozen more than ever in the ideas, the language and style of the past. As a result the estrangement between reality and the Western political establishment is growing more chilling every day. The only difference seems to be between those leaders whose lack of understanding and insight is so total that even their response to the conventional wisdom is subject to delay (like Nixon, declaring himself a Keynesian at the precise moment that the entire academic and financial world was shouting from the rooftops that Keynes was dead); and the other kind who, like Smuts, knew what was right and did what was wrong.

As the evidence of the bankruptcy of the old options becomes increasingly difficult to ignore, it is the second kind of leader who is in the ascendant. Endlessly appealing to what is politically possible, he is everywhere in retreat, displaying as much courageous resistance to the collectivist onslaught as that attorney general evocatively described by an American Senator of his day as "a left-leaning marshmallow." When Denis Healey takes what are regarded as courageous economic measures, we can be sure that in fact nothing has changed: external pressure rather than any sort of internal conviction still remains the main source of political action.

So politics is reduced to a combination of cunning and somnambulism and political leaders are transformed into political managers; tactics and survival become the standard by which they are guided and by which increasingly they are judged. When our leaders have eliminated the impossible, what remains, however improbable, is the course of action they will pursue. But in politics what is impossible is determined not by the nature of reality but by the nature of the prevailing ideas. Hubert Humphrey in his political autobiography has encapsulated the reason why the new leadership to fight the war of ideas will have to emerge from outside Parliaments, Senates, and Assemblies: "I had a choice: 'My own man and denounced by the President as irresponsible, or to muddle through. Really no choice if I want to be President and I do, how badly I do. . . .' "

After the war of ideas has been fought and the social climate changed, only then can we expect our reactive leaders who badly want—oh, how very badly they do want—to become presidents and under-secretaries of state and even ministers without portfolio, to react to political reality rather than political illusions. What is needed is not the old hero reincarnated as the new Savior, not the man who modestly declares that he is not a politician because he is really a Messiah, but pluralist leadership at different levels.

Solzhenitsyn has already provided a supreme example of the new leadership: in the struggle of people who have no faith against people who have faith in false gods, his has been the historic role of the prophet, of witness to something greater and high, pure and indestructible in man. He is neither an ally in the cause of increased expenditure on defense, nor a welcome reinforcement in the camp of free market economics, nor, for that matter, more ammunition for the ideological batteries of anti-communist humanism. Or he may be all these things at a secondary level, but to acclaim these aspects of his message is to misunderstand his uniqueness as the exorcist of the demons of our world. His message is a spiritual message, and to ignore this, and still praise him, is to reduce him to a political pamphleteer—the praise heaped on him nothing but empty sentimentalism.

His leadership is indeed political but only in the supreme sense, in Ivan Denisovich's sense: "Let the truth be told, and let things be changed! If words are not concerned with deeds and don't lead to deeds, then what good are they? They're no more use than the barking of village dogs in the night." [22] And his leadership begins with reclaiming lost words, with taking words which had long ceased to be words and had become slogans and "problems" filled with divisiveness and hatred, saturated with narrowness and malice—*the people, democracy, faith, equality, religion*—and returning them to us new, whole, truthful and alive. And then reviving forgotten truths of good and evil and of the relationship between the individual and society—"a human being is a physiological and spiritual entity before he is a member of society." [23] Let alone before he is a citizen of an all-pervasive state.

Unless individual freedom is recognized in these terms of the spiritual uniqueness of the individual, Declarations, Constitutions and Bills of Rights will be worthless pieces of paper, impotent in the face of advancing totalitarianism. "The writer is a teacher of other people," says Volodin in *The First Circle*, clearly echoing Solzhenitsyn, and properly understood, defining his aspirations "And a great writer—forgive my boldness; I'll lower my voice—a great writer is, so to speak, a second government in his country." And in the world. And in Solzhenitsyn's case, a second government offering moral leadership in a world where political morality is interpreted in the purely passive and negative sense of responsiveness.

It was inevitable that once the media experts and the gossip columnists had squeezed every drop of news value out of Solzhenitsyn, these self-appointed high priests of our secular age would get down to the serious job of debunking. "The true genius," wrote Jung, "nearly always intrudes and disturbs. He talks to a temporal world out of a world eternal. And thus he says the wrong things at the right time. Eternal truths are never true at any given moment in history. The process of transformation has to reassert itself in order to digest and assimilate the utterly impractical things that the genius has produced from the storehouse of eternity. Yet the genius is the healer of his time, because anything that he betrays of eternal truth is healing."

In an age as deprived of greatness as ours is, saturated with mediocrity, cynicism and compromise, the unease that the appearance of someone great has always produced, turned in Solzhenitsyn's case into an outpouring of undisguised censure and distrust that can only be explained by the pundits' fear that any phenomenon of a higher order would degrade *us*—or at least diminish *them* and disturb our sacred egalitarianism. So the *Times Literary Supplement* complained that Solzhenitsyn's books had been received by minds vigorously massaged to read them in a way which intensifies their political meaning and focuses an unnatural [sic] attention on their author. Across the Atlantic, William Safire in the *New York Times* called the man leading the fight against the entrenched ideas a reactionary. He also called him a religious fanatic and a Slavophile—but then somebody else had called him a KGB agent and a wife-batterer. Then he went on to "remind" us that Solzhenitsyn was "only a novelist," while proud cosmopolitans reassured those who found the voice grievous at first taste and had no time to digest it, that the author was essentially provincial, his themes outlandish and alien to our sunlit world where "such things do not happen."

And what was academia doing? Linguists were analyzing the lexical experiment in *The First Circle*, with specific reference to the Communist Lev Rubin's apostrophizing of Sologin; literary theorists were dissecting the cinematic and documentary devices of *August 1914*; and historians and Kremlinologists were exposing the inauthentic facts in the *Gulag Archipelago* and urgently debating the precise number of MGB and MVD executives shot as opposed to imprisoned after the death of Stalin.

Periodic saturnalias, during which the fool is free to attack and mock the hero, would only be countenanced—so the anthropologists have been telling us—by cultures totally sure of their survival. Solzhenitsyn and the fools have proved the anthropologists wrong.

Against such a monumental display of self-confident ignorance, polished triviality and worldly wise cynicism on behalf of the academic and media establishments, to say—as I intend to say—that the second layer of leadership would have to take the form of a "long march through the media and the institutions," will appear at best foolhardy. But if we accept that at the root of our predicament lies spiritual and intellectual error, and that ideas have consequences infinitely more decisive than the consequences of material forces, then the media and the academic institutions become of crucial importance in the war of ideas which has to precede any fundamental political change.

The power of government to mold public opinion is now shared, to a degree unparalleled in history, by journalists, commentators, authors and media professors. Intermittently the cry goes up from one end of the land to the other that all these pundits speak and write about public affairs without having the responsibility for the conduct of public affairs. But this lack of "responsibility" is an advantage: while there is little chance of leadership that does not merely refract the orthodoxy emerging among the practical men of politics, it can emerge among those who are not driven by the great causes of accommodation, flexibility and reelection to bow responsibly before every blowing wind.

When concepts like responsibility and accountability are reduced to pragmatic cowardice, unreflective conformism becomes all-important; then is it absurd to expect more from the ranks of the irresponsible? They will of course have to sneak through the net of an ideological conformism unequaled since the Dark Ages, and a spiritual inertia that simply has no historical parallel. They will have to be heretics in an age when porousness and bland receptivity have made heresy an impossibility. Free love, free verse and free reason have replaced free thinking. "We are free men and here is our corporal. Let us have our liberty drill. Let's disobey all together." [24]

It is said that the inhabitants of Tierra del Fuego have a single word which means "to look at each other hoping that either will offer to do something that both parties desire, but are unwilling to do." At this stage the only hope of ending this paralysis of modern political leadership lies with those who would undermine the stagnant system of ideas that permeates all. As politicians are increasingly operating on the principle of avoiding anything that will offend anyone, they respond more to "aroused minorities" than to majorities. So an aroused minority that will challenge the present consensus of ideas, will at the same time change the background against which the unwitting accomplices and the cowards that flinch have to "lead."

For the third layer of leadership we can take a clue from Machiavelli. "The people," he wrote in his *Discourses,* "are more prudent and sober and have better judgment than a prince." And another clue from a less machiavellian source: when in the *First Circle,* Nerzin has to leave his precious volume of poems to someone's safe-keeping, he turns to the half-blind and illiterate janitor, Spiridon. Spiridon will never be able to read them, but he is the keeper and transmitter of a wisdom that does not depend upon the number of books published or the number of books read. This wisdom is always there, but it becomes infinitely more difficult to draw on it in a cultural climate that perverts the spiritual essence of man by denying it all protection, air and nourishment.

This is neither an appeal to an entity as spiritually meaningless as the proletariat, nor is it a Tolstoyan claim that "common people" are superhuman; it is simply a restatement of the greatest political truth that is the foundation not just of democracy but of all religion, and that was so effectively summarized by Chesterton:

> That the four or five things that it is most practically essential that a man should know, are all of them what people call paradoxes. That is to say, that though we all find them in life to be mere plain truth, yet we cannot easily state them in words without being guilty of seeming verbal contradiction. . . . Now, one of these four or five paradoxes which should be taught to every infant prattling at his mother's knee is the following: that the more a man looks at a thing, the less he can see it, and the more a man learns a thing, the less he knows it. The Fabian argument of the expert, that the man who is trained should be the man who is trusted, would be absolutely unanswerable if it were really true that the man who studied a thing and practiced it every day went on seeing more and more of its significance. But he does not. He goes on seeing less and less of its significance.[25]

Precisely because the leadership needed today has to be provided by those who trust their eyes and not their ears, the people, even if they cannot challenge the root assumptions of a decaying orthodoxy, can lead the way in challenging the palpable, immediate abuses of noble theories and falsified ideas—as long as they refuse to be "interpreted" by pollsters and learned commentators and let their own eyes give the lie to what their ears have heard and go on hearing. After all, for the first time in history, the burden of the elite, of the traditional governing class, falls upon each one of us. Many died for the privilege. We can at least meet the challenge.

The role of the hero in myth has always been to see before others the death of what has decayed, to enter the pit, the labyrinth, the cavern, the ark, the wilderness or the symbolic netherworld—to penetrate darkness, confront it and draw from the mysteriously creative source within the individual and the collectivity, the power of renewal. The birth of the hero takes place just because tyrannical, oppressive powers already threaten mankind. Even at the very beginning of the world, Cadmus, before he can found a citadel, has to slay an already existing and already threatening dragon. Today the powers that threaten us are not ogre-tyrants but ogre-ideas. So we do not need Alexanders whose goal is action and whose deeds change the face of the world. We need culture-bringers who will shatter the crystalizations of the moment with their words and their example. Then the deeds will follow. In all the Grail quests, whether Gawain's, Perceval's or Galahad's, it is asking the right question that restores the land; then the waters flow again through their channel, and all the woods are "turned to verdure." And it is failure to ask the significant question that is alone responsible for "the illness of the King and the misfortunes of the country."

When the mythology of our time is created, assuming we learn again to create and to value myths, the hero who will release us from the menacing ideas will not be portrayed as one Godlike individual; but more as a kind of field of force, with a center of radiation surrounded by a series of rings, some nearer and others further removed from the center. The center is those men who with their lives and their teaching fulfill the supreme human responsibility—as Solzhenitsyn put it—"to preserve unspoiled . . . the image of eternity with which each person is born." They constitute the foundation of the collective human spirit; around them, that part of the intelligentsia that has passed through a spiritual filter and been renewed; and then the people who, stirred by aspirations born of the new ideas and the spiritual change, begin to manifest a new force, a new consciousness, and a new power.

2

OLD TRUTHS AND NEW HERESIES

In the *Winds of Change,* Harold Macmillan, the man who assured us that "the vision of a new Utopia," the Affluent Society, "was secure and will remain," [1] quotes Macaulay with obvious relish: "Now and then there has been a stoppage, now and then short retrogression; but as to the general tendency there can be no doubt. A single breaker may recede; but the tide is evidently coming in." And the tide was fully expected to bring with it not just eight-cylinder cars that leave well behind the six-cylinder ones, but eight-cylinder ideas that will just as automatically supplant the obsolete products of the past.

Faust's progress through life and through history was expected to continue along a line more or less straight and always ascending—a triumphant march of victories over the relics of the past. So we go on knowing the XYZ of everything, ignorant of the ABC of anything.

Oblivious of the fact that our dreams have been dreamt before, we connect the old dreams and the old truths with the real world much as Don Quixote connected knight errantry with it. Change has become the only accepted law of life and the faster and more frequent the surface changes, the greater the delusion of life and vitality; and the easier it becomes to disguise the decay and perpetuate the arrogance of modernity.

Political life does move in a cumulative manner but only for a while and within limits, until all that can be done has been done along that particular line. At the great turning points, such as the one Western democracies are now facing, new departures along new lines can take place only by recreating the past, rediscovering the old truths and reinstating them in the modern idiom. When the breakdown in the transmission of political truths is as complete as it is today, the maze of political life becomes a spider's web full of enticing false paths. But the laws of politics spring from the reality of human nature and they continue to operate even without the sanction of human recognition—after all, the laws of gravity worked just as effectively before Newton as after him.

The most important forgotten truth about political leadership relates to the public's attitude, rather than to the exercise of leadership itself. No one denies the political grayness among political leaders, but the general feeling is that it is better to be ruled by mediocrities than enslaved by Caesars. A look through history shows that mediocrities can enslave just as effectively as Caesars—in fact even more so, precisely because we are convinced that in mediocrity lies safety and sobriety. And even though the crisis and the dangers we face have been caused not by giants, Cyclops and sinister geniuses but by an enlightened mixture of moderation, scientific planning and regular guys, we persist in the belief that mediocrity is innocent, if not harmless.

But in politics there are degrees and kinds of innocence which are indistinguishable in their effects from the most vile intentions. A less innocent and credulous Brutus would not have played into the hands of evil, and helped to bring tyranny to Rome. He would have known that only approximate good lies within political reach—and not perfection on earth. It is not necessarily malign men who have been the precursors of disaster or who have helped to prop up modern totalitarianism. The men and women whom Stalin called "my useful idiots" and whose ecstatic adulation helped to disguise and so prolong the greatest and most abominable terror in the entire history of the world, were not evil, or malevolent, or indeed stupid.

And their modern-day heirs and assigns, who leave their judgment behind before they cross the frontier into modern China, and on the strength of seeing one or more of the handful of villages kept especially for the purpose, return to the West singing a unanimous pilgrims' chorus about the new civilization that has ushered in Paradise on earth, are not liars or criminals either—at least not most of them. But folly and naïveté are just as culpable as evil, when they help to perpetuate evil. How much more culpable then, and how infinitely more dangerous, is folly in office. The unreality of the world inhabited by political leaders and the complete divorce between human actuality and political abstractions—any political abstractions—are as much at the source of the Western political predicament today as they were of the political crimes in Brutus's time and, for that matter, of the large-scale atrocities of totalitarianism in our century.

Once desirable objectives are elevated into needs, they become political imperatives. "Where there is a need, there is an obligation." So Simone Weil told us, and when a need is perceived as a political obligation, the sense of compelling political necessity that it engenders in our leaders takes over from reality.

It was said that the Crossman diaries suffered artistically from want of a hero—or a villain. And it is true that neither the prime minister nor any of the members of the Cabinet can be cast in these exalted roles. Crossman's summing up of Harold Wilson—"just a man of routine carrying on with the agreed policy"—could with equal truth be applied to the rest of the Labour Cabinet. If Richard Crossman failed in his intention to light up the secret places of British politics, it is because he failed to expose the missing hero: the ideology behind the agreed policies. It is this ideology that provides the sense of political necessity to which routine politicians automatically succumb, drifting with the drift of things, further and further away from the actual world. The fact that this unacknowledged hero could equally convincingly take to the footlights as the villain, is the chief cause of the political predicament.

Unfortunately, human beings are only aroused by flesh-and-blood villains, and there is nothing villainous about political leaders who see themselves as the humble managers of successive economic crises and foist on us an image of cuddly, ordinary, harmless "people of the people," just when they are at their most powerful and all intrusive. "I am not a very educated man," Richard Nixon reassured us, "I listen to these clever fellows." And the "clever fellows," the government's experts, the academics and the ex-academics, produce their down-to-earth reports on incomes policy, the balance of payments or industrial restructuring, urgently debate technical feasibility and tactics, and draw politics deeper and deeper into the morass of insane rationality.

There is safety in numbers, we have been told, and when politics is reduced to a numbers game played by such ordinary chaps, who can disbelieve it? Of course the chaps may be wrong. In fact, Hubert Humphrey in an interview on CBS did not merely admit he had done things wrong—he *insisted* that he had done things wrong: "I am not infallible," he bleated, "I am fallible." The same aggressive humility and ordinary-chappery was displayed by Gerald Ford putting on funny faces on American television; Ted Heath talking with Michael Parkinson on the BBC and outdoing even that professional man of the people; Giscard d'Estaing storming the dining rooms of the petite bourgeoisie and ostentatiously dipping his biscuit in his *café au lait*; Golda Meir, pausing to assure us that she, little Goldie from Kiev and Milwaukee, wasn't really worthy of her lofty role. It is embarrassing, artificial, unconvincing; worse, it is ominous. Our public masters, alive to their small faults, tend to become wholly impervious to their important limitations, and to divert the electorate's attention in the same direction. Harold Wilson was unanimously admired for possessing perfect political pitch. But political pitch is the supreme gift of the *reactive* politician, and the more perfect the pitch the more automatic the bowing in front of great and "inevitable" pressures; just as the more precise the calculation of political odds, the greater is the reluctance to go against them.

The antithesis of the reactive politician was aptly described by H. L. Mencken: "Battling for his ideas in good weather and bad, facing great odds gladly, going against his followers as well as with his followers, taking his own line always and sticking to it with superb courage and resolution." [2] This creed has since the last war been dangerously short of practicing believers, and even conspicuously short of rhetorical followers. Political commentators find it difficult to withhold admiration from the party jugglers and the political tacticians. And when even Churchill was taken in by Stalin's eye for the immediate and the concrete, his powers of instant organization, his contempt for generalities and his grasp of relevant detail, this disposition to respect managerial gifts in political leaders and praise narrowness as virtue is not difficult to explain. It can be explained, but can it be excused? Especially when these gifts instead of being regarded as a useful adjunct of political leadership are being treated as its essence.

And so the dangers of accommodating, unperceiving mediocrity at the top go unacknowledged. "When I survey the French Revolution," writes Tocqueville in *Ancien Regime*, "I am amazed at the immense magnitude of the event, at the glare it has cast to the extremities of the earth, at the power of it, which has more or less been felt by all nations. If I turn to the court, which had so great a share in that revolution, I perceive there some of the most trivial scenes in history—a king who had no greatness save that of his virtues and those not the virtues of a king; harebrained or narrowminded ministers, dissolute priests, rash or money-seeking courtiers, futile women who held in their hands the destinies of the human race. Yet these paltry personnages set going, push on, precipitate prodigious events." [3] The coup against the provisional government in Russia in 1917 was hardly a tribute to Lenin's conspiratorial skill. The Bolshevik plans had been broadcast in the newspapers, and the date of the proposed uprising was known to every moderately well-informed person in St. Petersburg. It succeeded because Lenin struck against a hollow shell: Kerensky and his government.

When the stage is to all intents and purposes vacant and the body politic convulsed by doubt and confused action, then disaster does not need the helping hand of evil geniuses in positions of power. Deceived deceivers and sincerely deluded mediocrities will do just as well, especially when their faltering appeasement of the forces overwhelming them is presented under the cloak of bipartisan politics. It was inevitable, for example, that Eisenhower, obsessed as he was with avoiding partisan conflict (an activity that in his Olympian detachment he regarded as troublesome), would never succeed in putting into practice his proclaimed intention to return federal activities as far as possible to the states and to balance the budget. He was a victim of the liberal illusion of ultimate political agreement and rational harmony, and so refused to recognize that not to take a stand against the dominant collectivist forces is in fact to take a stand for them; and to maintain a bogus apolitical stance—he even went so far as to say in 1953 that "I wasn't a politician, and I am not yet"—when confronted with illiberal political forces, is in fact to precipitate by default their victory.

Eisenhower's temperamental distaste for political stands against "inevitable leftward tendencies" did not die with him. It is alive and well today and one of the most useful allies of collectivists everywhere. "I entirely concur with you in the necessity of agreement," [4] Melbourne wrote to Dr. Pewsey after one of his more controversial appointments had raised a storm of protest, "if it can be treated consistently with other more important objectives. . . . Uniformity of opinion, however desirable, may be purchased at too high a price. We must not sacrifice everything to it." But our political masters today have no qualms about sacrificing to a spurious uniformity everything, including resistance to the trend toward absolutist government.

It has been a constant feature of man's political history to attempt progressively to limit power to the capacity and virtues of the rulers. The old faith, born of long ages of suffering under man's dominion over man, was that the exercise of unlimited power by men with limited minds and self-interested prejudices is inevitably oppressive, reactionary and corrupt. Now this is another of the old truths that have been superseded by the collectivist spirit: no limits to the capacity ot men to govern others are recognized, and the concentration of control and more control, onward to the new despotism, proceeds unabated.

There is nothing to be said of the evils of the personal despotisms of kings, usurpers and conquerors, Neros and Torquemadas, that has not been said a thousand times already. But the illusions of collective despotisms remain unexploded. Collective government, however absolute, so long as it is democratically elected, is assumed to be incorruptible. In fact, when no limits are recognized to the function of government, the enormous expansion of state power and activity that follows carries with it, by definition, a formidable extension of its possible abuse. And the collectivist ethic takes political leaders beyond mere selfishness and gives them a creed. At least individual despots are soon worn out and personal tyranny is not directly transferable—nor is it independent of the individual who wields it. Power that springs from a tyrannical creed is both.

It is a short step from regarding the state as the provider of all man's needs to claiming that the will of the individual should merge in the will of the state. And once that fathomless abyss of *raison d'état* takes over, in the name of the general good, there are no moral limits to the actions that are deemed legitimate. When it takes over in the name of "the people" and the "brotherhood of man," it becomes possible not only to ignore any moral limits to state actions and measures, but to gain popular consent for them, however destructive of individual freedom they may be. There is one harmonious theme that runs through the cacophonous chorus of postwar leaders: the individual must surrender more and more of his rights to the state, which in return will guarantee more and more of what social scientists, psychologists and statesmen have decided are his needs.

And the source of our consent to the modern all-powerful institutionalized Robin Hoods is not Marx, but Bentham. The concept of utility, so this Newton of the moral world believed, would replace the obsolete ideas of justice, of right and wrong, while the state would legislate both morality and pleasure—and call them one and the same thing. From Bentham's "codifications"—does not this word, actually coined by Bentham, sum up the man and his illusions?—we can trace a direct line to the dominant assumptions of modern Western politics: that all pretexts of political conflict would permanently disappear if only unsatisfactory economic circumstances were removed. As more subtle and refined needs are discovered, unsatisfactory economic circumstances become more and more difficult to define—yet politics is reduced to a technocratic activity designed to eliminate them. So the elevation of desires to needs and the illusion of ultimate agreement become moral battering rams against any criticisms of the growing power of the state—the only agency that is seen as capable of satisfying these imperative needs.

When the state assumes the role of Providence, it becomes inevitable that every interest and every individual will begin to invoke its power in solving their problems and meeting their needs—in the public interest, of course. When leadership is defined as it was by Anthony Crosland as "getting things done," then any criticism that cannot be translated into action and the expectation—however illusory—of a solution to a social problem is dismissed as merely negative, and not "constructive." Locke described his work as "removing some of the rubbish that lies in the way to knowledge." Today, removing the rubbish would be regarded by indignant reformers as an irrelevant activity unless it was accompanied by a detailed scheme for "doing something about it." But detailed schemes are in a profound sense made to be distorted: a Lenin urgently creating parallel hierarchies of Soviet administration turns out to have been preparing the soil in which a Stalin grew, and Woodrow Wilson's New Freedom and Franklin Roosevelt's New Deal led the way not only to the Bronslow Committee and the first Hoover Commission and the Second Hoover Commission, and the Henry Jackson Subcommittee on National Policy Machinery—all of them providing in their reports a mine of splendid recommendations for strengthening the President's position as general manager—but also to the President's Budget Bureau, the President's MSC, the President's CEA, and to *All The President's Men.* And no number of Woodwards and Bernsteins, no amount of solemn moralizing, will put an end to executive abuses unless the functions of government are redefined and the limits of government by fallible human beings restated.

Society will not stop changing when think tanks and brain trusts stop producing blueprints of the desired change. It is the supreme hubris of modern "rational" man to imagine that no order and no change not deliberately planned by him can possibly materialize. And it is the supreme limitation of our reformers and model-makers that they are incapable of conceiving social improvements that are the result of human action but not of human design. "Liberty is essential in order to leave room for the unexpected. All institutions of freedom are adaptations to this fundamental fact of ignorance adapted to deal with chances and probabilities, not certainty." [5] Hayek is right. But only up to a point. It is indeed true that freedom and liberty are practical virtues that lead to much greater efficiency than any collectivist solutions which, however meticulously planned they may be, can never capture the intricacies, the diffusion and the millions of flows and relations of economic life—let alone of social, economic and political life together. But as long as freedom goes on being defined as a *practical* virtue, it will be impossible to reverse the modern trend toward democratic despotisms.

"The inability of science to solve life is absolute: this fact would be truly frightening were it not for faith." Marconi recognized this because, like most great scientists and unlike most men of simplistic logic, he knew that both our lives and the entire physical world are under the inexorable sway of polarity: the law of physics, chemistry or any other science is never found free from inherent opposite or contrasting principles. No man can escape in his life this cyclic pattern of flow and ebb, rise and fall, pleasure and pain; and no free political society can escape from irreconcilable choices and from conflicts about the ends, and not just the technical means, of political activity.

But without faith, there is a yearning in free men to sink all choice and all conflict into a common pool of control and direction. Collectivism and all its modern euphemisms—corporatism, social democracy, Giscard d'Estaing's "advanced liberal state"—are all appeals to hopes and dreams, promising to provide certainty and to obviate harsh choices. Without faith in a higher order and a higher harmony, it becomes emotionally unbearable for many people to accept that both the demand for certainty and the political promise that it will be delivered through greater—and then still greater—state control are illusions. "Only in our subjective experiences of conviction, in our objective faith can we be absolutely certain." [6] But the more trends—of exploding populations, growing food shortages, rising unemployment or increasing inflation—are discovered, the more insecure we feel, and the more we go on looking for trends and for ultimate solutions that will command universal support.

Considering the monotonous consistency with which power-holders have throughout history abused their power, you would think that the dramatic growth of executive power in response to utopian political demands would at least have been accompanied by an urgent debate on how to prevent men who have authority from abusing it.

> The strongest poison ever known
> Came from Caesar's laurel crown.

But neither Blake's old truth nor the practical problem that stems from it forms part of the cluster of "modern" truth and "modern" problems. We all know that even the noble Brutus suddenly turned into a savage and was the one to suggest that the conspirators should bathe their hands in the blood of Caesar's body; we all know that Caesar ended ominously, mingling Caesar the man with Caesar the all-powerful political figure; we all know about flattering parasites, wayward princes, court intrigues and regal vices. But they are treated as dramatic clichés or, by the less dismissive, as truths written for eternity. The present therefore feels no obligation to take notice of them.

It is no use pretending that poets can give direct answers to political problems. But great poets can illuminate the problems by illuminating the perennial truths about human nature. Then the politicians can take over. And in one case, two hundred years ago, they very gloriously did: in the *Federalist Papers* they laid the foundations for the most impressive political system in the world; acknowledging the vulnerability of the modern democratic state and aware of the fact that political leaders could be made neither moral nor wise, they relied on a framework of checks and balances to check their immoralities and balance their follies—to protect freedom from the "thirst of power, from rapacious and ambitious passions." The Founding Fathers knew that passions had become neither less rapacious nor less ambitious since Thucydides warned against them, and that the only way to secure against a gradual concentration of the several powers was to make ambition counteract ambition. Government was viewed not as the illusory cooperative enterprise it is supposed to be today, but as the enduring conflict of opposed interests that it actually is. John Adams, the supreme exponent of balanced government, regarded the art of Constitution-making as the establishment of "a multitude of curious and ingenious inventions to balance in their turn all those powers (legislative, executive, and judicial), to check the passions peculiar to them, and to control them from rushing into the exorbitancies to which they are most addicted." [7]

The separation of powers was the other dominant doctrine. Locke, Montesquieu and Blackstone had formulated it; the Founding Fathers put it into effect. As for the president, he was in theory subjected just as much as the three other branches of government to the Whig theory of political dynamics—his powers circumscribed, his ascendancy checked.

The 1912 election was the turning point. The campaign was dominated by the debate between Woodrow Wilson and Theodore Roosevelt on the proper role of the government in the economy. And for the first time the two opposing programs, Wilson's New Freedom and Roosevelt's New Nationalism, shared the underlying principle whose emotional and institutional legacy dominates Western politics today—the function of government as an instrument of economic welfare. Wilson won. And he became the first president to make the executive the supreme branch of government. By 1952, William Buckley was urging the Republican Party and the nation to "acknowledge a domestic enemy, the State." [8] By 1956, the first Republican President for twenty years had wholeheartedly accepted in practice the statist legacy of the New Deal. By 1962, the president and the nation [sic] were described by James MacGregor Burns as the victims of the "deadlock of democracy."[9] By Lyndon Johnson's time, the "czar"—a Roosevelt war creation—was set up to take control of the "War on Poverty" programs, and all departments were expected to take directions from the president's staff.

So what had gone wrong? Nothing that had not been foreseen by Tocqueville more than a hundred years earlier:

> No-one imagined that any important affairs could be properly carried out without the intervention of the State . . . the end which these various reforms had in view were various but the means they proposed were always the same. They wanted to employ the power of the central authority in order to destroy all existing institutions and to reconstruct them according to some new plan of their own device. No other power appeared to them capable of accomplishing such a task. The power of the state ought, they said, to be as unlimited as its rights; all that was required was to force it to make a proper use of both . . . these ideas were not confined to books; they found entrance into man's minds, modified their customs, affected their habits, and penetrated throughout society, even into everyday life.[10]

"Administrer c'est gouverner"—and when we look to the actions of governments to realize our visionary schemes and government is reduced to administration, nothing can push back the rushing flood of executive power, until the old truths of the Founding Fathers are seen again, not as bicentennial fairy tales but as urgently relevant insights into the present crisis and the present abuses. Otherwise the demand that we check executive power will remain a rhetorical flourish, and the executive's abuses will be explained away as the singular perfidy of the uniquely evil Richard Nixon.

The science of human nature is still awaiting its Galileo and its Newton. In the meantime, it would not be a bad idea to stick to the old truth of the Fall of Man that even Bertolt Brecht recognized. "The finest plans have always been spoiled by the littleness of those that should carry them out. Even emperors can't do it all by themselves." The result of resurrecting this old truth will not be to absolve Nixon, but to remind ourselves that the Fall of Man did not begin with Richard Nixon, nor with Ehrlichman and Haldeman, nor for that matter with Lord Lambton, John Stonehouse or Wilbur Mills. Then the truth about "public men"—which is after all only that they are the same men as private ones, and sometimes even more so—will be impossible to conceal any longer. And coming face to face with this truth and this recognition might start us back on the road to political health. When we finally accept that no man is as good or as incorruptible as the imaginary and impossible figure of the public man, we may begin to doubt the sanity of a political ideology that invests public men with far-reaching powers over private men in the name of equality, justice, fairness and similar lulling abstractions.

Then the terror of Lenin's "who-whom" will be remembered again, and not only when applied retrospectively to the Napoleons, the Hitlers and the Mussolinis. In the days when the existence of evil in man was recognized as a reality and not as a mythological invention, it was not necessary to invent contortionist interpretations to explain Hitler, to the point of explaining him away as not "fully human": Adolf Hitler was every bit as much a human as Blondi, his Alsatian, was a dog. Nor would it be necessary to explain Nixon as a uniquely evil man waging the greatest assault on Western civilization since Attila and the Huns; the explanation of a fallible, corruptible man invested with the powers of an Imperial Presidency would be sufficient.

Athena the Goddess of Wisdom advised Cadmus after he had slain the dragon and founded Thebes to sew the ground with the teeth of the dragon, a perpetual reminder to the Thebans that evil is a reality against which we must be continuously guarding; the dragon that has been overcome must again be vanquished, in repeated imitation of what the gods themselves did at the very beginning. At the moment, incapable of feeling the old truths of the old myths, we invent instead our own mythological hierarchies with the devil figures fluctuating according to the latest fashion, from property speculators and CIA agents to trade union militants and Nixon's merry men. Gleeful distrust of selected groups has replaced the truths about human nature in general. We have thrown up a screen to hide reality behind it, and seem unable to integrate into our political views facts such as those that emerged from the Church committee's investigations of intelligence activities. We learn, for example, that none other than the New Deal Saint ordered FBI Director Hoover to snoop on hundreds of Americans who had sent him telegrams in opposition to national defense, or approving of Charles Lindbergh's criticism of the president; and that it was the Johnson administration that pioneered the extensive use of the FBI for political purposes, and actually instituted the famous Nixon "name check," the collection of raw material about an "enemy," much of it misinformation supplied by *his* enemies.

The truth is that when the president is turned by the massive increases in government power into an elective monarch presiding over an apparatus too vast even to comprehend, he is transformed—the precise extent and speed of the transformation depending on his moral character—into a passable copy of the late Roman emperors, surrounding himself with "Berlin Walls" and other trappings of absolute power, including the spy systems that were a universal feature of the years before the Fall of Rome. Even the president, who at least in rhetoric and preelection addresses yearns for the Republic, finds that in practice he cannot turn back; and huge budgets become huger, government interference more interfering and the oppressive imperium more oppressive. "Have you thought how it felt to play God?" Lloyd George asked his son, referring to his experience as chancellor. How would the Welsh Wizard have phrased the question if he had been referring to the experience of the modern American president, or the modern British prime minister for that matter?

The Founding Fathers framed the American government with a visible regard for human passion and weakness. But Lincoln was the last president to treat human nature unsentimentally as a constraint by which policy could be determined without fear of surprise. Today, when human beings are treated as manifestations of general laws of "human behavior" to be empirically explained by the *soi-disant* science of sociology, appeals to regard human nature, the ambivalence of human motive and the mixture of good and evil in the same person as the most important constraints determining policy and the functions of government are dismissed as florid rhetoric.

When the Stoics said "There is no evil," they meant steel yourself against evil, and you may regard it with as much serenity as if it did not exist. When the modern collectivists assume there is no evil but only social injustice, they mean give up your power of choice, which of its essence involves the possibility of error, and your enjoyment of freedom, which necessarily involves the possibility of evil, and we shall deliver an earthly paradise where the state, as well as suffering and sorrow, will wither away, and the land will flow with milk and honey. This is what the Marxists preach and this is what the modern defenders of "the scientific and economic management of the economy" practice.

And this modern totalitarianism is not the heir of the authoritarian systems that existed for centuries—often without in fact producing totalitarianism. It springs directly from the fallacies of irreligious humanists: from the doctrine that Paradise should be made "earthly and fleshly because they could not make themselves heavenly and spiritual," [11] and from the belief that the function of the Angel of Revelation, who comes down from Heaven and throws Satan into the Bottomless Pit for a thousand years, should be arrogated to the state. So all problems have turned into political problems inviting a solution by state activity; and politicians have turned into technical experts skilled in political means. By this introduciton of the bogus neutrality of political expertise, the central problem of power—how tc avoid the abuse of political leadership without emasculating the central authority—can be conjured away.

Hand in hand with our naïve ignorance of this central political problem goes a mystic faith in the absolutism of the majority that has inherited the divine right of kings and the prerogatives of their sovereignty. And majorities, instead of democratically providing by popular demand realistic political ends, become all-encroaching, and can become highly illiberal. The supporters of the Volstead Act, quite democratically voted for, had no compunction about interfering, in the name of the majority, with the dinner menus of millions of citizens. What is more, there is little in the doctrine, and nothing in the practice, to preclude the abolition of majority rule by a vote of the majority—as history from Napoleon III to Hitler proves. It is in fact precisely those who idealize the masses most lyrically, who enslave them the more completely.

The most striking thing about Chairman Mao's writings is how much they reflect the tradition of Chinese statecraft reinterpreted to put the people, rather than the emperor, as the source of sovereignty and power. But would the Chinese People's Republic be any more oppressive if it were the Chinese Emperor's Republic? In fact no Chinese emperor ever claimed the ideological conformity and obedience that Mao demanded, or had authority and power as far-reaching and complete as the power of Mao's centralized state. And this is not an aberration of faraway yellow men; it is the inevitable practical application of a conception of democracy that is intellectually derived from Rousseau and which has nourished all modern totalitarian movements. Its chief preoccupation is to enforce the will of the majority and its principal indifference is by implication extended to the rights of minorities—whether private patients, employees who object to joining a trade union or parents who remain opposed to comprehensive education.

This notion of democracy that makes a romance of majorities is not just different from, it is diametrically opposed to, the Anglo-Saxon conception of democracy. This, deriving chiefly from Locke, is centrally concerned with the individual—with protecting his life, his liberty, his property, his pursuit of happiness not just against any group more powerful than he is, but *against* the majority, *against* the government and *against* the state. It is a short step from idealizing majorities to enthroning vanguard minorities that represent the majority really—except that the majority, because of "false consciousness" or a number of other ingeniously cobbled-up explanations, does not yet realize it. And it is an even shorter step from idealizing majorities to a total contempt for the institutions that have been developed over hundreds of years to achieve the democratic ends of majorities while safeguarding the rights of minorities.

"The question is not so much whether a minority of the electorate votes. The point is that only a minority of the voter votes . . . the average man votes below himself; he votes with half a mind or with a hundredth part of one."[12] Chesterton's truth is conveniently forgotten when governments in the name of their "mandates" gradually but relentlessly abolish individual freedoms. When government is reduced to the administration of mandates, and mandates to increasingly collectivist solutions to "imperative" social needs, representative institutions begin to be seen as cumbersome obstacles trespassing on the executive's powers.

The postwar shift of power form the legislature to the executive has been dramatic everywhere in the West. But it took Watergate to highlight the abuses of constitutional dictatorships. When during FDR's "One Hundred Days" the Congress, voting on legislation, was reduced to waving at it as it sailed by, impatient reformers the world over celebrated the impressive results produced by a strong executive. The celebrations continued when Lyndon Johnson repeated Roosevelt's feat. Indeed they were translated into more and more strident demands for institutional reforms—such as the reduction from two-thirds to three-fifths of the vote required to break a filibuster in the Senate—that would stalemate any minority opposition to increasingly interventionist legislation.

In Britain, in the meantime, recourse to delegated legislation, the guillotine and extra-Parliamentary administrative bodies proceeds unabated. And more ominously, less and less compunction is shown about publicly articulating scorn and impatience with the "anachronistic" procedures of Parliament that put off urgent action; what is even more ominous, less and less indignation greets such declarations of undemocratic intent. In fact it is no longer alarmist to assume that all that it would take today to make Mussolini's impatience with the "lachrymose" politics of a "paralytic" Parliament acceptable to a large majority of our political managers and an increasing majority of an increasingly bewildered public, would be a translation of his flamboyant Latinisms into the neutral language of pressing social needs and a few carefully chosen statistics of economic distress: "I prefer the work of the surgeon who plunges the gleaming knife in the gangrenous flesh to the homeopathic method which puts off action. . . ." There would be plenty of quibbling with the tone of the statement and even outraged rejection of the manner; but how many pragmatic reformers with urgently utopian political objectives, would disagree with the underlying sentiment?

The Watergate scandals made belief in the miracle of an omnipotent, omnicompetent and omnisaintly executive impossible. The miracle of an omnipotent, omnicompetent and omnisaintly executive has been revealed as a hoax, but the faith in earthly salvation through government action has proved too resilient for enough people to point to the connection between the hoax of the miracle and the much greater hoax of the faith. Instead, the true believers juggled slightly with the creed, and lo and behold, the miracle reemerged as compelling as it ever was—with Congress having proudly replaced the executive. Indeed, they did one better. They did not simply join the chorus of damnation on the executive—they became the cheerleaders of the shocked, the censorious and the morally superior.

But various time bombs were ticking away under the pedestals of the White Knights. Two of the most pyrotechnic were in the form of Gulf Oil Lobbyist Claude Wild and Representative Hays's secretary, Elizabeth Ray. Mr. Wild, who had been forced by Nixon's arm-twisters to contribute illegally $100,000 of Gulf cash for Nixon's campaign funds, was called by the Senate Watergate Committee, unctuously sympathetic over his plight, as a witness. But he proceeded to reveal that "there is a great deal of solicitation by the legislative branch too," and when it comes to that, by "all Senators on Watergate except Ervin." [13] And during his trial, the revelations about the extent of financial arm-twisting by lawmakers made the myth of an uncontaminated legislature fighting a contaminated executive impossible to sustain. Especially since Miss Ray had opened up another Pandora's Box full of amusing revelations about the lawmakers' sexual peccadilloes—and more to the point, about their abuse of public funds in the pursuit of the aforementioned peccadilloes.

Then the retreat into what may well turn out to be an infinite regression of explanations began: the revelations about watch lists, wiretaps and name checks during the Kennedy and Johnson years made it impossible to regard Nixon as exclusively and exceptionally venal; the revelations about senatorial and congressional financial abuses made it impossible to regard the executive as exclusively and exceptionally venal; corruption at Sacramento made it impossible to regard Washington as exclusively and exceptionally venal—although "Clean Up Washington" remains a good star to which political adventurers may hitch their wagon. But the inventiveness of the infinite regression is indeed infinite. So the cry went up in the United States, was echoed in Britain and reverberated all over Western Europe: "Roll back the government bureaucracy!"

The vacuity of an explanation that proclaimed that it was after all "the bureaucracy" that was exclusively and exceptionally venal, and the disingenuousness of the chorus that took up the cry, can be easily established by the absence of any concrete proposals to limit the bureaucracy. This would, after all, involve descending from pious platitudes to setting specific limits to what governments can and should attempt to do.

As the new antibureaucratic bodies set up to supervise the old bureaucratic ones turn out to be—as they inevitably will—exclusively and exceptionally venal, perhaps the infinite regression will take us back where we should have begun; we may be forced to recognize that it is human nature that is "exclusively" and "exceptionally" venal, although, rather confusingly, it is at the same time exclusively and exceptionally great. So only by eliminating the illegitimate functions of government will we be able to eliminate its illegitimate power and the illegitimate use of this power by business interests in the name of profits or by office-holders in the name of the people.

The claim that the major source of danger to the maintenance of free government is the selfish and conspiratorial ambitions of the few, variously defined from country to country and from age to age, is a customary piece of democratic rhetoric, normally of the kind that precedes the demise of democracy. Selective indignation and the profound moral asymmetry of such indignation are invariably accompanied by attacks on every feature of the political system that is not simply majoritarian, from the seniority system and the Electoral College in America, to those Parliamentary procedures in Britain that are designed to strengthen the rights of dissenting minorities.

If there is one quality demanded before all others for the preservation of a free government, it is patience. If there is one certain way to destroy this quality, it is the inculcation of unrealistic expectations from government action; as *le jour de gloire* fails to materialize, patience, notoriously limited among those who believe that the Kingdom of Heaven is at hand if only the state would stop getting sidetracked by time-wasting democratic procedures, runs out. And checks and balances presuppose patience and temperance; they are no substitute for them.

But modern man has surrendered the guidance of his life to the materialist passion and, having lost any sense of allegiance to God and his higher self, he has become the slave of the utilitarian values of Western culture. And these values—the rational determination of pleasure and pain and the greatest statistical good for the greatest number—are inherently collective, and by definition majoritarian: "The Sovereign People owe allegiance only to themselves; their enthronement must, therefore, result in their utter subjection to an abstraction—their own corporate existence, as embodied in the State and finally in a demagogue, who identified his and the State's will. Becoming Sovereign, the People had to become slaves; and the Totalitarian State, whether in its classless, socialist society or Third Reich version, is the full realization of their slavery." [14] Malcolm Muggeridge is right in predicting that when man's spiritual truth is forgotten, the heresy of the Kingdom of Heaven—or at any rate of Beria, Mao Tse-Tung, Che Guevara or Prince

Kropotkin—on earth takes over, and the mad activism that follows its pursuit inevitably leads to the salient fact of our century, the tyranny of the majority. Where Muggeridge is profoundly wrong is in assuming pessimism to be the spirit's great strength, and quietism the only alternative to state activism. Can there be a more massive misconception of man's spiritual life, a more glaring unconscious acceptance of the assumption dominating our culture and our politics, that the only possible discoveries are technological ones?

"Mahatmaji, you are an exceptional man. You must not expect the world to act as you do," someone reproached Gandhi once. And his reply was a magnificent rebuttal both of Muggeridge's despairing quietism and of the collectivists' jungle activism: "It is curious how we delude ourselves, fancying that the body can be improved, but that it is impossible to evoke the hidden powers of the soul. . . . If we may make new discoveries and inventions in the phenomenal world, must we declare our bankruptcy in the spiritual domain? Is it impossible to multiply the exceptions so as to make them the rule? Must men always be brute first and men after, if at all?" [15]

And if Gandhi's Vedic mysticism is dismissed as irrelevant to our complex modern societies, corroboration can be found in the writings of some of the greatest scientists, whose discoveries have actually been responsible for the existence of our complex modern societies. When Charles Steinmetz, the great electrical engineer, was asked what line of research he believed would see the greatest development in the future, his reply shows up all modern panaceas to be of the same order of significance for our predicament as a state-subsidized project to extract moonbeams from cucumbers: "I think the greatest discoveries will be made along spiritual lines . . . the spiritual forces have as yet hardly been scratched. When this day comes, the world will see more advancement in one generation than it has seen in the past four." [16]

In Galileo's time, the churches sought to invalidate science for being scientific rather than religious. Today, we are reversing the error by invalidating religion for being religious rather than scientific. In fact, far from there being a barrier between science and religion, there is a clear continuum between the two: "The old scientific ideal of *episteme*—of absolutely certain, demonstrable knowledge—has proved to be an idol . . . every scientific statement must remain tentative for ever." [17] Popper has shown that "the evidence proves," far from conferring on science a privileged objective intimacy with truth, it is actually based on an act of faith. But the illusion persists and flourishes that the exact sciences have solved the Great Riddles of the Universe, leaving nothing for any other form of knowledge to reveal.

The old truth that man consists of a spiritual, as well as a purely rational and materialist, part has become the age's arch-heresy. Marx assured us that "man makes religion"; so religion became an effect, never a cause—an expression of material conditions and springing from them. And every major and minor political statement by every major and minor political leader, Marxist and anti-Marxist alike, shows them to be Marx's spiritual heirs and assigns: "It has taken us a long time to realize," said Mrs. Thatcher in Chicago, "as a nation that unless we elevate the reduction of inflation to a first priority, moral values, our social and political institutions and the very fabric of our society will fall apart." [18] And instead of a swell of outrage, "a dismal universal hiss, the sound of public scorn," going up at such public expressions of dangerous delusions, we hear them and quietly move on; no, some of us actually stop and celebrate, eager to persuade ourselves that the right economic policies will be implemented *first* and our moral values resurrected later.

If the individualist Right are serious about their fight against the Marxists, they should begin by recognizing that the values by which we live and the ultimate ends we seek condition and are not conditioned by economic policies and material circumstances. Marx recognized the personal and social need for religion: he simply believed that his secular chiliastic utopianism, his do-it-yourself salvation, would do away with the search for the absolute by offering an earthly substitute. And the substitute will be accepted if the truth is not on offer. And at the moment it is not.

So the political defenders of the individual find themselves impelled, in the face of electorally threatening claims—by those with the inexorable thrust of all who believe themselves to be part of a victorious army—to adopt the claims for their own. It is a chain reaction, a vicious circle, and it has been going on for a long time. Our age began with the cult of the individual. Individualist materialism did begin as a solid daylight faith, but it was living off the spiritual treasures of the past. The fatuous optimism of the nineteenth century helped to dissipate these treasures, and gradually, and by the end of the First World War finally, the individualist tradition was torn to shreds. The utopian drive in man and his need to dream forward have proved as real as his preoccupation with his rational and narrow self-interest. Unless the modern heirs of the individualist tradition recognize this, the age that started with the cult of romantic and untrammeled individualism will end with the destruction of all individual freedom.

Only by acknowledging and stressing the spiritual element in man can individualist leaders hope to prevent the West from being swamped by *militant* utopianism which aims at forcing everyone into one pattern of community and one particular utopian vision. Only by bringing about a political and cultural framework in which politics is not seen exclusively as the satisfaction of the citizens' economic needs can they hope to save individual freedom.

Unfortunately for freedom, the case for its defense today is in the hands of those prosaically crying for a return to the closed, charmed circle of the Forsytes: to thrift, responsibility, stability, respectability, that is, to all the important but profoundly secondary virtues. If freedom and opportunity are taken to mean freedom to achieve the perfection of arrested development of a Forsyte and opportunity to preserve such perfection, we can deplore the fact that many people will choose slavery but we have no right to be surprised by the choice. People will fight for their city and their garden, but they will fight ferociously for cities yet to be built and gardens yet to be planted. The more complete the estrangement of our spiritual self, the more impossible it becomes to stand alone and self-sufficient and the greater the urge to reject ourselves and, like an unstable chemical radical, to merge with whatever comes along the way. And any cause will do—the postwar period is literally littered from beginning to end, and from Cuba to Cambodia, with causes.

And the defenders of freedom, whether conservatives, libertarians or social democrats, will go on being regarded as an aberration to be explained rather than a challenge to be refuted; more to the point, they will *be* just that. They will make no impact on the enemy because they cannot recognize an enemy whose fundamental world view they share: Marxist dogma and collectivist practice are a manifestation of the soulless anti-religious nature of Western liberalism; or if you want to put it another way, Western liberalism is one step on the road to Marxism. And the defense of freedom will remain halfhearted unless it is based on the ultimate value of the individuality of each human being—the *ultimate* spiritual value and not its functional value as a freely productive unit, or a freely saving member of the middle classes, or indeed a freely consuming member of groups A and B.

But modern conservatives are still suffering from the Burkean legacy: "The pretended rights of these theories are all extreme," writes Burke in his *Reflections,* "and in proportion as they are metaphysically true, they are morally and politically false." Had Marx written *his* Reflections he couldn't have put it better. Those conservatives and disillusioned liberals who are not content to dance along a precipice, surrendering more and more in order to survive at all, should begin by inverting Burke and declaring that freedom is morally and politically true, and socially and politically defensible, in proportion as it is metaphysically true and metaphysically defended. What the declaration loses in elegance, it gains in truth. And it can transform the anti-collectivists from an amorphous, scattered opposition, linked only by hostility toward the social-change merchants and negative feelings toward the counterculture, into a positive force: a force that will articulate the passionate need for a spiritual interpretation of the meaning of our lives.

Once the sluices of the dam that has for so long held back the life-giving spiritual truth are opened, the assault of collectivism on our freedoms will not stand a chance. At the moment it is our desiccated liberalism that does not stand a chance against a doctrine that sees itself, and is seen by many of its nerveless enemies, as the world's inexorable fate. The crude absurdities of the collectivist promises can withstand any number of facts and contradictions—the truth is embodied in the doctrine and there is a fact-proof screen between the doctrine and the realities of the world. Experience and observation are powerless against fanaticism. It is only spiritual strength that can resist it, because it is only the spiritually strong who can defy the faith of political salvation and expose its lies.

Reality has more than validated the anti-collectivist critique. It is no longer necessary to rely on warnings about the future effects of welfare states and on doctrinaire prophecy; there are mountains of statistical evidence and empirical facts proving the total failure of collectivist solutions. But they are not seen. And once we understand the nature of the enemy and the fatal deficiency of a defense based on data, however hard, we shall stop being surprised at the fact that they will go on not being seen.

Anti-collectivist muckraking, it is true, assembled a catalogue of failures so dreary that together with the independent "discovery of bureaucracy" by the liberal establishment, it led to many influential liberals—Daniel Moynihan in America and Peter Jay in England being representative of the new class of refugees—joining the "revolt against the state." They swelled the numbers, added prestige to the opposition and reverberation to its echo; they made anti-collectivism less bizarre, but they did not make it more victorious. Indeed, every single index of increased state power, from further nationalization in Britain to proliferating government agencies in America, keeps going up, however eloquent and specific the defectors' analysis of the numbing disasters of state action. In *Maximum Feasible Misunderstanding,* Daniel Moynihan revealed the truth about a major article of collectivist faith—the community action program of the War on Poverty. He concluded that "a program was launched that was not understood, and not explained, and this brought about social losses that need not have occurred . . . the government did not know what it was doing. It had a theory, rather a set of theories: nothing more."[19] (His painstaking exposure of his unequivocal conclusion was followed by a breathtaking prescription: "great care.")

In Britain, Bernard Levin, an early revisionist, was exposing collectivist failures and collectivist illusions at the rate of two a week: "Dying industries, making unwanted products, are to be resuscitated, not extinguished; though the mobility of labour is a vital element in economic progress, every assistance is given to those who want to stay where they are rather than go to where work is available; job-tenure for life is apparently to be the ultimate goal; inefficiency is rewarded and risk-taking discouraged; and the proposals in the Industry Bill for 'workers' participation' might have been and quite possibly were designed to ensure that firms which might wish to modernize and rationalize their operations will be unable to do so. This is not socialism; it is Luddism. . . ." (As a matter of fact, it is both, but like most latter-day anti-collectivists, Bernard Levin draws back from the only logical conclusion of his attack on increasing state power: the rejection of the myth of social democracy.)

Despite the glamorous additions to the ranks of the opposition, it continues to give the impression of a collection of people who, feeling routed, draw the lines and proceed to throw facts at the enemy in the expectation, visibly waning as time goes on, that the enemy will squirm. But facts in this particular battle are a boorish sort of wisdom. While the search for more facts becomes all-consuming, the truth flies off and the enemy marches on. The promotion of prosperity remains the supreme aim of Western societies, and so long as this is the case, the argument from fact and circumstance will continue—with a few ornamental appeals to "moral values" thrown in to brighten the rows of figures and soften the obsessive relish for material success.

"No one in our time finds it surprising," Solzhenitsyn concludes at the end of one of his bitterly humorous sketches, "if a man gives careful and daily attention to his body, but people would be outraged if he gave the same attention to his soul."[20] In the same way, no one in our time finds it surprising if the defenders of freedom give careful and daily attention to the material failures of socialism. But people—or rather that part of the people that forms the professional talking classes—would be outraged if, in defending freedom, the same attention were given to the spiritual failures of man that is now given to the material failures of systems. And yet it is in the spiritual rather than the strategic or the political retreat in which Western man has been engaged, that the ultimate cause of the threat to freedom lies.

So long as the demonstration remains intellectual, it will fail. The intellectual case against the paralyzing economic and political consequences of the omnivorous modern welfare state, buttressed with facts, data and statistics, really needs only to be stated to be seen as incontrovertible. But it has been stated; and it has not been seen as incontrovertible. Nor will it suddenly be accepted if the number and the intellectual weight of those stating it increases—however dramatically. Conservatives, complained William Buckley in 1959, had been unable to show the "nexus between individual freedom and property rights"; they had been unable to persuade the country that economic freedom was "the most precious temporal freedom." [21] The declaration of failure would have been equally true in 1969; will be just as true in 1979; and assuming Mr. Buckley is still free to utter such seditious pronouncements in 1989, it will remain true then—unless the ground of the demonstration has in the meantime been shifted.

The enemies of freedom, unlike its friends, have noticed that man is not driven exclusively by material self-interest. And while Margaret Thatcher and Franz Josef Strauss ressurrect Samuel Smiles and the narrowest kind of middle-class self-advancement, we have the paradox of undemocratic ultramaterialists recognizing and shamelessly exploiting "man's need for a transcendent ideology." Of course for Lenin, who coined that particular phrase, the need was about as transcendental as man's need for a ruthless, disciplined, secret and centralized body of men to launch the Revolution. For him, just as for Marx, the need for religion was an illusion, a lie, created by economic conditions; but then Lenin, like so many of his present-day assigns, had always had a simple faith in the superior efficacy of the lie, almost any lie, to the truth.

The superior efficacy of the lie is not to the truth, but to the parody of realism which the muckraking champions of freedom today parade as truth. And while the prodigal sons of nineteenth-century liberalism refuse to recognize that their secular faith has been played out and there is no turning back, the new masters of political theology will go on convincingly posing as the embodiment of truth in history.

When a lie as emotionally powerful as this is pitted against the folly, nervelessness, lack of understanding and insight of the modern Western leaders, its success is assured. Secular religion against the truth of religion is powerless—but against "realism" it is all-powerful. And yet the pragmatic champions of Western values—even those who do realize that men's self-transcending emotional needs are real needs with political spillover effects—fail to recognize the power of myth as political propaganda, great at all times but irresistible when it reverberates in a spiritual vacuum.

So they watch with growing nausea as Nyerere, forever canting about the dignity of man while at the same time driving his own population by straightforward methods of mass coercion into collectivized villages, is given a standing ovation at the Mansion House; and they listen with growing disbelief as the Khmer Rouge who expelled the entire population from Cambodia's capital city when they took over the country, go on being discussed as rather impatient agrarian reformers. But so long as truth is wearily treated as that age-old will o' the wisp, and seeking it as a rather fruitless exercise in a pluralist society, the moralistic displays of hypocrisy will become increasingly blatant and the nausea will be given plenty of opportunities to grow. But it will not be followed by greater understanding, until at least those who are alive enough to feel nausea and disbelief, stop deluding themselves that we can expose the hypocrisy and defend freedom by logic alone.

"There is a portion of enthusiasm assigned to every nation," said Swift, and if democratic leaders ignore it, totalitarian ones will exploit it. And what is true of language in general is true of political language: it can move us toward what is good; it can move us toward what is evil; or it can fail to move us at all. But policy is directly affected by the language of politics, and when political leaders choose to communicate with the electorate by debauching it with economic baits, they pave the way for black-magic politicians who, unlike the present technocratic ones, will offer action in language that can move.

If the ability to generate diffuse enthusiasm without brandishing economic baits got Hitler going, it is the same kind of ability in leaders such as Churchill that smashed him. Even nationalism, such a potentially fanatical and catastrophic emotion, does not have to be aggressive: de Gaulle appealed to it, used it, and got the French out of Algiers at the same time. But today disoriented leaders are trapped by the myth that the people will only respond to a specified proportionate increase in their standard of living; and they are bending before any wind that they believe might help blow them into executive office. So the ancient question goes unanswered: if the trumpet give an uncertain sound, who shall prepare himself to the battle?

Has political leadership ever been more hopelessly and obviously incapable of recognizing and seizing the latent resolve in Western countries for a profound change away from the old political panaceas? Politics today is supposed to be free from all poppycock; it is proudly described as factual and realistic. In fact, since World War II, Western politics has been profoundly surrealistic. Surrealist painting relies for its effect on the dreamlike association of incongruous images that are themselves meticulously detailed, realistic and immediately recognizable. Modern surrealist politicians start by painting in minute statistical detail their future achievements. From R. A. Butler's promised doubling of Britain's standard of living within twenty years to Denis Healey's promise of a lowering of the inflation rate to 10 percent by the end of

1976 with a simultaneous reduction in unemployment, the setting of specific, mutually contradictory and never-to-be-reached economic objectives has been the distinguishing characteristic of Western political life. So political language has been cast adrift from its source in reality, and political statements have been reduced to a vile combination of spurious thrills, portentous words, smears and innuendo: "The country needs fresh and virile leadership. Labour is ready. Poised to swing its plans into instant operation. Impatient to apply the New Thinking that will end the chaos and sterility. Here is Labour's Manifesto for the 1964 election; restless with positive remedies for the problems the Tories have criminally neglected. . . ."

Virile, restless, instant, impatient, positive, poised, swing—abracadabra that creates just the right air of heady significance and surrealistic *frisson*-needed to prevent the electorate from noticing—or from caring if it does notice—that Mr. Wilson could in one and the same speech give an undertaking not to attack "collective bargaining" and a warning that there can be "no return to the wage free-for-all"; [22] or that Sir Geoffrey Howe would, again in one and the same speech, attack government interference in price-fixing as leading to "higher rather than lower prices" and extol the Price Commission which "in Stage Three . . . should have a wider role to perform." [23]

The painter Max Ernst would have been proud of our surrealistic political leaders. What is more, the fact that they draw their dream images not from their unconscious but from their PR men adds a touch of incongruity, which he would have envied. Of course, public relations is not a new profession and its connection with politics is not a new connection. What is new is its new status in politics: from the minor status of technicians, publicity men and fund-raisers, PR men have climbed to participation in policy-making. As a result, policy is subordinated to the necessities of the image, and actions that involve risk shunned in the interests of "voter appeal" and of preserving the leader's image of humble infallibility. A PR man, in the words of one of the pioneers of the tribe, "helps to mold the actions of his client as well as to mold public opinion." [24] He does indeed. James Hagerty, the PR brain behind the marketing of Eisenhower, the beloved nonpartisan leader, did not merely provide most of what the world learned about the president, he was also the source of most of what the president learned about the world. This additional screen between political leaders and reality, superimposed on their instinctive reluctance to confront reality, leads to a perpetual postponement of hard political choices, to rule by lies and evasions, deceptions and "opportune" cowardice. And when it becomes obvious that reality can no longer be evaded or deceived away, their chief concern—and their PR men's exclusive one—is not how to avoid the imminent catastrophe, but how to be in the best political position to attract the maximum political advantage from it when it comes.

The surrealistic corruption of political language is the unavoidable result of the corruption of political life. If "lofty" oratory sounds out of place, it is because "lofty" leaders have been reduced to bureaucratic managers, and politics to the values of the consumer society and a technocratic culture. "Poetry and passionate speech are the sources of the life of every language." Goethe was right, but it is no good training passionate orators against the spirit of the age. Not even Aristotle's *Rhetoric* could prolong the great age of Attic oratory once the great age of Attic politics and Attic culture had died. The no-man's-land between appearance and reality, expression and substance, word-gesture and personality, becomes ever widening. And when the speeches of politicians and the manifestos of political parties are passed through the filter of language and reality, they leave behind dregs of folly and residues of false pretenses.

The power of ideas, emotions, language and the elusive side of man are ignored and action, however rough, coarse and inappropriate, idealized. There is no doubt that human action has increased human welfare. But the improvement has followed not from naïve blueprints—invariably foiled by events—but from *individual* resolution, *individual* faith and *individual* enthusiasm.

The one fundamental political truth that can be found in the work and teaching of all the really great spirits, from Christ and Buddha to Shakespeare and Solzhenitsyn, is that you cannot remake the world without man's first remaking himself. To improve man's condition is not to improve man, and without improving man you may be able to change the mask of the world but not its face. Yet it remains one of the great heresies of our age that man can improve society without first improving himself.

In literature, the same dehumanizing tendency has been at work. The only really positive hero of postwar Western literature is Frodo Baggins in *The Lord of the Rings.* Instead of a hero with whom we could identify, who would move us or entrance us, we are confronted with characters who are little more than repositories of perceptions, reflexes and sociological laws. In the absence of unforgettable heroes with uniquely individual destinies, the social panorama disintegrates into sterile social realism. And once man is reduced to a product of man-made circumstances, all sense of the superhuman and supernatural in the universe, of the truth hidden from us in clouds and darkness, is lost. This is the folly, the hubris, of man that Euripides warns the world against in all his surviving tragedies—and that has obsessed poets ever since. Icarus flies too near the sun and crashes to earth. And in all myths, we are made to feel that it is precisely because the hero is begotten by God that he must be "devout" and reverential. When he succumbs to the arrogance of egomania, the end is always disaster.

The more we see ourselves as the center of existence, the less able we are to create a balanced spiritual system; and the more likely we are to see ourselves as "star-cross'd" protagonists with "environment" taking the place of the stars, and the less willing to admit that the fault is not in our stars, but in ourselves. This is the beginning of searching for causes of failure always outside ourselves; disembarrassing ourselves of conscience and moral responsibility; and ultimately being dissolved into a featureless mass. Scientific determinism leaves us even less scope for free choice and responsibility than crude divine predestination. Chromosomes, glandular secretions and conditioned reflexes took over from the Olympic gods as the determinants of man's fate—and turned out to be the most unyielding puppeteers of all. In the meantime, we are all eagerly awaiting for the behaviorists, who have already denounced belief as superstition, to produce a comprehensive explanation of the phenomenon Man.

The main victim is the sense of the uniqueness of the individual. And there can be no freedom without that. The democratic leader ideally intensifies the individuality of his followers; it is the tyrant and demagogue who intensifies mass energy into a mob. For him, the people are nothing but a potentiality of response to leadership. And the more we see our life as response to external conditions rather than stimulus from our individual souls, the greater is the reaction against all social constraints—the more, that is, the perspective of our lives becomes sociological—and the greater is the predilection for a barren "authenticity" that leads to the bullish antihero, the trousered ape and the violent rebel. Even more ominously, the more fragile our sense of self becomes, the greater our readiness for self-surrender, and the better raw material we make for any totalitarian adventurer who comes along.

Once man is assumed to be the product of his social environment, "natural rights" become empty sounds; and individuals become phantoms. And the only way phantoms and apparitions can find freedom is by absorption in the whole—in society and, by an easy reductionist step, in the state. If human psychology can be altered by transforming social conditions, if indeed, as the Archbishop of Canterbury assures us, bad housing is a "root cause" of violence and juvenile delinquency, then there are no limits to the improvements that can be brought about in individual character by state action.

This heresy of presumptuous rationalism casts its shadow over the whole of Western politics. And the seeds were sown not by Marx and the Marxists but by as impeccable a Western liberal as Locke: in the

Essay, he portrayed the individual as beginning with a blank mind, and molded by the impressions he received, and human beings as sufficiently malleable that they can be educated to desire socially approved objects. So here we have the sketch of the road to the good society through education and state action.

When philosophers launch their systems into the world they cannot of course be held accountable for the implications which others may draw from them, or for the policies to which they may lead. But the implications were clear. And they were drawn, often with picturesque elaboration; in the "new theology," solemnly propounded in the United States in the last decade of the last century, the individual was held to be so enmeshed in the social environment that the human soul could not be saved unless society were saved first. The new theology is equally solemnly propounded today, except that we have in the meantime dispensed with the soul. By 1900, the new theology, and the social justice movement, and the social novelists, had given communal birth to the new discipline of "social science," which began immediately, and has not stopped since, to pour forth theories, reports and draft reform programs.

The only way out of the maelstrom is through remembering the old truth we have forgotten: man is neither a Meccano set nor a creature of detachable parts, nor a set of qualities, tendencies and dispositions, nor still an empty function of desires and pursuits. His reality is not in his actuality but in his spiritual potentiality, and it is as a precondition of his spiritual growth that man's freedom has to be defended; all other reasons are secondary and derivative. But if man is spiritually free, then he is capable of choosing evil. And as long as he remains spiritually free, there can be no earthly utopia through state action; nor can everything, from emotional stresses to crime, be reduced to "mental illness"—to be cured by behavior-modification-drugs or by the latest state-dispensed psychiatric treatment.

"At the moment," admitted Noam Chomsky, "we have virtually no scientific evidence and not even the germs of an interesting hypothesis about how human behavior is determined." Yet the social engineers and the psychiatric establishments go on spending billions of dollars (in New York State alone under Rockefeller, taxpayers have come to pay one billion dollars a year for mental "hygiene") carrying out research into "behavior modification." And they proceed to apply their findings, unperturbed by the fact that sociology and psychiatry have failed to produce any empirically supported propositions about human behavior that are not trivial.

But what makes one convinced that the entire sociological/psychiatric industry, the politicians who support it by generously voting billions of taxpayers' money, and the bureaucrats who produce the industry's grotesquely worded reports have all eaten together of the insane root that takes the reason prisoner, is statements such as the one made recently by Brock Chisholm, the former head of the World Federation of Mental Health: "The reinterpretation and essential eradication of the concept of right and wrong . . . are belated objectives of practically all effective psychotherapy. . . . With the other human sciences, psychiatry must now decide what is to be the immediate future of the human race. No one else can. And this is the prime responsibility of psychiatry." [25] And unbelievable though Chisholm's statement may seem, even more bloodcurdling is the statement of Dr. Lawrence Kolb, recently appointed head of the New York State Mental Hygiene Services, who praised Soviet psychiatry for "the facility with which effective decisions and actions are made in regard to the economic, social, legal and vocational life of the patient." [26] Such statements are made every day, and reported and presumably read, and nothing happens. And nothing will happen until it is realized that "social ills" are not the result of the economic and social order, nor can they be reduced to mental illness and eradicated through behavior-modification techniques. They emerge from the depths of human freedom—man's spiritual freedom to create evil by a perversion of the will.

3

THE IMPOSSIBLE STATESMANSHIP

In *Heartbreak House,* Shaw's vision of England was of an unmanageable ship manned by a gambling crew heading through wild seas for the ruinous rocks. That was 1919. Today, it is not that the crew is gambling and the ship unmanageable—more that the ship is overmanaged and the gray-suited sober crew guided by a navigational theory that rests on the assumption that the earth is flat.

Changing the crew is not going to solve the leadership crisis as long as the ship's navigational principles remain unchanged. In the same way, changing the rules of recruitment, selection and conduct of the crew—electoral reform, Bills of Rights or state subsidies to political parties—will do nothing to soften our predicament. The leadership crisis can only be solved when it is understood, and it can only be understood when it is traced back to the navigation theory and to the theory's central assumption. The equivalent of the flat-earth assumption in Western politics today is the belief that the state, through planning, Acts of Parliament, judicial inquiries, civil servants and exploding budget deficits, can reform *all* unsatisfactory conditions—a role hitherto attributed only to God, and then only by religious fundamentalists.

Hence the impossible statesmanship, the expectation that somehow Whitehall, Elysée or Capitol Hill leads to Damascus. And more generally—and this does sum up the *zeitgeist*—the conviction that you can arrive at the truth through facts (a conviction unshaken, however many times we have arrived at fantasy and nightmare instead), and at deliverance through power (a conviction equally unshaken by the number of arrivals at servitude and the proliferating number of totalitarian states founded on this very principle).

The most dangerous effect of the impossible statesmanship in terms of the leadership crisis is that contempt for the practitioners and their craft increases in direct proportion to the increase of the demands on the state. The more impossible the demands, the more overblown the tests of success that political leaders have to pass, the more merciless the switchback of anticipation and disappointment, and the more dangerous the frustrated expectations. And as politicians, faithful to the prevailing ideas, go on promising Paradise on Earth—however many times its realization is tantalizingly deferred—contempt for them grows.

The public's schizophrenia about what is expected of politicians, and is thought of them, is mirrored in an even more fundamental schizophrenia about what is expected of the providential state and what is thought of the inevitable side effects—meddling bureaucracy, punitive taxation, exploding public expenditure, galloping inflation. Public debate is characterized by such a bewildering multitude of voices on such a vast array of controversies—ranging as a rule from the peripheral to the trivial—that amidst the clamor and the confusion, the modern mind, lacking a central focus, seems to have lost the ability to connect.

The most damaging breakdown of the connecting faculty in political life has occurred in the relationship between freedom and equality. The eighteenth century was when the individual claimed and proclaimed his freedom in all spheres—freedom was the watchword of the Enlightenment. But by the end of the century, the ideal of freedom was no longer that of extending national and individual liberties, but that of expounding human happiness and social perfection throughout the earth. With the constant expansion of economic life in the nineteenth century, the notion of prosperity acquired an almost sacred sound, and with the rise of socialism, equality began to be identified with a removal of economic differences: it became a battle cry, the rod and staff of social reformers, a manifesto of humanism.

As for the conflict involved in the surrender of freedom for the sake of a promised economic equality, slow and almost imperceptible shifts in the meaning of the two concepts have led to the prominent present-day delusion that the two are to all practical intents and purposes identical. "If freedom is combined with a reasonable amount of equality," writes that impeccable social democrat John Dewey, "and security is taken to mean cultural and moral security and also material safety, I do not think that security is compatible with anything but freedom." Having redefined the two concepts so that they refer approximately to the same condition, he proceeds triumphantly to assure us that there is nothing incompatible between the two. Now if Mr. Dewey and the countless academics, artists, media men and entertainers who regularly indulge in similar malapropisms were running a grocery store instead of peddling ideas, Mr. Ralph Nader and the Consumers' Association would be hopping and shouting to ensure that there was no cornflake missing from any package sold at the store. But you can't eat ideas—so there is virtual critical immunity for purveyors of intellectual untruth.

At the intellectual level, the theoretical illiteracy involved in evading the conflict between freedom and economic equality is rather elementary. And yet even among the critics of increasingly coercive redistributive measures, it is not freedom that is universally regarded as the main victim of egalitarianism, but material progress. The economic cost of egalitarianism is great, but it is hardly primary. If people's aptitudes, capacities and motivations were broadly similar, then in an open society, incomes would be largely equal. But history—both the history of countless individuals who rose from poverty to prosperity the world over, and the wide differences in prosperity between religious and ethnic groups in different areas—clearly shows that contrary to the expectations of Tawney and his fellow Fabians, equality of opportunity does not result in substantial equality of incomes. But as long as the equality of men is taken to mean that we are all of us much of a muchness, except for differences of money and education, and that the poor are like the rich minus the money, then a malevolent and variously defined force has to be postulated to explain the persistent economic differences. And who better to fit the part than the more prosperous themselves, whose incomes, it is tacitly assumed, are extracted at the expense of the rest of the population, rather than earned?

So as the establishment in the West of open societies with "the career open to talents" has failed to result in economic equality, the call to reduce differences by political action and to prevent their reemergence by more political action has become irresistible. But political action entails the use of state power. And more political action entails the extension of state power. What has been left out of the calculations of earnest egalitarians is that the growth of state power in the pursuit of economic equality leads to the extension of the worst inequality of all: the inequality of power between rulers and subjects, the only inequality that is inherently and unavoidably coercive.

Coercion, through the restriction of choices, through confiscatory taxation, through economic quotas and through the politicization of economic life, is today the prerogative of the state. And the implications of this are uniquely sinister. As the quest for an impossible equality intensifies and is accompanied by growing demands for "social" justice—that is, the elimination of *all* differences and *all* sources of discontent—the result is an ever-accelerating flow of new regulations, with administrative orders gradually replacing new laws.

"It is seldom," wryly observed Hume, "that liberty of any kind is lost all at once"; and the impossible statesmanship that has been the creation of an age swooning with passion for a centrally imposed equality, may not be a dramatic way of ending individual freedom, but it is a sure and dependable one. The assumption that a man's relative economic position, as well as his health and education, depend on the state, began by being a prescriptive statement—almost a moral exhortation on the state to do something about economic differences. The tragedy is that that statement is in all Western countries today becoming an increasingly descriptive one: the politicization of life has come to mean that a man's income and vital social choices do indeed, as a matter of observation, depend more and more on the state, and are increasingly prescribed by politicians and civil servants. The prizes of political power are enhanced, and the stakes in the political fight and in the decisions of the executive and the bureaucracy are becoming so great, that more and more individual energies and resources are diverted to political life—sometimes from choice, often from necessity, and finally as a matter of course, unworthy not merely of protest, but of comment.

A strong distinction between a "public" and a "private" sphere was one of the main characteristics which Pericles singled out in his Funeral Oration as essential for a free society: "We are free and tolerant in our private lives; but in public affairs we keep to the law." This distinction is becoming ominously blurred in the West today, and government regulation of everything is accepted as an inevitable outcrop of other wider, and greater, purposes. When Locke wrote that governments are trusts, he was being hopeful rather than descriptive; unfortunately today not only are the government and the state regarded as trusts and agents of the peoples' interests, but they are also invested with a moral force which makes it increasingly difficult to restrain and control their excesses.

If Robert Walpole had been told what the number of jobs within the gift of ministers would be 233 years after his death he would wonder at his own moderation. And if Gladstone knew in 1833—when he initiated the Northcote-Trevelyan study that led to the creation of the Civil Service Commission, intended to end the corruption and inefficiency created by the old patronage system—what dimensions these and other new and refined abuses would have reached 145 years later, he might have spared himself the trouble. Theoretically at least, Parliament can check and correct the excesses of the civil service bureaucracy. But the executive's patronage nominees on the proliferating public boards form a rapidly multiplying parallel public service, subject to no identifiable public checks. Maurice Edelman, who raised the matter just before he died, in October 1975, asked the prime minister how many jobs were at the disposal of ministers and got one straight answer from the secretary of state for industry—the rest resorting to the time-honored dodge of claiming that the cost of obtaining the information would be disproportionate to its value.

"No absolute monarch, no monopoly capitalist," Edelman concluded, "could have greater scope than the Secretary of State." [1] And he ended with a plea for Parliament to take note of the problem. Parliament, of course, did not. The House of Commons may be traditionally regarded as the guardian of private freedom and the public purse, but in practice, however much MPs may pontificate on the evils of excesses of public spending, the specific pressures they exert are in the direction of increased spending. Yet in theory, Parliament's primary function is not to rule but to prevent misrule.

The rise of the state plutocracy is a truly cosmopolitan phenomenon. The average annual income for someone working for the federal government in civilian employment in the United States in 1972 was about $12,500; the corresponding income for someone working in private industry, about $9,000. And for collectors of picturesque details, the two richest counties in the United States according to average family incomes are Montgomery County, Maryland, and Fairfax County, Virginia—the two bedroom counties for the federal government. Those resistant to figures and more susceptible to visual images should take a walk around Washington—a city which exists for government and nothing else, which works at politics by day, talks it by night and so could act as a whitewashed symbol of the relentless takeover of life by politics.

The symbol goes unrecognized; and it will remain unrecognized as long as we refuse to come to terms within ourselves with the reality it symbolizes: the condemnation of grown men to what Milton, in his attack on the state in the *Areopagitica,* describes as a "perpetual childhood of prescription." What is worse, it symbolizes our enthusiastic acceptance of the condemnation in the name of comfort and security—the two supreme preoccupations of the courtier. The common human tendency to remain childish, to regress to childish patterns of behavior, has been invested with a political creed, with a state in the role of the Father, and the "system"—which is somehow always assumed to be capitalist, whatever the actual degree of state mix—in the role of the Wicked Stepmother. So whenever the Wicked Stepmother creates problems—and any discrepancy between norms proclaimed by social scientists in their infinite wisdom and reality is by definition a problem, indeed a *social* problem—Father has to step in and save us.

Logically, the inadequacies of the theories that proclaim the interventionist state as the means for better control and less unpredictability are so obvious that they hardly warrant the painstaking refutation they have received. And in practice we have seen again and again life break through the fictitious walls of our state-manufactured security and make nonsense of all our impressive-sounding programs to perfect the world. Between 1960 and 1974, for example, the total level of expenditure on social welfare programs in the United States increased from $50 billion to $170 billion—a $120 billion increase. Now, according to the Bureau of Census there are 25 million poor people in the United States, defined as people with an income level of $4,137 or less for a given year for a family of four. If we take those 25 million poor people and divide them into the $120 billion increase—not the whole thing, just the increase—we reach the conclusion that if the Department of Health, Education and Welfare had simply taken that money and given it to the beneficiaries directly, they would have given each and every one of them an annual stipend of $4,800 a year—which would have meant for every family of four an income of $19,200 or, to put it another way, would have turned every poor family into a relatively rich family. And which would have had the additional, and far from insignificant, advantage of laying permanently to rest that quip about private affluence and public squalor that must surely rank among the most oft-quoted as well as the most misleading of Galbraith's pronouncements—a hardly insubstantial claim considering that the man has made a jet-set living and a worldwide reputation out of such inanities.

But the poor are still here. You may wonder where, if the poor are still here, is the money? Well, a little bit of it is with them, but the bulk of it is in the pockets of those busy devising strategies, plans and blueprints for eliminating poverty and equalizing incomes—the social workers and the councilors and planners and the social engineers and urban renewal experts, and the administrative assistants to the assistant administrators. And before it gets into their pockets and before the music stops, the grip of the state has been strengthened and the value of the currency further eroded. Similar horror stories of the phenomenal waste involved in most taxation and welfare policies proliferate across the Atlantic. In Britain, for example, the yield to the state of surtax rates above 50 percent is less than one percent of total tax revenue. Now to the individual surtax-payer, a rate of 83 percent on earned and 98 percent on investment income must be a remarkable incentive to tax avoidance—the quintessentially unproductive activity of our age—as well as to straighforward dishonesty or emigration, all of which, if nothing else, must have certainly caused a direct loss of tax revenue considerably in excess of the surtax yield.

Then why does it demand an act of political courage even to utter these facts and why when they are uttered, are they ignored? There is, of course, a reason—but those who seek it in conspiracy theories are seeking in vain. The doctrine of state salvationism began to gain currency in the early nineteenth century. And comforting though it might be, one cannot explain two centuries of intellectual and political history by stupidity and dishonesty, let alone by a 200-year-old self-perpetuating conspiracy. So a need has to be assumed in the souls of men which has blinded them to the doctrine's fallacy. But the nature of the need cannot be discovered by submitting the structure of the fallacy to an even closer or more rigorous logical analysis. Analyses are intellectual counters, while the fallacy that lies at the center of the welfare state doctrine—the belief that the achievement of economic equality through political action is a passport to salvation—is an emotional counter with all the force of a symbol. And logic and facts, words and figures, are notoriously powerless against symbols.

The visual symbolism of political salvation has not been very profuse; and I doubt whether an attempt to turn the solid monstrosities of the Department of Health and Social Security or the Department of Health, Education and Welfare into visual symbols of the creed would be overwhelmingly successful. But the ingenuity of the verbal symbolism has been quite spectacular, probably the most imaginative contribution being Nkrumah's parody of the Sermon on the Mount: "Seek ye first the political kingdom and all things shall be added unto you." Perhaps by looking at what Nkrumah and his Western counterparts have achieved by the acceptance of this grandiose fallacy, we will be able to understand the nature of the human need that gave rise to it in the first place. What they achieved is a certainty about the meaning of history and about their own place in it. And certainties, however fictitious, are always in demand to overcome uncertainties. When the feeling of security in "a world full of gods" is lost with the gods themselves, and when faith, as the substance of things hoped for and the proof of things unseen, becomes increasingly impossible, a new meaning to existence and a new sense of order has to be found, if man is not to fall back into the abyss of his despair and nothingness. The activist redemption of man and society through political action has become the symbol of this substitute meaning and has, at a great and growing cost, partially met man's need for meaningful order.

One of the main ways in which the impossible statesmanship came about is the expectation that in the absence of a belief in some ultimate order, it would meet man's need for a meaning over and above affluent survival. By handing over all individual moral initiative to the government, man could participate in a massive philanthropic national effort that transcended selfish pursuits and, to a considerable extent, partisan politics. And the illusion persists that a bureaucracy accountable to a majority of voters and susceptible to the pressure of organized minorities is not exercising compulsion. The consecration of the word *social* confirms the illusion, with the result that anything proposed or undertaken in the name of "social justice" or "social conscience" is instantly sanctified—even when it denies the supremacy of the rule of law, ignores the reality of individual responsibility, and so makes justice impossible and conscience meaningless.

The automatic response to any problem today is to baptize it a "social" problem and call on the state to provide a solution. And the degree of one's compassion and the level of one's generosity are to be measured by the vociferousness of one's demands for the state to take action to remove the problem, and the intensity of one's indignation if the state fails to do so immediately. But the idea of *compulsory* compassion and *nationalized* generosity is moral nonsense in terms of the ethical development and spiritual growth of the individual.

It is on this sense of personal responsibility that the conception of democracy rests—and on its negation that the practice of totalitarianism is founded. Those who look to the state to supply them with a sense of moral purpose and who remain convinced, despite mounting evidence to the contrary, that the state is the only effective source of social help and the only effective agent of a just society, are ideal raw material for the totalitarian takeover.

The despatches from research institutes and specially appointed royal commissions are getting gloomier all the time. They show, among other things, what a Labour MP, Raymond Fletcher, expressed, with fewer figures but more feeling: "So it goes on . . . but you realise late on Saturday afternoon when you begin your visits to the disabled, how powerless you really are and how little legislation can do to bring about the complete social justice to which you were once blazingly committed. You recall how Trotsky once set your mind afire with a vision of a world turned upside down and refashioned nearer to the heart's desire. But you have simmered down over the years, into an obscure social democrat, still dreaming, but only able to dream." [2]

"Hot" socialism may have melted down to lukewarm social democracy, but the daydreaming and the chimerical vanities of political activism persist, with the failures used as proof that our impossibilist politics has not been impossible enough. The tragedy is that those critics of the welfare state who draw the logically correct conclusions from its failures, base their attack on a view of man that is empirically, let alone metaphysically, false. Their theories of ethics, based as they are on enlightened self-interest, fail to explain why a man should sacrifice his life in the defense of his family—let alone his country, liberty, beliefs. So they fail to account for the self-transcending tendencies in man, and to explain why the myths of collective political salvation, lifeless as they are, go on casting their dangerous spell.

Man intuitively knows that he is part of an ungraspable, unified and undivided whole. Except that today he is caught up in the collective delusion of believing that the whole was grasped when it was identified with something as transitory and as arbitrary as the political collectivity. Marx regarded socialism as the highest level of atheism; if atheism "affirms man through the denial of God," if it is "the negative affirmation of man," then socialism, he said, is "man's positive affirmation." [3] As long as the "negative affirmation of man" continues to dominate Western life (and calling atheism agnosticism is not going to fool anyone), man's positive affirmation (and calling socialism social democracy is continuing to fool us only at a growing cost to democracy) will remain a complementary psychological need, and will prevail in all its ultimate totalitarian horror. And the fact that the theology of socialism has been discredited in the West will not make the slightest difference—in the same way that it does not appear to matter greatly that, according to Solzhenitsyn, one cannot find in all of Moscow an orthodox Marxist.

Another effect of the negative affirmation of man that strengthens the collectivist politics of regulation, planning and intrusion is that man's instinctive desire for security and permanence becomes paramount. This vain pursuit of watertight certainty is one of the strongest allies of collectivist totalitarians. But even before the alliance has borne fruit and while democracy is still alive, it has a deadening effect on man—indeed it is modern man's supreme, life-denying hubris.

"In the olden days there were men who saw the face of God. Why don't they any more?" a young student—so the story goes—asked the rabbi. "Because nowadays no one can stoop so low," he replied. And yet "seeing the face of God," and feeling a kinship with all the things of life, holds the real promise that external security only seems deceptively to hold: it gives us the security of knowing that nothing is secure, and of accepting that hard fact without resentment, as one of the conditions of being alive. "It is important to have a secret," wrote Jung just before he died, "a premonition of things unknown. It fills life with something impersonal, a *numinosum.* A man who has never experienced that has missed something important. He must sense that he lives in a world which in some respects is mysterious; that things happen and can be experienced which remain inexplicable; that not everything which happens can be anticipated. The unexpected and the incredible belong in this world. Only then is life whole. For me the world has from the beginning been infinite and ungraspable." [4]

Today we lack the spiritual stamina to accept that the unexpected and the incredible belong in this world. We have asserted that nothing is greater than man and his deeds, and so have lost the sense of transcendence and with it the truth that wholeness and harmony cannot be attained through reason alone. So the "infinite and ungraspable" element of life has become psychologically unbearable; it has been reduced to a "haphazard" and "anarchistic" social order to be supplanted, according to a grand design fashioned by our political masters, and put into effect by the governing intelligence of their bureaucratic acolytes.

This fallacy underlies consciously or unconsciously the approach to the welfare state of the majority both of the electorates and the political leaders of the West—including those politicians who are eloquently proclaiming that the public sector must consume a smaller share of the nation's wealth and, when asked to be more specific, sonorously call for a cut in the fuel bills of the Bedfordshire County Council. But the mere contemplation of an attack on the welfare state is enough to daunt the stoutest political heart. Calling for monetary restraints and cosmetic cuts in public expenditure is one thing; being against specific welfare benefits is quite another.

The welfare state has become the Trojan Horse of collectivist totalitarianism, in two main ways. For a start, there is a gastronomic axiom, to which there are no known political exceptions, that *l'appetit vient en mangeant;* and an important political corollary, to which there are no recorded exceptions either, that what the public expects, permanently electioneering politicians will promise. But while there is an ascertainable limit to the amount of food an individual can absorb, there is no possibility of defining the amount of welfare needed by any individual citizen since there is no definable, let alone established, limit to the amount of improved health, education, housing and consumer protection that any individual can absorb. Demand is therefore potentially unlimited and since, at least until further notice, resources are not, but Exchequer money—for all practical political purposes—is, the trend toward state absorption of more and more of the nation's resources continues unabated.

The second way in which the Trojan Horse of the welfare state is betraying democracy and freedom can be traced back to another axiom, this time of economic rather than gastronomic theory: an economy cannot for long remain half-free and half-controlled, let alone less than half-free and more than half-controlled. The two sectors form a large part of each other's markets as well as competing for labor, materials, services and credits. The public sector, unrestrained by normal cash constraints, is able to attract scarce investment funds, force up interest rates, retain manpower and intervene in the economy in ways which are rarely without side effects that call for yet more administrative interference. And as economic knowledge remains hopelessly diffuse and no man or group of men can grasp the intricacies of economic life, state intervention, even when based on objective criteria, is more likely than not to be disruptive. Most of the time, of course, it is not based on objective criteria, but on political and often on crudely party political considerations. "It does not matter," a senior civil servant said, observing that Lord Rothschild had no pictures on the walls of his office; "if you want your masters to take notice of you, the only picture you will need on your wall is a map of Britain with the marginal seats colored in red."

Across the Atlantic, political leaders are seized by the same urge which in 1974 cost the American taxpayer—and this is only the *direct* administrative cost—$1.9 billion in payments to the major federal regulatory agencies. And as a small indication of a small part of the *indirect* cost, on June 30, 1974, there were 5,146 different types of approved government forms, excluding tax and banking forms. And individuals and business firms spend over 130 million man-hours a year filling them out.

Hunting the government waste has become a game which in the last few years everyone has joined in with a relish that becomes embarrassing when we remember that the game has many features in common with Russian Roulette. When multimillion-dollar apartment houses built by government planners at the behest of enlightened politicians have to be blown up a few years later, while in England the Housing Revenue Account deficit rose by 3,000 percent in ten years, the public, psychologically unable to cope with a problem that has become too big, too amorphous and too tragic in its implications, has turned instead to its farcical aspect. And the result has been a collection of extravagances and absurdities which could be called eccentrically diverting—except that for consistency's sake we would then have to begin calling the man who thinks he is a poached egg as well as the man who thinks he is a kettle, eccentrically diverting rather than insane. Any selection has to be personal and somewhat arbitrary, but there are certain items that no self-respecting collector can afford to be without: the $60,000 research project on the vital statistics of air hostesses; the $120-thousand inquiry into whether college students get sexually aroused watching pornographic movies while smoking marijuana; the £4,000-plus paid by Wandsworth Council to their "Toy-Library Co-ordinator"; the £77,000 nuclear bomb shelter to house forty *top* officials of Bexley Council; and the £114,000 ski slope abandoned by Knowsley Council when it was discovered that it would end up somewhere in the middle of the M6 motorway.

The trouble with this particular farce of government waste is that at another level it is also an act in the tragedy of Western democracy. And the solutions proposed by our political leaders will no doubt turn out to be yet another act in the tragedy. The essence of hundreds of speeches and thousands of proposals was unintentionally distilled and offered to the readers of *The Times* by the leader of the Liberal Party: "What we suffer from is not excessive public expenditure, but wasteful public expenditure. . . . . What matters is not so much the level of public spending as the results we obtain from each pound spent." [5] And while David Steel and his colleagues all over the democratic world go on clinging to the hope of balancing soap bubbles on hatpins, every week is dotted with legislative and executive measures that tighten the stronghold of government and bring closer the end of democracy. In 1975, the British Parliament enacted 2,227 statutory instruments and passed 58 major Acts. And the response to complaints about shoddy, ill-digested and often meaningless legislation entering the Statute Book was to set up two new procedure committees to recommend reforms. In the present political climate this means only one thing: facilitating through short enabling bills and guillotine motions the unhindered exercise of executive power, and further emasculating democratic debate.

"I am not a friend to a very energetic government. It is always oppressive," said Jefferson two hundred years ago. Today the elementary truth about government, that if it can do things *for* people it can also do things *to* people, is being remembered only long enough to appoint an Ombudsman or two to look after the victims of our refusal to act by it. And Ombudsmen, appointed from the ranks of exactly those public servants whose works they are expected to scrutinize, together with public inquiries reaching costly conclusions which the government can—and all too frequently does—gracefully ignore, are the public's only protection against ministers and civil servants giving increasingly portentous, and decreasingly democratic, impersonations of the General Will.

Increased powers are demanded, granted, abused and reinforced: in Britain the extra powers granted to the Customs and Excise for the purpose of investigations relating to Value Added Tax (VAT) were followed by new powers granted to the Inland Revenue to break into citizens' houses and seize any document said to be relevant to suspected cases of fraud; in another field, the Department of Health and Social Security has already been granted, and has already abused, odious powers of intrusion and spying in the cause of establishing whether women who claim to be forlorn are in fact cohabiting with a man; in another field still, the powers granted to local authorities to bully owners of houses into selling their property to them are being strengthened under the Community Land Act so that the public will be even more impotent against shameless municipal empire building. Private developers tearing down loved old buildings, destroying communities, and, through lawful but inexcusable methods, forcing house owners to leave their houses, were vilified. Government officials and local authorities doing all these things and at the same time wasting on a fabulous scale the nation's resources, are immune from attack: *they* can impersonate the General Will. And so cocooned have they become in their own self-justifying jargon that, judging by their aggrieved reactions to any criticism, some of them have come to believe that they actually *are* the General Will—and a pampered and well-paid General Will at that. The capital sum needed to provide inflation-proof pensions for all British civil servants has been estimated at £350,000 million, that is, three times all the existing private wealth in the country; their political masters have already had the law officially broken on their own behalf so that their pensions are now calculated on a notional salary some 60 percent higher than their actual one.

So the powers given, or nowadays simply taken, by Western governments in pursuit of equality have resulted in strengthening the most dangerous inequality of all: the inequality between us and our political masters. And measures increasingly totalitarian will go on being justified by arguments increasingly weak and dishonest, until the revolution of abandoned assumptions begins. Only when we abandon the most strongly held assumption of the impossible statesmanship, that the interests of Them running the state and the interest of Us being run by it actually coincide, will there be any hope that our horrified amazement at the waste and inefficiency of government, and at the continuous diminution of our liberties, will be translated into changes of policy and objectives.

The legislative situation in America and in Britain and the other Common Market countries has come to resemble in practice what is accepted in Sweden as constitutional theory. "The purpose of the law," wrote Carl Libborn, a foremost Social Democratic theoretician, "is to realize official policy. It is one of the instruments of changing society." [6] A deputy Ombudsman was even more explicit: "The law in Sweden is an instrument of the civil service, codifying its decisions." [7] And the sinister legislative trend to make offenses against the state more serious than those against the person was defended by Libborn as part of an attempt "to make the public realize that there is no antagonism between themselves and society and to make the individual realize that his interests are the same as those of the state." [8]

When material security is regarded as the gift of the state and is the individual citizen's paramount preoccupation, overshadowing all other values, then it is indeed the case that the interests of the individual and the interests of the state are the same. But then it is also the case that political servitude will be accepted as a fair price to pay for the continuation of material prosperity.

When welfare is celebrated as some hallowed religious dogma, any measure, however totalitarian, will be justified so long as it advances social security; and no threat to social benefits and the power of the welfare state will be tolerated—even if the threat comes from the assertion of individual freedom. So social security, having been turned into an indispensable component of the individual personality, has become a channel of subliminal manipulation; and the welfare state has paved the way to the new totalitarianism which, unlike the old-fashioned variety that rather messily depended on force, relies instead on willing submission in return for comfort, security and technological perfection. "Liberty will not be Catholic enough," Don Juan predicted in *Man and Superman*, "men will die for human perfection to which they will sacrifice their liberty gladly."

The old welfare-totalitarianism continues notoriously to thrive side by side with the new and subtler model. A study that looked at relative public expenditure levels in the Communist and the capitalist worlds found that, when allowances were made for different economic levels, the countries were indistinguishable in their expenditure on health and welfare, converging in their expenditure on education, and differing only to the extent that the capitalist countries spend more on traffic control and the Communist ones significantly more on police and internal security. "Electricity plus Bolshevism," Lenin once said, "equals Communism." But it turned out that the subservience of free human beings to a revolutionary amalgam of technology, politics and welfare could only be secured by a reign of terror, autocratic powers and a high level of public expenditure on "internal security." Many Russians could not—and cannot—forget that autocratic orders are "to be obeyed but not carried out"; and many exceptionally brave ones insist on remembering that they need not be obeyed at all. But once democracy becomes a fundamentally economic concept, as it unambiguously has become in Sweden and is increasingly becoming elsewhere in the West, then it means economic egalitarianism alone, and can be made to embrace any degree of tyranny provided more prosperity, more security and more social welfare are guaranteed. The opposition can be disarmed gently and effortlessly and the elected leaders assured the supreme political blessings denied to the despots of the Kremlin: compliant citizenship and an all-powerful unopposed bureaucratic establishment.

The first step toward making the slaves love their servitude is the inculcation of the belief that economic advancement is the overriding national priority and our primary personal preoccupation, and that economic security, sundered from values, is the most important objective for the individual. So gradually in Western democracies the panic over losing a washing machine has acquired the same kind of fear that hunger held in harsher times. The concept of economic security no longer means exclusively the absence of need, but the preservation of a particular degree of affluence; and the poor have become those who do not possess what others have. This may be like defining a horse and cart as a thing that lacks an engine, but it does have the great advantage for political technologists of establishing social needs in contexts where their imperative character cannot be denied. The conflicts and sacrifices involved in following certain policies can be safely obscured; and the people can die defending their social benefits.

So it has come to pass that gross national product statistics are the cosmic language of our age, *homo economicus homo faber* our fabulous image of man, and Sweden our tangible idea of Utopia. The 8.2 million Swedes, we are told, enjoy the world's highest standard of living; schools and medical care are free; there are no slums and unemployment is negligible. QED—the case for the realization of Utopia on earth has been proved. Can there be a more unambiguous illustration of Western man's spiritual stagnation and psychological sterility than his choice of Utopia? And is it any wonder that our world, having sought meaning in economics, is sick with meaninglessness?

But to accept the reality of man's soul and the truth of man's religious promptings is repugnant to an age that regards the soul as the product of chemical action and religious impulses as the result of glandular hyperactivity. And the spirit of the age will not let itself be trifled with, as Mrs. Alva Myrdal demonstrated when, in her capacity as *Ecclesiastical* Minister of Sweden, she proudly proclaimed: "We are dismantling the Church bit by bit. And where necessary we are using economic means to do so." [9] This is the official voice of Utopia. But the unofficial voice is finally making itself heard: "Anyone in this country, anytime and in any way, can be attacked and vilified by a bureaucracy that grows like galloping cancer," [10] said Ingmar Bergman before he exiled himself from his country after a tax ordeal that was exceptional only in that it was highly publicized. And sixty-eight-year-old Astrid Lindgren, who was hounded for taxes at the rate of 102 percent, turned instead to one of the oldest weapons against injustice—a fairy tale. "Once upon a time," the fairy tale began, "Pomperipossa lived in a country called Monosmania. She loved her country . . . no one had to be poor there. Everyone should have a slice of the welfare cake, and Pomperipossa was happy that she was able to contribute to the baking of that cake. One day, friends told Pomperipossa that she must pay 102 percent taxes. 'There aren't that many percents,' she told them. 'Oh yes,' they said. 'There are as many percents as anybody wants in Monosmania.' " [11] Western democracies are growing to look more like Monosmania every day—products of long centuries of a growing commitment to external realities and a fugitive unconcern for internal truths.

The greatness of the Renaissance lies precisely in its openness to the claims of both external and internal realities, after a long period of arrested introspection. But this unity of extremes did not last. And man set out on another one-sided road of advance, this time exclusively directed to the external world. The Renaissance view of the individual, implicit in the coming of Christ and the New Testament, as capable of taking upon himself the great universals and making them specific in his own being, soon lost its wholeness and was reduced to arid intellectualism and rampant materialism. "One half of humanity," wrote Jung just before he died, "fatten and grow strong on a doctrine fabricated by human ratiocination; the other half sickens from the lack of a myth commensurate with the situation." And the more lopsided and distorted our picture of man becomes, the more perplexed we are before the tyrannies produced by the arrogant, exclusive assertion of the rational and tangible side of man. We either identify ourselves with the tyrannies, or we cling all the more desperately to the collective delusion of guaranteed material security through our impossible statesmanship.

Men have rarely relinquished on their own initiative an approach to life that may have served them well as a transitional stage, but has ended by trying to pin life down to only one aspect of itself. "History teaches that men as a rule do not break with specialized processes without the help of disaster. The finer and more intellectually plausible the grip, and the longer the habit of a specialized development, the greater the disaster and catastrophe needed to free the human spirit from the drowning embrace of exclusive conditionings." [12] Laurens van der Post may well turn out to be right. But it is our duty to act on the assumption that he is wrong. And that we will be able to shake off the conditionings that have turned material prosperity to an exclusive goal before we are swallowed up in an all-powerful state.

Goethe's Mephisto in the guise of a court fool told the emperor that man's mind can bring money to light; and once man resolved to attach the value of gold to paper, the people, suddenly intoxicated by their cheap wealth, run into the wildest extravagances. What happened at the emperor's court is as nothing compared to what is happening daily at municipal committee rooms and annually at party conferences. But the root of the emperor's extravagances and our own, by now infamous, inflation is the same: a fundamental imbalance in our objectives, desires and priorities that springs from a profound unawareness of our true selves and leads to a weltering confusion.

> Take but degree away, untune that string,
> And hark what discord follows . . .
> And this neglection of degree it is
> That by a pace goes backward with a purpose
> It hath to climb. [13]

This "neglection of degree," this loss of the spirit for balance and proportion, starts within ourselves and can only come to an end if we heal the rift between internal and external realities—and open ourselves to the truth of both. Western democracies have reached the stage where they can no longer rely on makeshift rules to curb the worst excesses of a lack of balance in individual priorities. In the past, governments have been able to point credibly to an absolute obstacle for resisting the pressure of more and cheaper money: the gold standard, fixed exchange rates, balanced budgets and the limitation of the supply of "international liquidity" all had the same function for governments that strict rules and hours have for a drunkard. The demands of the impossible statesmanship and Lord Keynes's scientific sanction released Western governments from the shackles of mechanical rules, in the expectation that freed from arbitrary restrictions, they would be able to act wisely for the general good.

But only a temperate man may obey his instinct. With this in mind, many are advocating the construction of new rules—a new international monetary order, or the resurrection of the classical gold standard—to restrain intemperate collectivities. But it is too late. Men, who have always manufactured superstitions to suit their desires, are by now to all practical intents and electoral purposes, and despite theoretical assurances to the contrary, firmly in the grip of the seductive superstition that through more and cheaper money we can lastingly ensure material prosperity. So our only hope for stable money, says Professor Hayek, is to protect money from politics. But it is too late for that, too. The equally seductive superstition that the state can and should guarantee employment and prosperity for all is even more entrenched—especially as it is much more easily exploitable by our political leaders.

And the difficulty of forgetting is at least as great a handicap to new beginnings as the arduousness of learning. Except that at this stage in Western history, the fact that all conventional retreats out of what most of us still regard as a conventional—that is, an economic—crisis are blocked, may force us to recognize that we can no longer ignore imbalance in our values, or escape the urgently needed redress. Day by day our lives are threatened by a proliferation of collective values and by the enthronement of the state, like the city of Rome, in the place of God in man. The extent to which both these dangers spring from the worship of the material is illustrated to paradoxical perfection by the ex officio leaders of the revolt against asphyxiative government: the vilified capitalists and mechanics of the private sector who flee into the protective arms of the state at the least hint of commercial difficulty.

"There is something which is almost incomprehensible to the human mind," said Solzhenitsyn, addressing the American Federation of Labor in Washington, "that burning greed for profit which goes beyond all reason, all self-control, all conscience—only to get money." And he went on to illustrate what he called "the alliance between our Communist leaders and your capitalists" by discussing an exhibition in the Soviet Union of United States anticriminal technology that so engrossed the Russians they instantly put in orders for the whole thing—the problem being, as he wryly pointed out, that the American practitioners of *free* enterprise were selling their scientific paraphernalia not to the law-abiding for use against criminals, but to criminals for use against the law-abiding. If the defenders of the free market indignantly point out that such attacks misunderstand the disinterested nature of the marketplace, they should be reminded that a complete indifference to any principle other than the predatory defense of the market place is the surest way to guarantee its extinction.

In a culture as singlemindedly committed to material prosperity as our own, even the practitioners of free enterprise will defend it only to the extent that it does not endanger their principal commitment. When man's needs and desires are predominantly economic, then Jay Nock's first law of human behavior—"Man tends to satisfy his needs and desires with the least possible exertion"—applies with a vengeance. The more entrenched the impossible statesmanship becomes, the more true it will be that government-granted monopolies, rate regulation or lobbying for tax exemptions from tax reform are less exacting ways to secure profits than free competition.

And the more powerful the state, the more likely it will be that state patronage will become the easiest way to satisfy one's more ethereal needs and desires, such as chairmanships of commissions, membership of committees or chairmanships of nationalized industries. Indeed, in

Britain (and perhaps in America tomorrow?) no sooner does some tycoon retire from a life dedicated to private enterprise than he reemerges as the champion of nationalization. Lord Ryder, who emerged from an apprenticeship as a paragon of free enterprise to head the National Enterprise Board, claimed that those who attack Government involvement in industry, overlook "the following basic facts: i) it has been going on for a very long time, ii) it has been continued under successive Governments of different political complexions, iii) it exists in varying degrees in most industrial countries," all of which "basic facts" could also be cited, in the memorable words of Peter Jay, "on behalf of crime, disease, inflation and fallacious reasoning by those in important positions of public responsibility." [14]

There was a time when Cecil B. de Mille gave up a million-dollar contract because he refused to pay the sum of one dollar to a labor union with a closed shop. Cecil B. de Mille is dead, and no amount of free-market theorizing will breed his replacement. Even in business, the field of human activity that is par excellence the province of economic man, businessmen will stand up to the collectivist onslaught only when they abandon their stubborn moral ignorance and recognize that metaphysical man comes before economic man—otherwise individual freedom will continue to take second place to next year's balance sheets. And sooner or later the *Wall Street Journal,* which already contains very little that does not deal with government-business relations, will contain *nothing* that does not deal with government-business relations—except that by then the distinction may have become a historical curiosity. And those practitioners of free enterprise who are today vying with each other in their submission to the collectivist onslaught will no doubt be amply rewarded: The President of the United States Chamber of Commerce, who in 1973 loudly praised Ralph Nader's proposals—one of which involved the federal chartering of major corporations, with the government empowered to control the hiring and firing of executives—as designed to help business, will probably be designated The Hero of the State for heroically fulfilling norms and quotas; and the managing director of the Philips subsidiary who called for immediate government investment of £100 million minimum annually and for the appointment of a Minister of Electronics to "stimulate the whole electronics sector," [15] will quite likely be made the minister.

Already the efforts of generations of earnest reformers to protect the "little man" from giant corporations have made the little man, who is clearly regarded by Ralph Nader and his paler consumerist counterparts as a prime specimen of a bovine dupe, less independent and more defenseless than ever before against a state invested with greater and greater powers—in the interests, of course, of the aforesaid little man.

The little man has, in fact, discovered that bureaucracies, corporate and governmental, are combining their power to make his life more expensive, less free and ever more regulated. And it remains true, even though the truth goes unacknowledged even by its natural defenders, that in all countries in which the range of goods available is artificially restricted by state action, the range of political goods available is likewise restricted, and enforced by methods a good deal more unpleasant than economic decrees. But the modern capitalists, indifferent to the abstract ideas on which the practice of living as free men is based, are vying with each other in demonstrations of eager subservience to the interventionist state. And the more they beseech popular favor, the more they are vilified by the self-appointed keepers of the public conscience. Not long ago in London, a first-night audience at the revival of Brecht's *Happy End* burst into applause at the line about it being worthier to rob a bank than own one—a perfect illustration of the illusion that has dominated our century, that if only capitalist institutions would be abolished, then covetousness, acquisitiveness and the inequality and injustice that go with them would be abolished, too.

At the Twenty-First Communist Party Congress, just when the Soviet Union had set its course in the direction of private property and a consumer society, Komsomol leader Semichastny, a protégé of Khrushchev's power machine, was to declare that "manifestations of egoism and individualism, as well as other remnants of the psychology and morality of private property owners, must be eradicated in the Soviet Union." His proposed method was to set up rental shops everywhere, "so that those who wished to do so could hire a bicycle, a car, a motorbike, a motorboat and other things for a short time at little cost." [16] Those who insist on tracing the human greed for possession to private property, rather than private property to the human greed for possession, must have been distraught when Semichastny's pet method of "communal economy" first took on in the stronghold of capitalism: in America, increasingly, objects of daily use from brand-new automobiles to clothes and pictures are regularly rented or leased with no marked, or even perceptible, diminution of collective greed.

Yet the belief persists, and forms the basic emotional impetus behind the impossible statesmanship, that amassing private property or indulging in any economic activity that produces profits and personal riches is antisocial. And "antisocial" businessmen and corporations are censured as if they were absolute monarchs extracting the last precious coins from their subjects in an economy with a static supply of gold or silver. But ever since the Industrial Revolution, with mass technology to produce any item in as many copies as there is demand for, and with sustained economic growth, such accusations have made no conceivable economic sense. Yet we go on acting as if we were the Dobo Islanders: "They create situations," writes Margaret Mead, "in which the objective unlimited supply is redefined as being in fixed and limited quantity. No amount of labor can therefore increase the next year's yam crop and no man can excel another in the number of yams, without being accused of having stolen (magically) his extra yam from someone else's garden." [17] In the same way we publicly chastise our own yam-producers and conspicuous yam-consumers not because we believe—though the most shamefaced or ignorant among us claim they do—that they really deprive anyone else of their equitable yam share, but because they symbolize the yam obsession that we dimly despise and reject within ourselves. When Senator Jackson, sitting high in his committee chair, castigates in front of the TV cameras the twelve top officials of the America oil and gas industry, meekly astride their stools at the bar of justice, for their "obscene profits," he is in fact attacking a symbol that embodies the obsession of every single one of us with material prosperity.

We glibly talk and write of the destructive emphasis of our culture on the intrinsic desirability of making money and the virtue of making more of it than the next man, but we do not for a moment stop and identify this preoccupation with money, success and worldly recognition within ourselves. But by concentrating our energies on attacking the enemy without, because of what he reflects back to us, we do not rid ourselves of the enemy within. It is not the unacceptable face of capitalism that is unacceptable; it is not capitalism that is unacceptable; it is our own fatal neglect of the spiritual and long-forgotten part of ourselves that is unacceptable. It is this neglect that has made us turn the necessary but peripheral human preoccupation with securing a material basis for life to an obsession with economic growth and uninterrupted increases in our standard of living. To what end? "It is rather hypocritical and offensive," wrote Arnold Toynbee, "to advocate spiritual progress without considering the material basis for it." [18] Indeed it is. Except that the material *basis* of our existence has become its ultimate *determinant.* We cannot function without a material basis, in the same way that we cannot function without hydrogen. But while we have not turned hydrogen into the ultimate purpose of life, we have done precisely that to material prosperity.

Men have been reduced to isolated bundles of wants and satisfactions. The corollary of this false individualism that recognizes no moral obligation and acknowledges no inner sanction except that of one's ego, is a false altruism that demands nothing more than a mental pose in favor of the Utopia of a perfectly egalitarian society. And the greater the discrepancy between utopian objectives and actual social behavior, the greater the need for scapegoat sacrifices so as to maintain the social myth that our armchair altruists actually live according to their officially declared ethical beliefs. The assumption behind all scapegoat theories, irrespective of whether the scapegoat is witches, Jews, Negroes, capitalists or trade unionists, is that if only the offending group could be dominated, subjugated, mastered, eliminated or redistributed, all problems would be solved. But they would not. And for a political leader to sanction this illusion or make use of it as a means to his own ends, is to display the deepest moral ignorance or the most tragic unscrupulousness.

Every culture must have an explanation to offer to its members for their varying lots in life. For the Greeks, it was Fate, and even the individual gods were subordinate to her. In Northern mythology it was the Valkyries and the Norns or fairies who came to the newly born baby and created, inescapably, its fortune. Mythological explanations of the discrepancies in the fates of individuals may strike us as amusing nonsense. But today's political attempts to rationalize the discrepancies and make them emotionally tolerable in a godless world are cosmic nonsense that can only amuse those with a cosmically perverse sense of humor.

Men forgot that they were men, not gods, and took it upon themselves to invent a formula for the ideal society and to balance the scales of fate according to the formula—whatever the sacrifices, brutalities and atrocities on the way. So leveling became in our time the equivalent of fate in antiquity. But leveling is the victory of an abstraction over individuals. It could only take the place of God in our agnostic century after a phantom had been invented as the instigator of the leveling process: that phantom is the "people," more colloquially known as the "public," an abstraction in whose name previously unimaginable crimes have been committed. So the modern theory of human providence became the perfect preparation for the justification of arbitrary power and the onset of modern tyranny. In our fury to explain men's varying lots rationally, we have explained away man's essence; and with the disappearance of the religious feeling that vindicates respect for man as man, no perpetual challenge exists to the dominion of man over man.

The blind pursuit of the abolition of all discrepancies in the name of equality "transcends justice and morality"; and so subjective morality must not raise its puling litanies—about decency, and humanity, and charity, and tolerance, and justice, and liberty. The irony is that as Toqueville predicted over a hundred years ago, a society thoroughly imbued with the idea of equality will become increasingly envious as this principle becomes institutionalized. More than two thousand years before Toqueville, Aristotle had clearly set out in his *Rhetoric* the degree to which envy results when what we lack by comparison with others is small. It is our neighbors and equals that we envy, because it is their possessions and achievements that are a reflection on our own and that make plain the nature of our failure.

The hierarchies of degree have disappeared and the old social classes have broken up; but the urge of men to build themselves into little unofficial, self-appointed aristocracies within which they can feel superior to the mass persists. In exclusive clubs or private beaches by the ocean, in college fraternities and sororities, man's unceasing effort to get above and beyond the humbling brotherhood of men goes on. The torture allotted to the Danaids in the classical Underworld, of attempting to fill sieves with water, was nothing compared to the tortures allotted to "other-directed men" who base their lives on an optical illusion. Convinced that when others come on, they themselves go back, they are afraid of seeing their own good overshadowed by the good of others. And yet it is on this optical illusion that Western democracies have based their idea of social justice. "The poorest pensioner," wrote W. G. Runciman, "is entitled to a sense of relative deprivation based on the inequality between himself and the richest man." [19] This unique privilege of unlimited resentment, the essence of all slave moralities, became one of the main emotional sources of the impossible statesmanship, and has been confirmed and legitimized in countless political statements this century. As early as 1920, Woodrow Wilson predicted class warfare in America sparked off by the envy of the many at the sight of the few in their automobiles. And the militant indignation that Woodrow Wilson was sure he could detect in his electors' eyes has since been turned into public envy for the benefit of the public weal, and enthroned, heavily camouflaged, of course, in the welfare state.

Sumptuary laws against luxury go as far back as the Roman Lex Didia of 143 B.C., which laid down for the whole of Italy that not only the givers of extravagant meals, but their guests as well, should be punished. And demands for legislative restrictions of luxury and consumption—ranging from shrews and mussels in the Roman markets to long pointed shoes at the time of Charles V—persisted unabated until the end of the eighteenth century. By then, Voltaire could cite Colbert to substantiate his own belief that, with economic progress, luxury could actually enrich a state. But after a short interlude, demands for sumptuary laws reappear heavily reinforced with all the emotional power of the egalitarian ideology; for the first time the aim was not to punish the extravagant but to leave no one well enough off to *be* extravagant.

The aim struck a chord, because with a part of ourselves—only unconsciously remembered today—we all recognize that there is something profoundly sad about men who seek the meaning of their lives in buying the biggest drum they can find and beating it around the village.

But the appropriate personal reaction to them is not envy, but pity, and the politically appropriate action is most definitely *not* the kind of legislation that far from ending fairy-tale extravagance, makes it increasingly the exclusive province of the state.

Yet we remain oblivious of the truth that society, far from being the creation of political abstractions, is the projection of ourselves. Without transforming ourselves inwardly, more legislation may bring about certain adjustments and a few reforms, but what we are inwardly will always overcome the outward—however meticulously planned the outward may be. Unless the problem is shifted from without to within, from the externalities of political action to the life within ourselves, we will go on vainly trying to realize our mechanical concept of equality and justice by law—and increasingly by compulsion. "The turn toward inward development," writes Solzhenitsyn, "the triumph of inwardness over outwardness, if it ever happens, will be a great turning point in the history of mankind, comparable to the transition from the Middle Ages to the Renaissance. There will be a complete change not only in the direction of interests and activities but in the very nature of human beings, and a greater change still in the character of human societies." [2] It will be a great change indeed, a great turning point; and nothing else will do. Yet we persist in seeking both the cause of our destiny and the meaning of our lives outside ourselves, with the state cast in the role of beneficent deity, guardian of just measure and redistributor of lots.

Tolerant, civilized, cultured agnostics throughout history have movingly described their dread of theocracy. Theocracy was indeed the worst of all possible governments until our century invented secular theocracy. But our own civilized democrats fail to see—or worse still, having seen, fail to say—that lofty pretensions are no less dangerous in a secular state than they are in a theocratic power. All political power is potentially the perpetrator of the greatest evil; and the only way its dangers can be circumscribed is by ensuring that its claims are modest, commonplace and set within strictly limited objectives. Instead we have today invested political power with moral responsibility and ethical sanctions which simply do not belong to the political domain, and it has as a result become more meddlesome, more oppressive and more inhuman. "Everything they touch withers and dies, and they touch everything." [21]

All the evidence around us—from the grave labor unrest to the steadily rising number of individuals in need of mental treatment—should by now have been irrefutable testimony to the failure of the impossible statemanship to meet the real needs of our day. But in the same way that belief in the Rain Dance persists even though it is seldom followed by rain, we go on seeking the causes of our troubles in "inadequate" living standards and social security—at the same time as a new and much deeper insecurity and meaninglessness has grown as living standards have risen and social security has increased.

It is this avidity for political power which has led to our age's supreme delusion: the belief that we can recreate human society in the image of liberty, equality and fraternity through politics. And successive generations have, through an increasingly impossible statesmanship, worked at the machinery of human life and ignored the inner being of man. But freedom, equality and brotherhood will never be achieved through the external machinery of society so long as man lives only in the individual and the communal ego. When the ego claims liberty, it arrives at competitive individualism. When it asserts equality, it arrives first at strife, then at an attempt to suppress all differences and variations through the state; finally, as the sole way of doing that successfully, it constructs a tyrannical, machine-made society. As for brotherhood, for the ego even to speak of it is to speak of something contrary to its nature; so fraternity is reduced to "distant love," either the distant love of Zarathustra for the superman of the future, or today's favorite pastime, the proclamation of our love for all those who are distant, as a substitute for our failure to love those who are near.

We persist, with fatal consequences for all these three supreme ideals, to seek their fulfillment in the political sphere, but freedom, equality and unity are the eternal attributes of the spirit and the nature of the soul. When the soul claims freedom, it is the freedom of its self-development, the manifestation of the divine in man; when it claims equality, it is claiming that freedom equally for all, and the recognition of the same soul, the same godhead in all human beings; when it strives for brotherhood, it is basing that equal freedom of self-development on a common aim, a unit of mind and feeling founded upon the recognition of this inner spiritual unity.

To rob man of his transcendence, dispense with his soul and yet blindly insist on the political fulfillment of freedom, equality and brotherhood is the tragic arrogance of our age. And unless we renounce our arrogance and recover our spirit, the trend toward the despotic state will lead suddenly or imperceptibly to the totalitarian state, the source of most of the miseries of our century.

4

THE TOTALITARIAN TEMPTATION

The most astounding fact to emerge from the concluding volume of *Cecil King's Diary*—a fact not once mentioned in the endless post-publication commentaries that focused instead on the backbiting gossip—is the extraordinarily high proportion of bankers, ministers, labor leaders, trade union barons, press lords, back-benchers, tycoons and other public-spirited superior persons who are quoted concluding that parliamentary democracy has failed and that the answer to Britain's problems is some form of authoritarianism. In America, Dr. Henry Kissinger was quoted as saying that "the day of the United States is past and today is the day of the Soviet Union. My job as Secretary of State is to negotiate the most acceptable second-best position available." [1] And that one phrase embodied in a stark form much of the philosophy which guided his foreign policy. In Japan, at an exhibition on the progress of democracy, no less a person than the then prime minister announced that parliamentary democracy is "on trial," "its problem-solving capability challenged," and its future "a very basic problem." [2] Quite so. Only one wishes that all those diagnosing the mounting threats to democracy would do so with rather more fear and trembling and rather less blithe equanimity.

Anti-parliamentarianism and deep skepticism about the survival of Western democracy are in the air today as never before. And they are to be found everywhere: among the dark inhabitants of the underworld of fantasy and frustration; among the professional academic pessimists on Western Democracy, Industrial Civilization or indeed the Human Prospect (" . . . I am not therefore sanguine that public understanding and cooperation will make unnecessary a considerable exercise of coercive power. . . ." Thus Robert L. Heilbroner in *An Inquiry into the Human Prospect*); and among the blithely and fashionably glum ("Freedom and liberalism are aberrations in the history of the world. I believe that every country is under way to getting its own dictator. I see it as inevitable. We must either find it funny or sit down and weep." [3] Thus Gore Vidal.)

What *should* make us sit down and weep is that our political leaders themselves—children and beneficiaries par excellence of parliamentary democracy—are discussing its death throes, blissfully unaware that they are talking about their own suicide. We are in the position today when more and more politicians think they know what should be done but would hate the men who would do it. But political leaders, commentators and electors who speculate on these lines in private—even though they would *naturally* hate anyone who acted on their speculations in public—forget that nothing that cannot be founded on human freedom can ever be of value. No leader or avatar, no social scheme or system, no device or machinery, can ever bring about the perfected society and the terrestrial millennium. Because man himself is not a machine, nor a device, but a being and a most complex one at that; and mechanical schemes, however much they may claim to appeal to his highest moral tendencies, can never in fact save him.

The great success of modern totalitarianism has been to make thousands believe that as long as it is based on a moral principle and purports to embody a social ideal, it is not really totalitarianism at all. More: the holding and proclaiming of the ideal is sufficient to abrogate the need to live by it. The attempt to make us believe in the existence of a kind of untotalitarian totalitarianism, a new species of triangular square, as the patent medicine for all ills, has in the case of Marxism in general, and the continental Communist parties in particular, been conspicuously successful. And it has made not just the spread of totalitarianism, but much more ominously, the temptation toward totalitarianism, the political hallmark of the twentieth century.

The credulity toward the democratic rhetoric of modern totalitarians has largely dispensed with the need for overt and actual force, and may still prove to be the greatest ally of monstrosities yet unborn. Even among British and American intellectuals whose commitment to anti-communism has been the main difference between Anglo-Saxon and Continental social democrats, the "suspecting glance" is lost. So when confronted with that *nice* Signor Berlinguer who is so democratic and so honest and *so* efficient, they are emotionally ready to believe that he will actually turn Italy into that dreamer's paradise—a really *free* Communist state. What is consciously or subconsciously admired is the efficiency of totalitarian regimes—no votes to be taken, no motions to be referred back, no tedious, bone-headed constituents to be coaxed and cajoled. Often it is not merely the efficiency but the sheer power of these regimes that is the cause of envious admiration: "It's true that in the Soviet Union people disappear," exclaimed Beatrice Webb, accentuating the word *disappear.* And although our world is full of the shadows of millions of victims who disappeared, and abounds with the ghosts of dead ideals, dead moralities and dead political theories, the sacred formulas of the past are obstinately repeated, and the totalitarian temptation grows more irresistible.

The tyranny of ideas has turned out to be even more dangerous than the tyranny of instincts. Generations of intellectuals have been carried away in this century by the totalitarian ideas of statism in all its guises; they have espoused them with passion, pursued them as interests, sought to make them a system and lasting rule of life, pretended that they were the whole truth of life and so suspended disbelief and become unable to think freely about them.

Today, the heirs to these ideas continue to live in the habit of that enthusiasm. Those not completely anesthetized begin to feel less at ease with the result, but seem intent on perfecting its form, making its application more thorough, its execution more effective and its effects more totalitarian. The fact that this last will come as a surprise—even a very unpleasant surprise—to most earnest seekers after good, will not make totalitarianism any less totalitarian.

But until the long night begins in the West and all pure and innocent souls are abruptly jolted on the road to a belated enlightenment, they go on taking every opportunity to gush and coo over existing and nascent totalitarian establishments. They go on fighting to preserve the right of Third World totalitarian "freedom fighters" everywhere to "liberate" their people and establish in the process their people's democracy, their people's courts and their people's tyranny; they go on swallowing whole the European Communists' line and asking for second helpings; and they go on being struck by a curious form of paralysis affecting the vocal chords and the writing fingers, every time amazing evidence comes to the surface to the effect that oppressors tend to oppress, tyrants frequently tyrannize and professional hypocrites do occasionally lie.

The Italian Communist Party, they say, has clearly stated that it is moving toward a "West European model of socialism," that it accepts the principles of parliamentary pluralism, and that like its French counterpart, it is independent from Moscow. What they do *not* say is that at the same time all European Communist parties, without exception, claim a monopoly of truth and seek a monopoly of power; that all party members are subjected to the system of "democratic centralism," which should be included in Roget's *Thesaurus* as an antonym of democracy; that, not surprisingly, the "full and searching inquiry" into the reasons why the Soviet system degenerated into totalitarianism has been with ritualistic regularity postponed every year for the last ten years, while the Kremlin connection remains intimately related to the buoyant state of the party coffers; that Lenin did note in "Left-Wing Communism, an Infantile Disorder," that the best way to climb a mountain is by zigzagging; and that Communist parties *everywhere* are essentially conspiratorial organizations seeking total power by *whatever* means may be judged expedient at the time.

These days, however, Communist parties can afford to be very open, very cosy, very British sorts of conspiracies. Social Democrats on the Continent are less and less averse to forming "popular fronts" with them, while the British Labour Party is a "popular front" by definition and by a simple translation of Harold Wilson's quaint description of his party as a "broad church." As for Conservative, Liberal and Republican parties everywhere, they may not be "popular fronts" in terms of their composition but they certainly are in terms of their hypnotized acquiescence in the slide toward an increasingly collectivist and decreasingly democratic society.

The attempts to draw fine distinctions between socialism and social democracy, Titoism and Berlinguer's West European model of socialism, Stalinism and orthodox Communism, proceed unabated. The concept of Stalinism is particularly convenient for Western Communist parties, Western popular fronts and Russian purified Marxists, like Medvedev, who insist on believing that "the bitter Russian experience with socialism need not be repeated elsewhere," and that "it is possible for European countries to find their own way to creation of a just socialist social order." [4] But as Solzhenitsyn has shown, there never was any such thing as Stalinism—either as a doctrine, or as a part of national life, or as a state system.

Ultimately, the only valid distinction among political systems is between those which recognize that in relation to the true ends of human existence the state structure is of secondary significance and those which do not. "Render unto Caesar what is Caesar's—not because every Caesar deserves it," writes Solzhenitsyn, "but because Caesar's concern is not the most important thing in our lives. . . . When Caesar having exacted what is Caesar's, demands still more insistently that we render unto him what is God's—that is a sacrifice we dare not make." [5]

It is the demanding of this sacrifice that is the hallmark of modern totalitarianism and that makes it unique in world history; its inhumanity surpasses that of all its authoritarian forerunners not because it is based on worse physical constraints, but because it demands the total surrender of man's being to the system. Yet we in the West will be increasingly tempted to accept the terms of the surrender as long as we continue to regard a well-appointed life as the sole meaning of existence, with the modern Caesar-state as its guarantor.

When Bryan Magee, a staunch anti-Marxist Labour MP, can say of the rulers of the Yugoslav state—which is believed to have more political prisoners than any other East European state apart from the Soviet Union itself—that "what they are is attractive, civilized and generally benevolent authoritarians" [6]; when Robert Kaiser of the *Washington Post* comes back after three years in Russia to reassure us that Russian totalitarianism is less than total and that "the country's rulers do not insist on limitless power in all things" [7]; and when C. L. Sulzberger of the *New York Times* declares—and incidentally provides a textbook example of non sequitur—that he does not "consider it axiomatic that the evolving Italian Communist Party, which has produced one genius, Gramsci, a brilliant semiheretic, Togliatti, and the present reformer Berlinguer, must be condemned a priori" [8]; when those, and countless other committed democrats, who ought to know better, go on, as if in an hypnotic trance, poisoning the well of truth, is it alarmist to assume that unless we abruptly wake up and shake off the cumulative effects of these fashionable lies, we will in fact have to drink the bitter cup to its dregs?

Among those who recognize the dangers, many seem to forget that the boundary between totalitarianism and democracy is patrolled *first* by our own individual moral commitment to the reality—and not merely the rhetoric—of freedom and democracy, and only secondly by military divisions and nuclear capabilities. Rome fell not because of the floods of Teutonic barbarism without—it had, after all, triumphed for several centuries over all disruptive pressures—but because barbarism had taken over within.

If the fall of Rome haunts the political imagination of the West today more than ever, it is because we instinctively know that another kind of barbarism is now progressing to its culmination among us. It is, after all, the entire identification of the self with the physical life that is the primary characteristic of barbarism; and our modern barbarian has made the pursuit of accumulation, possession, comfort and convenience his standard and aim. He has, it is true, a mind, and thirsts for general information of all kinds, for such new ideas as he can catch, for mental sensations and excitations of any kind. He would like to think that certain ideals are activating his conduct, while in fact they are merely giving it occasionally a certain color: as, for example, when he is seen collecting signatures on petitions in defense of "freedom-fighting" mass murderers, or appearing on television to extol the rights of whoever happens to be the *dernier cri* among Third World dictators, and so get his regular dose of the warm, comfortable feeling of vicarious virtue.

The Western recoil from medieval religiosity led, it is true, to a time of great activity and of high aspiration: a time, especially, when humanity got rid of much that was cruel, evil, ignorant and odious by the power of the awakened intelligence and of human idealism and sympathy. But the blind swing of the pendulum from the wrong affirmation of spirituality to a wrong negation of the religious instinct in man has clogged modern life with material needs and has turned politics and government into a trade and profession for the supply of these needs. And our ideals, with no spiritual light to examine and illuminate them, have been turned into the life-denying systems and creeds which are everywhere in the ascendant. Yet in opposition to all the totalitarian signs, there are signs that the religious instinct is breaking through, purified and free of stultifying religiosity.

And this is the only force that can defeat the new barbarism: the force that is encoiled, springlike, in our hidden, higher selves. Not the force of the spirit which turns away from reason, the earth and her works, but of that greater spirit which surpasses and yet accepts and fulfills them. It is only a growing reliance on man's spiritual light that can ultimately bring about the reign of individual harmony and communal happiness that man has always vainly expected from each great new revolution of politics and society. It is only such reliance on our spiritual resources that can deflate the appeal of totalitarian solutions, which, in the name of rationality, would put an end to the Age of Reason and plunge the world into totalitarian mysticism.

At the moment it is the totalitarian solutions that appear real and rational, and the spiritual ones that are dismissed as nebulous and fantastic. It is not surprising. Political solutions rely upon a reality which is patent, solidly founded and already accomplished. Spiritual solutions can easily be made to seem unreal, unsubstantial, things of thoughts and dreams rather than live actualities, because they are trying to embody a reality that is not yet accomplished. In the same way, seeking the causes of our ills, and specifically of the totalitarian threat we are facing in the West, in external, identifiable enemies, is far easier than accepting the truth of a cause that is a stranger among the facts of our everyday existence and the terminology of the political debate.

So we have become addicted to conspiracy theories. It may indeed be that, according to the methods set out in the Warsaw Pact's secret long-term strategic plan, "a second power" is being organized in Britain, "based on the left wing of the Labour Party, the industrial trade unions and the Communist Party of Great Britain, and designed to usurp the functions of 'the first power,' namely government and Parliament." [9] But "the first power" is already busy usurping for itself functions and powers which are outside the legitimate scope of any government and Parliament—and the arrogation of such functions makes the distinction between a "first" and a "second" power increasingly academic.

The principal tactical aims of the Russians, according to Lord Chalfont, are to "accelerate the moral and spiritual decline of Britain." [10] Apart from the inherent absurdity of an officially atheist state commenting on the spiritual decline of another state, only those whose conception of spirituality is based on throat-clearing preliminiaries can say, without their breath being taken away, that a nation's or an individual's spiritual decline can be brought about as a result of an enemy's tactical aims and deliberate attempts. Spritual decline can never be instigated by an outside aggressor, and it has always preceded, never followed, conquests, falls and overthrows.

Today, spiritual decline, or more accurately, spiritual blindness, lies at the center of the totalitarian threat to the West. The blindness is ours, although it remains undoubtedly true that the blind can both more easily refuse to recognize the brutality of twentieth-century totalitarian regimes and also be more easily manipulated by them toward surrendering political and economic positions. But it is *our* spiritual blindness that first made totalitarianism tempting. And it is to this blindness that all the specific reasons that make the totalitarian temptation particularly real today must be traced.

One of the most important of these specific reasons is also one of the most prevalent myths of our times. Unmistakable in Freud, and even more so among today's Freud-vulgarizers, is the idea that man is essentially driven rather than driving, acted upon rather than an active agent in his own destiny. In Freud, it is the Unconscious that is driving us. In others who have taken Freud's ideas over into social and political realms, it is the institutions, or technology, or history, or the "inevitable" class struggle that is doing the driving. This transposition of the principle of causal determinism from classical physics to human affairs, this doctrine of historicism, as Popper called it, expresses in all its versions the same feeling of being swept into the future by irresistible forces. So the psychological preparation has been made; and many of us are ready to hand over the wheel. The totalitarian solution, after all, offers a better life *now* and strengthens its appeal by fostering such disgust for the world as it is that *any* other state becomes preferable.

Once the totalitarian solution has been imposed, no problem in living can be acknowledged. Hence the non-existence of psychoanalysis, or any other private psychotherapy (only public "mental" hospitals are provided by the state) in the Soviet Union. Communist theoreticians started with the assumption that all problems are due to the inequities of the capitalist social system and ended with the conviction that the problems had obliged them and ceased to exist, thus making the existence of private psychotherapy unnecessary—and, indeed, illegal.

Seeking the causes of our ills and dangers in systems and environments is by no means the prerogative of Communist theoreticians. It is not just revolutionaries who pose as social therapists. Politicians, consumerists, journalists and sociologists are, every day, discovering new evils, encouraging new fears and proposing new remedies which almost invariably involve outlawing what is feared and setting up a Public Inquiry Committee to investigate the new evil. What is dangerous about this daily cultivation of more fears is that it is part of the general "therapeutic" approach to life, the reclassification of a vast number of occurrences—from phobias and divorce to homicide and addiction—as "illness."And when life is reduced to a series of problems, fears and arbitrarily defined illnesses, expert engineers of society and of each individual "physiochemical" machine are expected to provide expert and universal cures and solutions.

All totalitarians, long before they become the enemies of civilization, are the products of its discontents. They embody our frustrations, fears, problems and hatreds. And the more fears to be quieted and problems to be solved, the greater the need for a rallying point, a dispenser of hope—a savior. And the belief in an outside, *political* savior is fostered by the therapeutic approach to life, which ignores man's spiritual needs and aspirations and forces him to seek the meaning of his life outside himself.

Our spent selves and worn-out societies will go on seeking renewal in increasingly totalitarian solutions unless we recognize the healing reality of the rejected forces within ourselves and seek to make them conscious—before they take revenge for man's centuries-long neglect by inflicting on our lives still more collective monstrosities. What is within us must manifest itself outside. So war, tyranny and oppression will remain, and if banished for a while will return, so long as they have not become psychologically impossible. And yet our unbounded hopes and struggles to discover and impose external solutions to man's age-old problems persist, even though the truth is that some of the things that men and women have desired most ardently for thousands of years are no nearer realization now than they were in the time of Rameses. There is little reason for believing that they will suddenly stop eluding us, but—this is another important reason that makes totalitarianism particularly tempting today—the modern mind seems inherently incapable of grasping the concept of political insolubility. All problems are assumed to have an obvious solution if only the right men could be in control to implement it. And all modern solutions invariably involve investing officials with authority to enforce them. And however often they fail, the reality of the political insolubility of certain problems will remain unacceptable unless the possibility of their ultimate spiritual resolution is recognized.

Until then, men will remain psychologically defenseless against any modern totalitarian presenting them with a set of principles heralded as obvious enough to be accepted by all men of goodwill; precise enough to give unambiguous guidance in particular situations; and clear enough to cover all problems that may arise and to obliterate with a sweeping gesture whatever struggle, distress and sense of loss we have been undergoing. The details of the particular political apparatus that will so sleekly achieve this earthly Utopia will not, of course, be deemed worthy of the public's attention. No amount of life's ill luck and haphazard tribulations can in fact compare with the absolute misery that an ultimate and "infallible" central power can inflict; but this truth will make little impact against the promises of deliverance from uncertainty and from life's undeserved blows.

Related to the conviction of solubility is the belief that it is somehow possible to order totally the economic and social life of a country and yet not interfere in the private lives of its citizens. "What would the mass do if it had not its own interpreter, expressed by the Spirit of the People?" Mussolini talked about the mass and the Spirit of the People; our modern leaders talk about the public and the mandate of the people. But when there are no strict limits set to the parts of our lives that can be included in our leaders' "interpretation," the effects of interpreting the people's mandates can be just as totalitarian as the effects of interpreting the People's Spirit.

Today we persist in believing that the power of the electorate to turn out the government should be a sufficient safeguard. This power is indeed what we understand by democracy. But the corollary is the electorate's expectation that the new government will provide what its leaders have promised. When the process of changing governments stops being a pendulum move and becomes an evil circle with both the promises and the disappointments monotonously recurring, the public begin to feel swindled. And the question begins to be whispered: at what point does the price you have to pay for parliamentary democracy become excessive? And the obvious answer is not always the one automatically given.

"We have had the Socialists in power since 1969 and we discovered that nothing changes. Our frustration is great. We have lost confidence not only in the Social Democrats but in any Government." [11] What is sinister about this summing up by a West German student leader is that it can no longer be dismissed, as it could have been in the sixties, as an isolated outburst by a student activist.

It is becoming increasingly difficult to believe the endless parade of deceptions and mendacities with which our political leaders have for years now sought to divert our attention from reality—and to get their hands on the plums of office. And the greater our sense of powerlessness to affect either their lies or their policies, the greater is the totalitarian temptation. It is fashionable today among influential liberals to trace this feeling of powerlessness to what they call "saturation politics," [12] conveniently forgetting that it was they who, believing that the government could solve all problems and usher in the Great Society, ushered in instead the saturation politics by which Western democracies are now plagued.

The feeling of powerlessness is growing. In the sixties they called it alienation, and although *alienation* has become a sixties word, it is by no means a sixties concept. From Calvin's depiction of man the original sinner, alienated from God for all time, to the modern notion of man alienated in a particular form of social organization, alienation has been omnipresent. It is, after all, just another name for that basic, atavistic feeling in human nature of not being "at home" in the world, a kind of cosmic homesickness. It most certainly was not born with modern technology.

Alienation is not new, but in terms of the totalitarian temptation it is dangerous in two new ways: in the unprecedented absence of any spiritual conviction to mitigate the emptiness of secular materialism, and in the unique way in which it manifests itself among the leaders of the intelligentsia.

Resentment, railing against the emptiness of life and craving for a new faith have been, through the ages, practically the sine qua non of the typical intellectual. What is different with the present variety is that unlike his alienated predecessor, he is not "disaffiliated, disinvolved and disengaged"; he is *committed*—and frustrated when his relevant and meaningful solutions are not instantly implemented. Dwight Macdonald ironically summed up the predicament: "We were right, but they (the masses) wouldn't listen. Nothing is more frustrating for an intellectual than to work out a logical solution to a problem and then find that nobody is interested." For modern intellectual leaders are leading not the quest for truth but the quest for records, figures and—above all—solutions.

The confusion between logical solutions and practical action, on the one hand, and actual results, on the other, is one of the major banes of our time. We have made a mystique of practicality and in our devotion to it we have failed to notice that whatever other virtues it may have, it most certainly does not produce results. Practicality, in our political culture, has become so exclusive that other aspects of human experience are denigrated or ridiculed. But our problems are never exclusively "practical"; so their resolution and the results we long for will remain out of our reach as long as we are content to be the slaves of expediency and to admit as the only law of our thought and action the yoke of immediate and temporary utilities.

The mystique of practicality, and the manic activity to which it leads, are two of the most powerful elements in the trend toward totalitarianism. It used to be only the fanatic who was convinced that life and the universe conformed to a single formula, that he had it, and that it was, therefore, his duty to impose it. But today's practical men have become today's fanatics; and the fact that they lack conviction does not make them a bit less fanatical. Unquestioning, ununderstanding, they rush as if in a race with time to apply their defective formulas on the real world. So palpable, immediate, existing, *practical* evils are being multiplied by the practical actions of practical men. And as man has no affinity for social chaos, and will pay any price for social order, the scene is set for the most energetic, practical men to take over and impose their own brand of cohesive collectivism—no less totalitarian for being based on workaday formulas rather than revolutionary vision.

"Government," said Franklin Roosevelt, "includes the art of formulating a policy, and using the political technique to attain so much of that policy as will receive general support; persuading, leading, sacrificing, teaching, always, because the greatest duty of a statesman is to educate." [13] That was the rhetoric of the practical politician. Today our political leaders have dispensed with the rhetoric and the educating, and have reduced their political credos to the second and more dangerous half of Roosevelt's view of government: its duty to provide "practical controls over blind economic forces and blindly selfish men," and "to solve for the individual the ever-rising problems of a complex civilization."

It is not quite clear at what precise moment the idea that a "complex" civilization requires to be run from the top by an official aristocracy of special knowledge, entered into the heads of politicians, but it has certainly dominated political thinking and political action since the Second World War. If Roosevelt, the prewar pioneer of "complex" politics, or any of his postwar successors had been asked to sit on top of the cosmos and, together with their guild aristocracy of knowledge, manage everything in interstellar space, they would have demurred on the not unreasonable ground that they did not have the slightest idea where to begin. Yet they have assumed quite unblushingly a role no less portentous: managing millions of human beings, each one of whom is as phenomenal as the cosmos itself.

John Kennedy has expounded in some detail the principle on which the assumption of this role is based, a principle which, if seriously accepted, would make nonsense of democracy: "The trouble is that the problems are so complex," he told Benjamin Bradlee, "and so technical that only a handful of people really understand them, and so the average man discussing those problems falls back on a bunch of outdated, if not meaningless, slogans like 'sound dollar' and 'fiscal integrity,' and these old slogans are losing their value. Without complete information, which is necessarily limited to a few because of the complexity of any given problem, the average American is forced to rely for information on what he reads." [14] And this statement, which encapsulates the most undemocratic of all political untruths—that there exists a handful of people with complete information and complete understanding of our "complex" problems—would be endorsed by most politicians today. Otherwise they could not continue for one more hour in their self-appointed role of managers of our destinies.

"I have an earnest proposal to make," wrote the biologist Lewis Thomas. "I suggest that we defer further action until we have acquired a really complete set of information concerning at least one living thing. Then, at least, we shall be able to claim that we know what we are doing. The delay might take a decade; let us say a decade. We, and the other nations, might set it as an objective of international, collaborative science to achieve a complete understanding of a single form of life. . . . As to the subject, I propose a simple one, easily solved within ten years. It is the protozoan *Myxotricha paradoxa,* which inhabits the inner reaches of the digestive tract of Australian termites." [15] *Myxotricha paradoxa* remains a mystery, but in the meantime, undeterred and undaunted, we have been proceeding toward the totalitarian planning of human beings.

Even before the war, Roosevelt could announce that he would be satisfied if 75 percent of his experiments produced beneficial results, with an insouciance about the 25 percent of acknowledged failures, and a facile self-satisfaction about the 75 percent of highly questionable successes, that should have been unacceptable if the subject of his experiments had been Australian termites. And John Kennedy, that paragon of postwar leadership, could declare: "The United States has to move very fast to even stand still." [16] When the Red Queen asserted the same thing, Lewis Carroll and his readers recognized that it was nonsense—at what precise point did nonsense become practical politics? In this atmosphere of purposeful, manic activity—activity which politicians on the other side of the Atlantic were quick to emulate—the administrative discretionary state is daily growing more omnivorous.

The most ominous development of all—and this lies at the core of the totalitarian temptation—is that our powers of indignation are diminishing and our consent to coercion increasing. The history of our century has demonstrated that consenting to coercion may be a logical impossibility, but it is by no means a political one, especially when coercion is masquerading as idealism and morality. For people who can accept no conclusions unless they are freshly concocted in scientific laboratories, Professor Stanley Milgram's experiments into "how people will defy authority in the face of a clear moral imperative" could be used as a scientific symbol—and there are many who recognize no other kind—of Western society's vulnerability to authoritarianism. "Ordinary people," concluded the professor, in *Obedience to Authority,*"simply doing their jobs, and without any particular hostility on their part, can become agents in a terrible, destructive process. Moreover, even when the destructive effects of their work become patently clear, and they are asked to carry out action incompatible with fundamental standards of morality, relatively few people have the resources needed to resist authority." Professor Milgram deplored the power that science and scientific trappings had over the great majority of those he used in his experiments; they unquestioningly yielded their moral responsibility to an external authority. And the whole civilized world did not merely deplore; it was "amazed," "dismayed," "astounded." But then was it not the same whole civilized world that has been urging us for decades now to hand over the responsibility for our lives to the state so that it could bring—or legislate—out of us what is best?

The government, surrounded by specialists, experts and think tanks, has been invested with the same illegitimate scientific authority that was deplored in the experiments. And even more, modern government is somehow expected to embody the best minds of the nation, its noblest aims and its highest aspirations. Of course, nothing of the kind can be asserted of the modern politician in any part of the world. What he does embody and represent is all the average pettiness, selfishness and self-deception that is about him; these he represents well enough, together with a good deal of moral ignorance and timidity. His authority, and the authority of modern government in general, is the authority of the laboratory; and the constraints political authority relies on are the offer of rewards and the promise of sybaritic paradise on earth. For a time that continued promise did indeed lull to sleep man's deep yearning for meaning and truth. But the history of the last third of our century has consisted of a series of falsified political predictions, and all the predictions have been falsified in the same direction: paradise persists in eluding us. And the new totem—a washing machine not yet paid for—is no longer fulfilling, or silencing, man's deeper needs, especially as it becomes more and more difficult to meet the payments.

So political authority is everywhere in decline, and contempt for our political masters seems to be increasing in proportion as their powers are growing. And the revolt against authority has spread to language, music, art and the very ideas of objectivity and rationality. Any intermediary authority, institutional, ethical or artistic, is categorized as authoritarianism and dismissed as dogmatism.

The individual has been liberated from the tyranny of conventions, and in theory, he can stand beyond them in an autonomy of perception and judgment. But what started by being a necessary social and psychological space in which to breathe has ended by being a vacuum. The totalitarian paradox of our age is that the dethroning of the intermediate cultural and moral authority has left the individual naked against the magnified power of the state, and political authority bereft of the means whereby it can be given legitimacy.

"The peculiar, unique and deepest theme of the history of the world and man, to which all others are subordinate, is always the conflict of belief and unbelief. All epochs, in which belief rules, under whatever form, are illustrious, inspiriting and fruitful for that time and for the future. All epochs, on the other hand, in which unbelief in whatever form, secures a miserable victory, even though for a moment they may flaunt it proudly, disappear for posterity, because no man willingly troubles himself with knowledge of the unfruitful." [17] All spiritual life is what Goethe meant by belief, and never is belief more vigorous or more true than when it revolts, in the name of spiritual truth, against the usurpations and pretensions of ecclesiastical powers. Of all perversions, the perversion of what is highest and most sacred is the most unpardonable.

But the spiritual revolt against the arbitrary mediation of the priesthood between God and the soul was drowned in the secular influences that had come to its aid; and a denial, not merely of outward creed and institutions, but of all religious belief, was the sterile result. So our individualistic age threw away belief together with stereotyped conventions. But no society can survive without two established principles of order: a general standard of truth, to which individual judgments can subscribe, and a principle of social order which must equally be founded on a universally recognizable truth of things, and which will justify and yet control the claims and desires of individuals. Both these supreme social needs of our age seemed to be impeccably satisifed by science: a truth of things that depended on no doubtful scripture or fallible human authority, but provided clear, fundamental principles about our world, and so could guide our individual judgment; and a verifiable standard which provided an outline and the means for the progress and perfection of the individual and of society, and by which human life could be governed.

But this attempt to impose by mechanistic laws a synthetic intelligible meaning on life, and then to seek to govern according to these laws, has been irresistibly driving us toward a totalitarian society in which the individual, deprived of his freedom for his own and the general good, will have his whole life determined at every step by the well-ordered mechanism of the state. The fact that this does not sound as nightmarish as it should, is an indication on how far we have already traveled.

What was the culmination of the rational, individualistic age—the triumph of science and the establishment of general laws by which life could be organized—is threatening to become the cause of the death of individualism and of that individual freedom of thought which made the discovery of universal principles possible in the first place. Our age, which gloriously began with the free individual's revolt against arbitrary, ecclesiastical and political conventions, could reach its menacing consummation in political systems of such tyrannical, mechanistic rigidity that they demand the total surrender not only of our freedom but of ourselves.

Scientific, administrative and economic experts have already become the new High Priests, who know us better than we know ourselves, and are gradually delivering us from our cumbersome, erratic self-will. In America, it was Roosevelt's Brain Trust which consolidated the power of the expert, with his ready accommodation to practical considerations, as an essential adjunct of the government of the country. And gradually, and since the Second World War consistently, on both sides of the Atlantic, it has become the prerogative of the experts to set the very terms in which the issues are perceived, and to define the contours of economic and social problems. "A few years ago," wrote H. L. Mencken, "all the New Deal Isaiahs were obscure and impotent fellows who flushed with pride when they got a nod from the cop at the corner; today they have the secular rank of princes of the blood, and the ghostly faculties of cardinal archbishops." [18]

Worse, the experts have begun to believe in their own panaceas and to forget, hauled as they often are from their classrooms into the political maelstrom, that there is a vast difference between an experiment made in a test tube and one made on a living nation. The appallingly narrow specialization of professional disciplines has meant that semi-ignoramuses who have managed to become doctors of science find themselves in the center of political life, invested with all authority. And as knowledge and power have become to an astounding degree differentiated functions, political leaders have to resort increasingly to the knowledge of a bloated army of experts. And it is not only power and knowledge, but knowledge and thinking that have become differentiated functions. Experts at the call of the man who hired them seem to leave their capacity for independent thought well behind them. They become mental technicians, so hypersensitive to what they, and their masters, call the realities of power, that they form today a very significant factor reinforcing the reactive nature of political leadership.

So the distinction between the practical men of power and the intellectual associates of power, who could bring some critical detachment to bear on the exercise of political leadership, has become extinct. Despite the academic credentials of the British Cabinet and the rush of professors to Washington, the relation between power and the force of mind has rarely been more remote—and never has this remoteness been as dangerous as it is today. Political power pays scant deference to *intellect*—although it does constantly defer to whatever it is that Professor Galbraith, Professor Balogh and their breed purvey. Indeed its deference seems reserved for ceremonial occasions, and preferably televised ones. Symbolic of this decorative use of intellect by power was the dinner held by President Kennedy in the spring of 1962 for Nobel Laureates—when he charmingly remarked (the charm was his; history does not record whose was the remark) that there were now more brains at the White House table than at any time since the day when Thomas Jefferson dined alone.

The rational collectivist society, whose essence and justifying ideal is the strict organization of life by conscious *reason,* is actually destroying the source from which it sprung; under the dominion of overvalued reason that rejects its own evolution into a deeper spirit, reason itself has been reduced to insipid practicality. And unless we allow reason its spiritual consummation, the collectivist trend will end by pressing personal freedom out of existence—and reason will disappear with it. Because without the freedom to think and the freedom to realize its thought by action in life, reason cannot do its work: it can neither evolve nor seek out its own ultimate truth. So its function will increasingly be to give coercion a system to administer and to give the state a plan for its actions and a rationalization for its brutalities.

"Our age," wrote Jung, "has shifted all emphasis to the here and now, and thus brought about a demonization of man and his world. The phenomenon of dictators and all the misery they have brought springs from the fact that man has been robbed of transcendence by the shortsightedness of the superintellectuals." [19] Transcendence is not, as the superintellectuals suppose, the opposite of the here and now, nor is it the irrational religious impulse that dominated the dark confusion and brute violence of the Middle Ages. It is a higher spiritual living for which the clarity of man's reason is in fact a vital prerequisite, and into which reason and intellect will be taken up, transformed and brought to their invisible source. For reason lives not only in facts, but in possibilities; not only in realized, but in ideal, truths. And there is an important sense in which the thinker is a special custodian of moral values which are vitally related to his own search for truth: Voltaire striking out passionately for the Calas family, or Zola speaking out for Dreyfus, are classic cases of the supreme function of the committed thinker.

The *trahison des clercs* begins with a different kind of commitment: not the intellectual's commitment to the pursuit of truth and the defense of those values that make the pursuit possible, but his commitment to the consummation of what he regards as "truth captured." It is this commitment that has transformed countless intellectuals into zealots overcome by the most irrational of all the vices of reason—its subordination to the purposes of power. Today *engagé* intellectuals, to the extent that they are pledged, committed, and enlisted, are reinforcing all the totalitarian tendencies of the age.

And it is not just tin-pot intellectuals who are susceptible to this obsession with action and results. When the bankruptcy of the humanist solution is recognized, and the need for a spiritual dimension rejected, or worse, perversely understood, the cure for the evils of the age is sought in power not just by charlatans and ignoramuses, but by many of the highly gifted and loftily idealistic as well. Yeats was one who saw the need for a spiritual dimension as "the revolt of the soul against the intellect," and ended up writing the songs of Franco's Irish contingents. Ezra Pound revolted against the "intellectual malaise," "cultural isolation," and "defunct academic standards" of America; but chose instead to satisfy his thwarted spiritual impulses by sanctifying Hitler. Stefan George was another fine artist who succumbed, and ended up stamping the swastika on the covers of his books.

Historically, Marxism is by no means the only ideology to which action-prone intellectuals have looked for salvation. And anti-Marxist Western political leaders should stop pretending—or still worse, believing—that the totalitarian temptation can be resisted with the aid of nothing but a copy of Professor Hayek's *Road to Serfdom* and another of

Professor Friedman's *Capitalism and Freedom.* Right-wing dictatorships in South America are sustained by a fanatical ideology which can detect Marxist conspiracies in the *Wall Street Journal;* if nothing else, this should remind democratic leaders in the West that not only is anti-Marxism a totally ineffective basis from which to resist the onslaught of totalitarianism, but it can potentially become a totalitarian force itself. Because there is in every man an instinctive reaching out for something absolute, infinite and ultimate.

Man cannot for long live in a spiritual vacuum; indeed, the spiritual iconoclasts are always the first to set up their "One and Only" surrogate god to fill it. Can there be a more striking demonstration of this tendency of the intellect to create a dogma and worship it as God, than Freud's substituting in the place of the God he had lost the image of sexuality, an image that for him was no less compelling, insistent or exacting, and of which he spoke with almost mystical emotion? In the world of politics, it is "class-consciousness" and "the voice of the blood," or the collective god in human form, "Our Leader" and "Father of the Proletariat, Son of All the Peoples," that have been given the absolute attributes and intrinsic meaning of spirituality. And in politics, the new anointed do not simply proclaim their doctrines of worldly redemption in the wildest mystical language; they give body to their strained, skeletal theories with corpses. But democratic leaders will remain powerless unless they have first had a refresher course in human nature, and come to terms with that aspect of man which both the facile optimism of the Enlightenment and the laboratory logic of the social science departments leave out: his hunger for the absolute. In our immediate experience this hunger delivered three great nations into the hands of tyrants and thousands of intellectuals to all-consuming authority. Only when we understand the nature of the need that lures men to extremes, and makes them treat a modest truth as a revelation and equate a minor mistake with fatal error, will we able to grasp the power of the totalitarian temptation.

Hayek himself has recognized the need, but his solution is yet another example of ideological vanity. "We must," he writes, "make the building of a free society once more an intellectual adventure, a deed of courage. What we lack is a liberal utopia, a program which seems neither a mere defense of things as they are nor a diluted kind of socialism. . . ."[20] Hayek has sought to establish a balance between "muddling through" and ideological formulas promising to provide unity and purpose. But the "principles" of a liberal social order that he has formulated are far too weak to satisfy man's hunger, and the utopian virtues he attributes to human freedom are simply unreal when man's reason is seen as the ultimate foundation of his life. Because reason when it is struggling to understand and live life creates either a series of more or less empirical compromises, or else general laws and fixed ideas that can be applied in practice only by doing violence to life and renouncing man's drift toward higher possibilities. Reason is either empirical or doctrinaire; and to bridge the gap between ideas and life is simply beyond its province and power. So the attempts of those few libertarians who do not actually steadfastly disdain all moral discussion to mitigate incoherence by offering "maxims" and "principles," without providing catchwords and ideological blueprints, are bound to fail.

The hungry sheep that have for so long been keeping their muzzles down in search of riches and more abundant pastures, are looking up with growing regularity. For the time being they only fall in love from afar with dictators and their autocratic regimes—especially the Third World variety. In the same way that so many quite intelligent heirs to the ideas of Jefferson and Lincoln fell in love with Mussolini, thousands of committed Western democrats have fallen in love with Nyerere—the "romantic" philosopher of the "ideal society," whose rhetoric of democracy and revolution has become a sacerdotal cloak over his tyrannical regime. "He is a democrat," we are told, "who believes that democracy in his kind of society can reach its truest expression only through a one-party state." [21] With such a rich vocabulary of deception, we can perfect our distinctions between falsehood, imposture, fraudulence and delusion—and in the process completely lose our grasp of reality. So that Hugh Jenkins, the Labour MP and ex-Minister of the Arts, could seriously declare—and continue to be treated as a democrat—that democracy should no longer be considered as a matter of one-man, one-vote, one-vote, one-value, but rather that those disposed to greater activity, whether in the trade unions or in politics, should properly be regarded as enjoying greater weight.

Freedom, like *democracy,* continues to act as a detonator word, releasing explosions of emotion in everyone within hearing distance. Except that with the progressive atrophying of those powers of discrimination which have in the past enabled us to distinguish the false from the genuine, "freedom fighter" has been adopted as an unchallenged description of anyone taking part in a resistance movement, however brutal, against the established political system of a country. It was a poet who first used the phrase—"Their freedom fighters staining red the snow"—and it is poets, thinkers and philosophers who still have the most profound influence on our lives. But life has always writhed out of the hold of their ideas and transformed them into something their originator would not recognize, or would indeed repudiate, as the very contradiction of the principles which he sought to manifest. When J. G. Herder expounded his belief in the dynamic and unique "life-spirit" of an ethnic community, and in the profound, almost mystical logic of its unfolding, or when D. H. Lawrence produced *Apocalypse,* commending thinking with our blood, or even when psychiatrists of the late nineteenth century developed their theories of eugenics and euthanasia, and called them "mental hygiene"—could anything have been further away from their thoughts than *Mein Kampf,* let alone Auschwitz and Treblinka?

Inspiration and justification for the most brutal and inhuman political actions have always been sought—and found—in the first principles of philosophers and intellectuals. And the more readily we accept the claim that man's ultimate destiny can only be fulfilled through politics, the more inextricably bound intellect and action become. Indeed, political history has been not so much a case of philosophers becoming kings, but of kings and their modern totalitarian equivalents perverting philosophy by turning it into political action. Rousseau's political theory found no purer practical expression than in Napoleon's attempt to transform the theoretical ideal of liberty and equality of people and nations into reality: the revolutionary construction of a chain of free republics with decorative classical names—the Batavian Republic, the Cisalpine, the Helvetian, the Ligurian and the Parthenopean.

By building on his idea of the social contract a generally valid system not fashioned on a specific state or nation, Rousseau laid the basis for a universal nationalism and the totalitarian state, since only the national state could serve as a concrete unit for the ideal. And even socialism, which at first seemed destined to sweep away all nationalism and national states in the irresistible current of its internationalism, could only be realized in practice through the strengthening of individual states. Marx may have taught that the worker has no fatherland, but applied Marxism has once again demonstrated the impossibility of any intellectual utopian system, including the most abstract and universal, being realized except through the all-powerful central organization of the totalitarian state. Trotsky summed up the frustration with democratic reality that besets intellectuals as they come in touch with the high reaches of power: "There is a limit to the application of democratic methods. You can inquire of all the passengers as to what type of car they like to ride in, but it is impossible to question them as to whether to apply the brakes when the train is at full speed and accident threatens." [22]

But political passengers are never in agreement as to what type of car they like to ride in. And the more complex and differentiated Western democracies become—with all the increased risks of breakdown inevitably implied—the greater is the need for the continuous regeneration that only independently and autonomously functioning individuals can provide. Yet our political leaders go on seeking in institutions, rather than in individuals, the solutions to the Western predicament. And those among them most prone to what in political circles passes for ratiocination, are trying to tame to their political uses what in our effete times passes for philosophy.

The undemocratic implications of this tendency are most eloquently—and most unintentionally—illustrated in the latest book of that exemplary democrat, Eliot Richardson.[23] "What kind of people should our institutions nurture?" is the principal question he asks; finding a social challenge that evokes a communal response—what he calls the "moral equivalent of war"—is his chief hope; and greater citizen participation in collective decisions so as to combat the "complexity explosion," his central recommendation. Only in an age which—rhetoric apart—denies the spiritual uniqueness of the individual would the question *what kind* of people should our institutions nurture be regarded as a legitimate question to be asked in a democracy by a democratic leader. However admirable the answer may be, it is the *asking* of the question that contains the seed—and more—of the totalitarian threat. Political leaders have no place formulating political aims about human character—however unexceptionable these aims may be. Nor have they the right to ask the kind of question that leads to such answers, and to the inescapably undemocratic methods that have to be followed if the answers are to be turned into realities.

As for Mr. Richardson's hope, moral equivalents to war are precisely the stuff mobs and fanatics are made of. All individual differences are suspended, and all individual impulses, aligned through narrow blinkers, point irresistibly in the same direction. Once one is in a marching column, it is extremely difficult to keep out of step. And finally we are offered that perennial wonder cure for all life's ills—greater citizen participation in collective decisions. The precise way in which this secular equivalent of the Real Presence is supposed to work its political miracles has never been elucidated. Nor has it ever been explained what precisely are the benefits of participation in collective decisions that should never have been collectively made in the first place.

The more blurred the division between the public and the private spheres becomes, the more automatically we slough off on the state our concern for others. The altruistic emotions in man are just as real as hunger, rage and fear. Yet elections are fought, political promises made, states governed—and increasingly misgoverned—on the assumption that these emotions are non-existent, and that men if left to themselves would be concerned with nothing but their self-gratification. So we go on delegating our concern for others to an impersonal state, and seeking solutions to social problems at the hopelessly futile level of political action. In this Age of Excuses, we go on seeking fault everywhere but in ourselves—indeed, regard it as socially irresponsible to do otherwise.

Even churchmen have in large numbers surrendered to this dominant illusion of salvation through political action. And among those who have not, many have given way to the opposite illusion that pervaded the formal and soulless religion of much of the Christian Middle Ages. They have turned "The Kingdom of Heaven is not of this world" into the most misused quotation from the Gospel, and have in its name opposed not only reform but life. By focusing on death they have deprived physical life of its most powerful channel of connection with spiritual life, and have thereby strengthened modern man's tendency to regard material need as the only need and material impoverishment as the only impoverishment. They are therefore partially responsible for what Walt Whitman called "the great fraud upon modern Civilization . . . the melancholy prudence of the abandonment of such a great being as a man . . . to the toss and pallor of years of moneymaking with all their scorching days and icy nights." [24]

The inevitable concomitant of this fraud was the pouring-out of much of man's vital energy, cut off as it was from the formative power of integrated spirituality, into the impossible task of transforming man and the world through political action. The belief in the political perfectibility of the world has imbued many of those possessed of it with an equally strong belief that they are also in possession of the secret instructions concerning the route to its achievement. And the more obvious it becomes that the secular Promised Land is receding instead of approaching, the greater is the intolerance toward those who have reservations as to the instructions about how best to reach it.

What then are the democratic defenses against the totalitarian temptation? And what, if anything, can modern leadership do to alert us to it?

First of all, most vitally—and, alas, least probably—it has to be equipped with the imagination and emotional power to capture the full extent of the danger. And this can only be done if we recapture the sense of the existence of evil which has been replaced in modern times by "the forces of society," "the accidents of history," and the dictators' psychopathology. Two world wars and the Gulag Archipelago should have shown, even if nothing else had, how thin are the walls which separate our quasi-civilized world from lurking chaos. The Promethean gift of consciousness in man meant that he was free to choose between good and evil. And our modern world is full, not just of men who do evil with evil intentions, but of dreamers, visionaries and men of action who do evil with the best intentions.

At the end of the last century Dostoevsky cried out what Solzhenitsyn, his spiritual heir, is crying out today: "Tyranny will become first a habit and then a disease. . . . Blood intoxicates, and minds will be open to the worst abnormalities. Such degeneracy can take place that abnormalities will seem like pure joys. . . . The opportunity for going on such a rampage often infects a whole people. Society despises the hired executioner, but not one who is provided with unlimited power. . . ." Dostoevsky's broken Promethean heroes are to be seen everywhere—increasingly more broken and less heroic. But we persist in our striving for political omnipotence, while political omniscience is taken for granted among many of our socio-democratic leaders. And we continue to play down, in the interests of "reason," the darker realities of life.

In English law, ignorance is no excuse for breaches of the law. In political life, ignorance and unawareness are not only inexcusable but the immediate cause of the most dire consequences. "I don't understand why people who were involved let that happen," said Mr. Ford of Watergate, wearing his moral ignorance like a Boy Scout badge. "It was so unnecessary, so nonessential, that it just stuns me when I look back." [25] In Greek myth and legend, man's unawareness invariably evokes the vengeance of fate; in American politics it is clearly regarded as straight-guy decency. Dr. Kissinger's critics leveled his failure to communicate the Communist threat as one of the major charges against him. What was more dismaying than Dr. Kissinger's failure to communicate the threat was his failure to grasp it; what is more dismaying still is the failure of both his critics and his friends to realize that real though the Communist threat is, infinitely more threatening is the lie in the soul of *our* civilization, and in the suppressed soul of each one of us.

But our statesmen go on proudly declaring that they have no imagination for evil, and increasingly reducing politics to crisis management. And in the fourth quarter of a century that should have taught us all how explosive the combination of short-term crises and pious desires can be, we are still pleading ignorance.

Ironically it is modern science, which in its technocratic guise has made modern totalitarianism possible, that is one of our greatest hopes for halting its spread. Rationalistic and physical science is being gradually overtaken by a mounting flood of psychological and psychic knowledge which will before long compel a new view of man, scientifically incompatible with all the simplifications, systems and abstractions that have dominated our century. The work of scientists from Einstein to Schrödinger has revolutionized the concept of matter, to the extent that the hard and fast distinction between the physical and the metaphysical no longer holds. The mystic and the physicist are now closer than ever, in relating the one to the All—the soul to the Spirit. And science, which almost succeeded in slaying religion and the religious spirit, is on the way to making doubt of eternal life as impossible as doubt of existence now is.

The triumph of science so far has been to master the forces of material nature by *knowing* them. The development of new, and the recovery of old, mental and psychic sciences is the next stage to follow the perfection of the physical sciences and to complete our mastering of nature—which, as we are prone to forget, includes *human* nature. But this can only be done by the expansion of human consciousness, by the recognition and development, that is, of those powers of knowledge which stand above the logical mind and go beyond the strictly rational part of our nature. Human nature includes man's divine potential, and so is greater and profounder than his purely intellectual consciousness; it can never be understood—let alone mastered—by the arbitrary constructions of human reason. And yet until recently the very concept of consciousness had been banned from the vocabulary of science as another occult fancy.

But the signs are unmistakable: the mechanistic trend in the material sciences, and in what is after all supposed to be the science of the psyche, is at an end. What is uncertain is whether there is still time for the modern mind to assimilate the new knowledge before the onslaught in the West of political systems based on the old. And not merely on the old, but on a perversion of the old, that treats man as consisting only of 90 percent water and 10 percent minerals.

Ultimately, our greatest hope against the totalitarian temptation lies precisely in the fact that man is *not* only 90 percent water and 10 percent minerals; that there is in every man—in some more concealed than in others—a soul spark which refuses to submit and longs to discover its larger truth. It is because there is such a larger truth to be discovered, and because, contrary to Sartrian absurdism, man does not invent his own nature as he goes along, that oppressors have never been able to breed out of man his deep, psychic need for freedom. Giving systematic oppression the varnish of rational necessity may make men accept servitude submissively, and even gratefully—this after all is the temptation we are fighting against. But authority, however totalitarian, is never secure, precisely because there is in man a quality, an energy, a soul, that is literally indomitable and that makes men different from ants, cows and domesticated fowls.

Today we watch men namelessly crowding one another in our big modern cities; we picture all the bits of human thought that are constantly adrift, floating around from mind to mind, and turning up simultaneously in New York and Timbuktou; we observe how effortlessly we can collectively change our music, manners, dress and entertainment all around the earth in a year's turning. And we begin to feel that the absolute separateness of each one of us—our whole, dear notion of one's own self and one's own soul—are nothing but a myth, and that, after all, the purpose of our species is a collective one. Well, it is not. However striking the resemblances with the kingdom of the ants and however picturesque the analogies with colonies of wasps, they are essentially meaningless. We may at times appear—all three billion of us wired together—like a stupendous animal engaged compulsively in a single, universal, fixed task. And in a sense we are. But the task is profoundly individual and has nothing to do with the collective building of a human anthill.

It is to this task that our deepest commitment is owed. We are not committed by our genes, as ants and wasps are, to drone away, all together, at the same fixed activity, at some immense, collective work, its outlines hidden forever from our sight. But we are committed by the seed of that divinity which we *all* embody—and which we call our soul—to unfold gradually our own individual, spiritual truth, and through this truth to fulfill our part in the truth and law of the collective existence. The power of this truth-seeking tendency in man has not been equally strong at all stages in our history: the impulse slackens, becomes lost in dead conventions, is renewed, modified and variously embodied in different forms and different activities. Anything we do collectively, whether it is tumbling out over Europe to build cathedrals in the twelfth century, or landing samples of ourselves on the moon in the twentieth, however compulsively we may be involved in it, is transient and secondary; it is only the physical embodiment, constantly growing and changing, of the underlying truth of things, constant and eternal, that we are committed and impelled to discover.

This process of discovery is supremely individual—a celebration of unpredictability and surprise. All the high points of our civilization have been not in the workaday fitting together of things, connecting and communicating of details, but in the abrupt, unaccountable individual moments of the "Eureka" cry. It is then that the infinite blends itself with the finite, and eternity looks through the window of time—it could be a medieval stained-glass window, or it could be Newton's equations of celestial mechanics. And we simply have no idea what window eternity will choose to look through tomorrow.

This is the supreme denial of totalitarianism: the condemnation of man to his present, and by definition, inferior potentiality. It may seem safe, rational, comfortable and secure to lead a collectively planned existence, but the self, which is growing in us but into which we have not yet grown, can never rest content with an inferior potentiality. Our aim is to become ourselves, to "exceed ourselves"—not in the tragically misconceived Nietzschean way of idealizing the will and the intellect, but by awakening our real, because our highest, self and nature.

Ants in their anthill somehow manage to coordinate and synchronize all the movements and needs of the anthill's crawling parts. There is physical effort but no mental conflict. Man alone is subjected to mental conflict, and is therefore at war not only with others but with himself. It is because he is capable of this war with himself that he is also capable of that which is impossible to ants and domesticated fowls; an inner evolution, a constant self-transcending. But this conflict and progress of ideas applied to life, which is the agent of man's perfectibility, is also the ultimate cause of his responsiveness to the totalitarian temptation. Human ideas are, after all, mental translations of the forces and tendencies of life itself, as they are manifested in the form of needs, desires and interests. To the extent that it is our material needs, our desire for security and our economic interests, that dominate our life, the temptation grows strong to ignore the aspiration of our soul toward our inner evolution and our higher potentialities, and to listen instead to the siren songs of modern totalitarians. And our soul goes undefended.

Man's rebellion against hunger and poverty is as old as the myth of Prometheus, and so is his rebellion against ignorance. But the aim of life is to be found neither in our victory over poverty nor in the triumphs of the human mind. These victories, vitally important though they are, are only a basis for the revelation in our inner and outer life of the transcendent and universal spirit, which is one and yet various in all of us. The totalitarian temptation rests and feeds on the elevation of instrumentalities into ultimate objectives. Effective resistance to the temptation can spring only from the glowing realization that what is essential for survival is not what gives value to it.

5

LEADERS, IMAGES, AND PHANTOMS

"A family with the wrong members in control," was George Orwell's summing up of Britain's leadership problems. Today, Orwell's conclusion is echoed across the democratic world. It is hardly surprising. Man cannot live without some kind of idealism, and in our secular age our political dream of a rational and mechanically perfectible society demands for its completion the advent of a socio-democratic messiah or avatar—or a committee of them to match still better the sober glamour of our ideal future. Except that the cause of the present leadership crisis is not that the wrong members are in control but that the wrong ideas are in control of all the members. And the wrong ideas will continue to be in control as long as modern man remains in the grip of the prevailing secularized mentality. So it is doubly futile to look at the members in political control for a change of direction. But as it is they who provide the *visible* leadership of democratic states, and as visibility has never mattered more than it matters today, this chapter will be devoted to our political leaders; despite the fact that, as I have stressed throughout the book, today more than ever our leaders are our followers.

We shall hold up a mirror to our political leaders; and what we shall see reflected is not only them, but ourselves: creatures only half-tamed, whose great moral task is to hold in balance the angel and the demon within. For we are both, and our leaders are both, and to ignore this duality is to invite disaster. Especially as the modern politician does not merely reflect and represent the average reason and temperament of the time, but is almost invariably nearer the minimum than the maximum of what is possible. Fear of launching out into the uncertain and new is even more entrenched among men whose self-importance is exclusively derived from the world of established appearances.

The most common fallacy in the philosophy of leadership has been the belief that a well-trained ruling class could be created, wise and disinterested enough to realize the ideal society. And the more politicized life becomes, the more important it is that those in power are as wise and disinterested as the theory of the planned, directed state automatically assumes they will be. It is a tribute to the resilience of the theory that it has survived a massive accumulation of evidence against the existence of such men.

Demands and schemes for political leaders belonging to a special class, or indeed breed, that has overcome all human limitations are very old. Plato set the stage and many fools—often otherwise extremely intelligent—walk on.

George Bernard Shaw's program for a new class of public servants "specially trained and tested as lawyers and doctors are and registered as 'naturally capable of functioning efficiently' in municipal or national office," [1] encapsulates all the worst fallacies about the exercise of political leadership. But his obsession with efficiency ("one efficient sinner is worth ten futile saints and martyrs") is a very modern obsession and a very modern misunderstanding of the role of leadership. And it persists despite the fact that no other century has suffered as much as the twentieth from "efficient" tyrants. "We have changed our system from Aristocracy to Democracy," Shaw wrote, "without considering that we were at the same time changing as regards our governing class, from selection to promiscuity. Those who have taken a practical part in modern politics best know how farcical the result is." Shaw's exasperation with politicians and his attempts to overcome their limitations by training and breeding programs, ludicrous though they may sound, follow naturally from one fundamental principle: that the domain of politics is the whole of life and that only through politics can life be transformed. Despite the egalitarian "force of history" rhetoric implied in talking of politics rather than politicians, people like Shaw recognized that politics and what can be achieved through the political process are inexorably tied up with the practitioners themselves—the petty bureaucrats, self-interested MPs, and narrow civil servants by whom Shaw himself was surrounded.

So he, and all the *illuminati* who followed, have only three options open to them:

1. Demand the limitation of the scope of politics to correspond to the limitations of men.
2. Invent fanciful programs of educating political leaders so that a race of political saints will emerge, uncontaminated by the weaknesses that membership of the human race entails.
3. (And this has turned out to be the winner.) Deny the existence of the inescapable incompatibility between collectivist politics and *human* political leadership—a denial that is not only fatuous but dangerous, since we become increasingly vulnerable to the first messiah who offers us some splendid prospect, some Caesarian, all-embracing certainty.

We laugh at the medieval vision of a world ruled by chivalry—of politics reduced to a noble game with edifying and heroic rules and of worldly salvation through the chivalric virtues of the nobility. Shallow and fantastic though this vision may have been, the vision of the secular mind of our age—if only we could for a moment step out of our period—is not only shallower and more fantastic, it is infinitely more sinister. We have replaced the chivalric fiction with the fiction of the "moderate politician." And having played down the role of the individual in politics, and the overwhelming role of ambition and the urge to prevail in the average political leader's makeup, we have assumed that moderate politicians will not countenance immoderate measures.

It is not a moment too soon to recognize the fact that moderate politicians, as much as the other variety, will bend before any wind that might help blow them into Downing Street, the White House or the Elysée. And as one harmful, unjustifiable, ridiculous, hypocritical and dictatorial policy after another is sanctioned by our political masters, we no longer have any excuse for assuming that laws and measures even more inconceivable can be ruled out, provided our leaders believe that here lies the road to office, status and what today passes for power.

Wisdom—the ability to see through the fallacies of the conventional wisdom, and the moral courage to say that they are transparent—is precisely the quality most heavily penalized by Western political systems today. The little boy who saw, and having seen proclaimed, that the emperor wore no clothes, should be the patron saint of all true leaders. But not only has no political leader since the war extended the accepted boundaries of the political debate; it is very rarely that a politician has had the courage to state the obvious within these boundaries. And then the impact—and this stresses the latent power of visible political leadership—can be devastating. When, for example, after the February 1974 General Election in Britain, Sir Keith Joseph made a speech in which he pointed out that if inflation was to be brought down, unemployment would have to be allowed to rise—a fact which every astute financial journalist in the country had been saying for years—that one speech, once the uproar had subsided, changed the terms of the political debate on these issues. But on the whole, Western politicians today are following with a vengeance the advice that Iain Macleod gave to his younger friends in the Conservative Party: "Don't stick your necks out unnecessarily, don't take up too many unpopular causes all at once; wait for the climate of opinion to change—as change it will." [2]

This approach to politics has so thoroughly dominated the exercise of political leadership in the postwar period, that we tend to assume that we understand the logic which makes its universality inevitable. The logic, however, only becomes obvious when we seek the clue to the modern politician's motivating force. To say that the common leitmotiv in the lives of political leaders, from Alexander the Great to James Callaghan, is the desire to win power, to be recognized and applauded is, of course, a truism, and like all truisms, only partially true. The danger today is that never before have the politician's self-esteem and need for recognition been so totally dependent on political office. In the past, politicians were independent personalities first and ministers second, and often only for a short time. Now that this has been reversed, politicians see in ministerial office their exclusive means of power and status. And as the pursuit of office becomes their paramount driving force, they are inevitably prone to overadminister, overgovern, underestimate the limitations of the political medium, and interpret the public interest as a bench of green leather—or whatever is the color equivalent in Continental and American assemblies.

So politics becomes—and Watergate was only a graphic demonstration of a political fact—the continuation of warfare by other means, a matter of outmaneuvering antagonists and winning games. And although the effects of politics without values are felt by all of us, its suicidal emptiness must surely be felt most acutely by the political practitioners themselves. It is this that makes them more dependent than ever on the applause of the audience and on the need to espouse policies with automatic "audience appeal." But once vanity's desire for recognition has become paramount, the political leader will find her a very expensive mistress. She will beautify herself for every national gigolo and caudillo and change her fashions according to the latest taste of any part of the electorate, however small, that makes its wishes loudly known. And they are the vainest who woo the lowest taste of their time while hotly pursuing Destiny's call, and appealing to the "verdict of posterity" and to "historical justice."

Walter Bagehot warned against "the government of immoderate persons far from the scene of action, instead of the government of moderate persons close to the scene of action." Today all warnings should be against the government of moderate persons determined at all costs to stay close to the scene of action. "Lack of power is what corrupts," said Pierre Trudeau, athlete, traveler, philosopher and highly personable man, enshrining, according to many, all the civilized democratic virtues.[3] But Trudeau missed a step in describing what lack of power does to our political leaders. What it does is not so much to corrupt them as to disorientate them; and it is that which corrupts. Politicians have always been Janus-faced entities switching from a private identity to a public one: and the more definite and coherent the private identity, the less disorientating the effect of the loss of the public persona. Today not only does the public persona seem to have completely eroded the private identity; much more alarmingly, the suspicion grows that, in an increasing number of cases, there is little for the public persona to erode or take over. When this is the case, and the politician becomes identified with his political mask, he will, not unnaturally, do anything not to have his mask torn away. And then there never is an "opportune moment" for a politically courageous stand. So the political leader *de nos jours* yells, makes fierce faces and emits strange shouts, but we all know that it is only for show, and nobody—let alone our politician himself—is going to get hurt.

It was courage which Pericles identified in his Funeral Oration as the first quality that made Athens great. It is courage that Western political leadership most conspicuously lacks and most urgently needs. Not the often hysterical courage evoked by the presence of an enemy; not simply the golden mean between rationalism and cowardice; but the courage that Plato defined as the knowledge of what is not to be feared. This is the supreme knowledge; but it can only spring from an inner harmony within the individual, not from his impersonal role or his objective political function. With this knowledge goes a refusal to succumb to fear, or to the passion for security—whether it is the fear of loss of office or the security of public status. Without this knowledge, the public man is at the mercy of expediency and circumstances, and public acclaim or mere political survival becomes the motive force of his actions. And the greater the power attached to his public persona, the more the political leader lives in a world of make-believe and the more dependent he becomes on the continued existence of his world.

It is only wishful ignorance of this truth that can explain the gasp of censorious shock that went up from one end of Western political lands to the other when Richard Nixon spectacularly demonstrated the unhinging effects of the grotesque concentration of executive power in the hands of one man, and the ruthless lengths to which that man would go to prevent its "untimely" loss.

Political authority, sociologists and anthropologists tell us, is impervious to the logic of everyday life, and to be effective must command the motives which spring from beyond the area of calculated stratagems and spoils, from the symbols that remain ineffable and unknown. And yet we have reached the point when all three bases of authority—logic, spoils and symbols—are alarmingly precarious. The alarm springs from the fact that no democracy can survive the collapse of political authority. The question now is how long authority can survive when national symbols are becoming less ineffable and more feeble day by day; when the expectation of a stable, let alone a growing, supply of material spoils is increasingly based on faith alone; and when it requires only the most elementary logic to establish that many of the legislative and administrative measures pursued by Western political leaders in the last few years, far from mitigating the dangers Western democracies are facing, have actually increased them.

The growing contempt for politicians is not only gradually bringing about the collapse of political authority, it is also leading to a dangerous decline in the quality, and narrowing of the range, of those willing to seek office. A situation arises where political leaders are chosen among an increasingly narrow circle of men, uniquely ambitious, insensitive and conformist. Chesterton may have been exaggerating when he claimed that as democracy means getting those people to vote who would never have the cheek to govern, the people who ought to govern are the people who have not the cheek to do it. But there is no doubt that comical though the prospect of a country run by its most diffident people may be, the state we are reaching at the moment is just as comical, especially as what was first coined as a witticism is becoming dangerously true: "The wrong sort of people are always in power because they would not be in power if they were not the wrong sort of people."

At the same time that the status of the actors has diminished, the importance of the play has increased. Political power is no longer the Platonic supreme mission or the divine duty of medieval thought, and yet in order to meet the excessive demands made on the political process, it makes greater encroachments into private life today than ever before. And so since the war, hand in hand with the conviction that the progress of sociology, psychology, systems analysis and Keynesian economics have made it possible for government to accomplish things which no government ever dreamt, let alone attempted, before, has gone a growing contempt for politicians, as it became inescapably obvious that they were failing to meet these massive expectations.

But it is essential in a democracy that politics be regarded as an honorable and not merely an unavoidable profession. Yet all the evidence is that the politicians are growing more suspect every day, symbolizing as they do the wretched gospel of failure that has become the distinguishing characteristic of Western political life. And the people's hold on their democratic beliefs is slackening with every diminution of political authority, until perhaps the Roman cry, "Authority in the Senate, Power in the People," is heard again in a dangerous reincarnation: "Authority in No One, Power in the Bureaucracy."

For the time being there is a general, unmistakable feeling abroad that as far as our leaders are concerned, "our expectation hath this day an end." The uninterrupted postwar trend toward treating government like a science, as exact as chemical analysis, has reached a stumbling block. The trend, accompanied as it has been by the development of the political arts of showmanship, compromise and maneuver, reached its symbolic culmination with Harold Macmillan. He brought to a head all the elements of sterile, technocratic leadership that had long existed in isolation; he threw them all together, and in their fusion they revealed in its full glory a new form and style of leadership that was not merely accepted as a standard to be followed, but gradually as the only sort of leadership expected to work.

"One of the most remarkable men, Harold Macmillan—I've always had a great admiration for him as a Prime Minister—while we had great, almost historic duels and the House used to fill up whenever it happened, even on the Committee stage of a Finance Bill . . . I think he was a great Prime Minister." [4] Could there be a more deadly tribute than this one, from the man who carried Macmillan's political wizardry and fudging of all issues to a degree that finally snapped credibility? Macmillan and Wilson—the self-satisfied patrician, aping what he thought was the idiom of the masses, and the purposive, white-heat, full twentieth-century citizen—between them they emptied British politics of all political principle. But it was Macmillan who first vulgarized political leadership, and then made the vulgarization respectable.

The day after the 1959 election, before British politics had fully assimilated the irrevocable shift in style and priorities, Trog produced a cartoon for *The Spectator* showing Macmillan seated at the Cabinet table with the other chairs filled by washing machines, refrigerators and cars: "Well, gentlemen," he is depicted as saying, "I think we fought a successful campaign." It has been quite a few years now since any cartoonist would have thought a cartoon on similar lines funny. Fighting elections with washing machines and refrigerators has been the order of the day for too long to seem incongruous. The shrinking scale of politics and politicians has been accepted as inevitable—as has the apparently limitless willingness of political leaders to debase themselves before the glittering prizes of supreme office.

The refusal to have recourse to principle, and the distrust of what the human mind and the human imagination can achieve, have been enshrined in the don't-make-trouble philosophy that has dominated Western politics under the unexceptionable guise of "unity." "The watchword of the democratic party will be unity," trumpeted Macmillan in 1946, during the speech that launched his campaign for a new name and a new policy for the Conservative Party, "and unity will command self-sacrifice in every class, rank and calling." Party unity was also what Harold Wilson saw as his first and highest political duty, and his undeviating lack of candor, coupled with the Olympian detachment with which he viewed the gradual collapse of Britain and the rapid debauching of the English language, made it possible for him to fashion frail bridges of words and keep his party together. Unity has been the leitmotiv of Jim Callaghan's career too; and standing, as he does, for nothing except the tactics of politics, he has been able to find forms of words that, meaning everything, can mean anything, and so whatever else he may have been untrue to, he has never betrayed his passion for unity. Unity was also the siren song that led Jimmy Carter astray: he fought and captured his own party, but in the process of bringing it back together, he was captured by it, and began to sing all the postwar political canticles, and to sound and look as exhausted as the clichés and parodies of clichés that he was mouthing.

What, then, is the meaning of "unity"? From where does an appeal to unity draw the strength that has turned a legitimate and unavoidable concern with conciliation into the beckoning light to which postwar leaders have been irresistibly drawn, and in the reflection of which they have constantly succumbed to the temptation to deny reality? The clue, as so often, lies not in the world of politics but in our culture—and more specifically, in the cultural climate of our all-questions-are-open-questions society. When Oscar Wilde called truth something so personal that the same truth can never be recognized by two different minds, and when Nietzsche declared that "it is only moral prejudice to assert that truth is more valuable than appearance," I wonder whether they could have suspected that their precious, *fin-de-siècle* statements would become the gospel of our proudly pluralist age—dominating the climate to which politicians have been reacting. When the various interests and ideas of the political world are morally neutral, then different political beliefs—including, at the extreme, Communism and Western democracy—are treated as nothing more than subjective attachments to be managed in such a way as to reduce tension. In a cultural climate which attaches no independent value to the pursuit of truth because it attaches no value to absolute truth the modern political leader will best achieve his functions if he has no ultimate values to which the all-consuming pursuit of an illusory unity might have to be sacrificed.

"If there is one thing worse than the modern weakening of major morals, it is the modern strengthening of minor morals. . . . It is the great peril of our society that all its mechanisms may grow more fixed while its spirit grows more futile." [5] And what Chesterton prophesied has indeed come to pass. Secondary objectives, such as unity and reconciliation, are treated as primary, and second-rate skills in management and administration extolled as uniquely important. But not only has unity failed to lead us to the land of political milk and honey, it is also becoming increasingly difficult to achieve. For unity is based on certain common and commonly accepted valuations, and these are in turn paper currency based on a fast diminishing proportion of gold. The gold is the spiritual truth on which Western civilization and its culminating principle of liberal democracy are based, and on the reserves of which they have been feeding. It is from this truth that our democratic standards and values have emerged, lived and been modified into readily applied empiricism and common sense. Today the ultimate spiritual values have been so thoroughly eroded that the process has been reversed, and we expect pragmatism and common sense to be the ruling principles of our political life. And through an artificial unity we hope to prevent the complete breakdown of those common premises on which our society is based. But once the reserves of gold at the center dry up, our vaunted empiricism is worthless and common sense itself in danger.

"Britain has lived for too long," announced Callaghan with that touching lack of self-awareness that seems to be his trademark, "on borrowed time, borrowed money and even borrowed ideas." [6] It really does make reason falter to hear a man who has in his long political life never been heard to utter anything other than the ritual phrases, and sing any other than the ritual songs, accusing Britain of living on borrowed ideas. The truth is, of course, that it is not just Mr. Callaghan who has been living off borrowed ideas, but all Western political leaders who have refused to make a turn into their own minds, have silenced their inner doubts, and have surrendered to the collective aura that ritual repetitions of the belief in political salvation have created. Our surrender to the contemporary political mythology springs from the belief that when it comes to our personal opinions, we are answerable for their uprightness, not for their rightness; this fallacy, underpinning our cultural pluralism today, automatically absolves us of all responsibility to go on trying to recognize the good, and to express in our opinions no less than in our lives the highest truth that is in each of us.

The present clamoring for unity—both in its everyday guise of party political unity and in its idealized preoccupation with collective unity—has its source in one of the highest aspirations of humanity: to transcend the struggle and opposition of ideas, impulses and interests which have plagued our history. But, as there is no discoverable common collective reason, the solution everywhere in the ascendant is to get rid of disorder, strife and waste by renouncing freedom and subordinating the life of the individual to the life of the collectivity, the beliefs of the individual to the beliefs of the collectivity—and the principles of the individual politician to the policies of the party. This is to substitute the arbitrary rigidity and straight line of mechanical reason for the vigor, richness and difficult curves of the process that springs from individual freedom. And the artificial unifying remedies, based on mechanical devices and the sacrifice of personal principles, do not merely fail to lead us to the political Promised Land; they also retard the spiritual progress of the individual for which he needs all the freedom he can get—both to stumble in action and to err in knowledge.

We are seeing everywhere how easily our Western pluralism is bending under the pressure of an imposed uniformity. Only a society unified by belief in a spiritual truth can ultimately practice tolerance; for only then are individual pursuits of the truth, and individual or group disagreements, sanctified by the conviction that, however different our three-dimensional approaches to a four-dimensional truth may be, such a truth, far from being an hallucination, is the supreme reality. Only a spiritual, a greater than rational, individual enlightenment can impose harmony on our self-seekings, antagonisms and discords. Because only a spiritualized society—which far from denying reason is actually built on reason transformed and lifted to a higher power—can bring about the reign of unity and equality which political leaders are vainly seeking today in an artificial uniformity, and which men have always, just as vainly, sought in each great new turn and revolution of politics and society.

The inner spiritual change needed is difficult. But if this is not the solution, then there is no solution, and if this is not the way, then there is no way except an outwardly symmetrical totalitarianism, within which our devitalized individuality, dwarfed and robbed of its freedom, will slowly perish. Pundits, commentators and electorates alike have for years now been calling for political leaders with a "coherent vision," clear principles and definite ideas about the sort of future they want for their country—without being remotely specific themselves about the vision, the principles and the future they would like to see promoted. Well, there is only one vision that can legitimately inspire political leaders, without at the same time goading them to turn the vision into reality through state action: it is the vision of a society which has put an end to the division between life and spirit, and has discovered the true aim of human progress in a new turning inward, toward man's soul.

Human society has never before seized on the discovery of the soul as a means for the discovery of its own being. Religion has never been more than an appearance: it has looked at man's life, mind and body as mortal members which have only to be dropped off, for the rescued spirit to flee away into the heavens beyond. But then man need never have left the heavens beyond if he had no divine business here, in the world of physical, vital and mental nature. The vision of a spiritualized society is as far away from theocracy as it is from secular totalitarianism. And this is why the first function of a political leadership informed by this vision would be to recognize that man, as he grows in his true spiritual being, must have as much free space as possible; his growth and experience of himself can only deepen and increase through his freedom to err, and to choose wrongly. So the first step of a political leader who did have such a coherent vision of what his country might be—and those who insist on calling for leadership that will supply a "coherent vision," but disagree with this use of the words, should be asked to say quickly and in plain words what kind of vision, compatible with freedom, *they* have in mind—would be to remove all the fetters and yokes that buy their results at a heavy cost to human freedom and to man's spiritual progress.

"Political leaders," Jimmy Carter informs us, "must be willing to tackle economic problems head on, without timidity or fear." This is the view of leadership which feeds on our economic monomania, on our arrested spiritual development and on our leaders' chronic inability to remember where tackling economic problems head on—with or without timidity or fear—has led Western democracies so far. It is the view that has driven politics into the realm of mere administration; it has turned the Giscard d'Estaings, the Trudeaus and the Callaghans into increasingly authoritarian managers of political events, never permitting any commitment to ideas to deprive them of the executive ecstasy for which they long. "While you run the mile," said Aneurin Bevan, "there is no time to take your pulse." While running the mile remains the sole acknowledged aim, both of the individual and the collective life, then this is indeed the only possible approach to political leadership.

Sociologists divide the art of governing into the science of problem-solving—the instrumental function, as they call it—and the art of keeping the group together—the expressive function. When social objectives are seen as exclusively economic, then the instrumental gifts of man-management and administration completely eclipse every consideration of a leader's expressive role. As a result, the public is assaulted on all fronts by bureaucratic authority, increasingly meaningless and oppressive, without any positive payoff for this continued erosion of freedom—an unstable situation which makes totalitarianism both more tempting and much easier to impose.

But even in our pragmatic century the man of ideas has not always been beaten by the manager. De Gaulle is the rare postwar example of a democratic leader combining expressive with instrumental qualities. On paper, often ridiculous; in practice, irresistible. He had what political leaders conspicuously lack today—a sense of history and clearly worked-out ideas about leadership and politics; amidst the rubble of a derelict civilization, the vacuity, fantasy and triviality of a moribund culture, he helped revive France.

Gandhi was the other outstanding example—although in a very different cultural context—of a twentieth-century leader whose influence, unsupported as it was by any sort of ceremonial trappings or material resources, rested on the three main weapons of unalloyed leadership: personality, example and oratory. It would be absurd for any modern political leader to seek to emulate De Gaulle, and still less Gandhi—although the idea is worth entertaining, for the sheer pleasure of picturing Callaghan or Carter in loincloth, blessing the crowds from the lotus position.

There is only one reason for singling out De Gaulle among postwar leaders, and it has little to do with the use of De Gaulle as a model of leadership and still less with the particular causes he espoused and values he incarnated. If I have isolated De Gaulle's leadership, it is to prove that within the Western democratic framework, and in our own postwar period, it is still possible for a political leader to transcend his reactive nature and *create* his own role while remaining scrupulously true to the principles of freedom and democracy—provided he has the courage and the conviction necessary to ignore the hallowed rules of the political game as it is being played at the moment.

"When are you going to take action, *mon Général?*" asked one of his aides when people began to call for his return. "*J'attends la catastrophe,*" was the reply. Well, *la catastrophe* is here; all but those who have had every rudiment of imagination bred out of them recognize that our predicament contains every possible catastrophic element, and more, and that we are in it *now* and not about to meet it over the next hill but one. And yet there are no signs anywhere in the democratic world of a political leader prepared to arrest the stampede toward suicidal collectivism in practice—and the descent to the senseless in rhetoric. It is this complete absence of any effort towards a new and personal understanding of the Western predicament on behalf of our leaders that makes the conclusion inescapable that, if we wish to change what the thermometer registers, we should concentrate on altering the temperature instead of blaming the mercury.

"I did check in three weekends, how many different subjects you have to deal with, pronounce upon, write or act on or get something started, take decisions, and they were about 500 each weekend in the usual four or five boxes." [7] Only a man as far advanced in self-deception as Harold Wilson could possibly count the number of decisions he took each weekend, the number of Cabinet meetings he attended (472), and the number of parliamentary questions he answered (*more* than 12,000), and then go on to talk with still more perverse pride about the "compulsion of taking decisions" and "the great pressures you are under when you have got five or six or seven things all at the same time . . . acting or reacting one on top of another." And neither he nor any other Western political leader seems able to make the connection between this managerial view of political leadership and the disastrous state of the countries over which such leadership is exercised.

Political leadership has maneuvered itself into a cul-de-sac, and there is nowhere to go along the established way. We can either curse the stumbling block or transform it into the cornerstone of a new conception of politics. "Can I ask you finally what do you go home and say in moments of economic crisis?" Lord Armstrong, the former head of the Civil Service, was asked in 1974, and his reply should become the guiding light for a new approach to leadership: "Thank God, the government's influence is so little." Only by asking ultimate, or at least penultimate, questions will politicians be able to give ultimate or at least approximately right, rather than systematically false, answers. "To invent you must think aside" [8]—and to lever ourselves out of our own political deadweight, we need a fixed point, an Archimedean support, outside two-dimensional politics. Those who believe that the solution is to be found in National Emergency Governments with urgent recovery programs, are effectively proposing to carry the artificial remedies which have stifled our powers of healthy action to their utmost. The leadership needed is not the leadership of impressionable politicians overwhelmed by anything tangible and loud, and unable to think except in terms of crises and emergencies, but of men who refuse to accept the facts standing around as coercive, and allow instead the inner realities of the current conditions to dictate their decisions.

So-called charismatic leadership is, in fact, based on the distinction between what happens in the minds of men and what happens on the political ground—between the cultural outlook and the political facts and figures. Charismatic leaders depend on their ability to attract support by incarnating the desires of their followers, rather than on constraining them by the threat of force or the offer of rewards. And here lies the great potential danger to freedom and democracy posed by charismatic leaders: "The natural leaders in distress," wrote Weber, who first introduced the term, "have been holders of specific gifts of the body and spirit; and these gifts have been believed to be supernatural, not accessible to everybody. The concept of 'charisma' is here used in a completely 'value neutral sense.' " There is little chance today of believing charismatic gifts to be supernatural; but the "value-neutrality" of charisma is as much a danger now as it has ever been. A charismatic leader is guided by the unexpressed desires of his times and shows the way to the attainment of that which everyone blindly craves; but cravings *are* blind and charisma is indeed neutral, so the attainment may result in good or evil, in the healing of an epoch or in its destruction.

The inaudible murmurings in our souls are longing for a conscious expression: a charismatic leader can use his political creativity to help our times only if he strengthens and protects our freedom to seek by ourselves the directing light and the harmonizing law of our lives. If he incarnates these unconscious longings himself, rejects the need for individual, spiritual fulfillment, and focuses them instead on an external enemy—black, Jew, capitalist or any picturesque permutation of all three—the murmurings, far from being hopeful beginnings of our effort at greater consciousness, will turn out to be dark portents of more universal catastrophies; the leader's political creativity will have been used to create political nightmares. But for both the reason-mongers who deny the existence of a psychic reality and those Christians who confine spiritual truth to a supernatural or historical reality, the possibility that the ultimate threat to our freedom comes from the undercurrents of our psychic life is anathema.

Recognition of this truth does not mean that we should stop trying to improve the institutional safeguards of our freedom or that we should stop fighting against our totalitarian enemies, or indeed that we should stop denouncing their lies. What it does mean is that by becoming aware of the nature of the ultimate threat we will more clearly understand where our enemies' strength lies; our gropings toward reform at the institutional level will be less ill-informed, and our expectations of what can be achieved through such reforms more realistic. At the moment every feature of Western political systems is under attack—not excluding, in Britain, Parliament itself, which was described by Mr. Short, when he was actually leader of the House of Commons, as an impediment to effective government.[9] Others, who lack Mr. Short's indecent frankness, are advocating reforms most of which would simply accelerate the concentration of political power—in the name, of course, of progress and democracy.

The *Reader's Digest* would fulfill a great service for modern Western democracies if it condensed and distributed with every ballot Suetonius's *Twelve Caesars*, an intimate narrative of twelve men wielding excessively concentrated political power. Nero, who started well, became progressively irrational. Domitian, an intelligent man of some charm, let the innate human cruelty flower monstrously upon succeeding to the Principate. And even the stern Tiberius's character was ruined and transformed by the violent influence of absolute power. Human nature has not changed since the first century A.D. as much as we naïvely like to believe. It is only the political technology at the leader's disposal that has changed—and made his power potentially even more absolute.

The long retreat from ideas and principles heralded by Machiavelli reached its consummation in the "scientific approach" to leadership, and its supreme expression in the person of Henry Kissinger, who is undoubtedly the archetypal exponent of the genre: the politician as sub-Machiavellian technocrat, a technocrat not even of politics but of administration. Relying on think tanks, intelligence units, research and strategy teams—all regarded as essential adjuncts of modern leadership—he seemed increasingly blinkered by the quasi-scientific material called to his political aid. So blinkered, in fact, that even justice and human dignity were reduced in his mind to questions of efficiency: "No system," he said during one of his continual press conferences, referring to South Africa, "that leads to periodic upheavals and violence can possibly be just or acceptable."[10] What is alarming is not so much the idea of the then official Defender of the Free World committing the sin of reductionism of ultimate values—but the fact that he was blissfully unaware of having committed any sin at all.

Across the Atlantic, the force-feeding of our leaders by an ever-burgeoning technocratic bureaucracy with data and information of a hitherto unequal abundance and precision is just as unremitting. "I have yet to see a Minister," wrote Richard Crossman in his diaries, "prevail against an inter-departmental official paper without the backing of the Prime Minister, the First Secretary or the Chancellor." Civil Service committees which parallel Cabinet committees, he went on to explain, meet beforehand to go over the agenda of the Cabinet and reach provisional conclusions—which turn out to be remarkably permanent. So one of the most important aspects of political leadership, the ability to shed new light on problems already examined a hundred times by political technicians, and to distinguish what is essential from what is merely important or actually trivial, has been done away with. And political leaders, fascinated by the machine, forget to ask where the machine is taking us.

"The more the narrow interests of the present," wrote Schiller, "keep the minds of men on the stretch, and subjugate while they narrow, the more imperative is the need to free them through the higher universal interest in that which is purely human and removed beyond the influences of time, and thus once more to reunite the divided political world under the banner of Truth and Beauty." The need to free politicians' minds from their complete subjugation to the narrow interests of the day was recognized by Winston Churchill when as Leader of the Opposition, he refused exact allocations and restrictive covenants within the Shadow Cabinet. Heath, in explaining why he rejected Churchill's method, claimed that it was contrary to the electorate's expectations of specialized knowledge from ministers and prospective ministers. It would have been truer to say that for a very long time electorates have not been given any other choice from politicians in opposition, let alone from those in government. The result has been a growing tendency to treat Party Political Manifestos as substitutes for thinking and "imperative" Civil Service data as substitutes for principles.

"But politics, like it or not," Sir Dingle Foot has assured us, and many have concurred, "is always a matter not so much of principles as of personalities." [11] Leaving aside for a moment the fact that it is not, contemplation of the "personalities" dominating Western politics today is not likely to make the blood race, the eyes glow and the step quicken. What it is likely to do is induce a state of deepening gloom. This is not because of the absence of any originality and political creativity among our leaders—universal though this absence undoubtedly is—but because of the far more dangerous absence of independent-mindedness among them. Their political lives are bounded not merely by conventions of political form, but by the stalest conventions of political thought and the most meaningless conventions of political expression. This applies to the small number of "first-rate" minds no less than to the rest, and is precisely for this reason the single most ominous feature of modern leadership.

It was this capacity to remain blinkered against reality which so forcibly struck Tocqueville in his analysis of the *Ancien Régime:*

> It was not surprising that the nobility and middle classes, so long excluded from all public action, should have displayed this strange inexperience; but what astonishes far more is, that the very men who had the conduct of public affairs, the ministers, the magistrates and the intendants, should not have evinced more foresight. Many of them, nevertheless, were

> very clever men in their profession, and were thoroughly possessed of all the details of the public administration of their time; but in that great science of government, which teaches the comprehension of the general movement of society, the appreciation of what is passing in the minds of the masses, and the foreknowledge of the probable results—they were just as much novices as the people itself.

Today the technocratic veneer on the modern politicians' ignorance has turned them into muted, identikit figures compared to whom the typical political figures of the past show up as clearcut and idiosyncratic as characters in Dickens. But there is nothing more dangerous than to have the conventional ideas of the political novice supported by brains and a stock of mental skills, superior to the conventional.

We have long suspected that we could not unequivocally trust intellectuals in politics, however attractive and imposing they may be. The American people not only suspected but acted on the suspicion when in 1972 they rejected that final degradation of the Stevensonian tradition of intellect detached from reality, George McGovern, even though this meant delivering America into the hands of Richard Nixon. What we are now discovering the hard way is that not only intellectuals, but practical men of practical intelligence can be fools, as the careers of Harold Wilson, Giscard d'Estaing and Pierre Trudeau—to mention only three out of a fast-multiplying breed—and of the highly intelligent, practical bureaucrats at the center of political power, prove.

Democracy is based on the assumption that the important functions of government are simple enough to be understood by everyone: it is this which makes the present emphasis on expertise and complex centralization so irrevocably undemocratic. This is not intended to idealize wisdom brought out of the forest, let alone to glorify illiteracy, but to isolate lack of reflectiveness as the worst illiteracy of all. Ernest Bevin was a semi-literate man who found the simple business of writing a letter arduous; but he was an instinctive, though limited, political leader. Harry Truman is another postwar leader who, though not highly educated, refused to take any notice of the research bureaucracies on offer, and based his political decisions on simple political insight, understanding of human nature and instinct for the "right thing." Both he and Bevin had the confidence to assume the responsibilities of power without hiding behind mammoth research backups. They were undoubtedly often wrong, but not as often and, more important, not as wrong, as today's infinitely better-informed and elaborately advised professional politicians. These may be able to function in short periods of normality, but are hopelessly inadequate once the machine—partly as a result of their own efforts—begins to break down.

"What I fear," said Woodrow Wilson during the 1912 campaign, "is a government of experts. God forbid that in a democratic country we should resign the task and give the Government over to experts. What are we for if we are to be scientifically taken care of by a small number of gentlemen who are the only men who understand the job? Because if we don't understand the job, then we are not a free people. We ought to resign our free institutions and go to school to somebody and find out what it is we are about. I want to say I have never heard more penetrating debate of public questions than I have sometimes been privileged to hear in clubs of working men."[12] This is not the false idealization of the working man, so unconvincingly perpetrated by Harold Wilson when he cultivated his Yorkshire accent, or by Tony Benn when he progressively doctored his *Who's Who* entry to hide the disgraceful truths of his Westminster, New College Oxford education.

What Woodrow Wilson meant when he extolled the wisdom of the common man was identical to what Thomas Jefferson meant when he wrote to his nephew in 1787: "State a moral case to a ploughman and a professor. The former will decide it as well, and often better than the latter, because he has not been led astray by artful rules."[13] And what they both meant was made unequivocally clear by Wilson himself when he unceasingly placed what he called "character" above both intellectual and practical abilities. No twentieth-century political leader has a greater claim to be considered an intellectual than Woodrow Wilson; and yet he continually returned with prophetic foresight, both in his writings and in his speeches, to the same theme: "Character is far more important than intellect to the race as to the individual. . . . Oh, how I wish I could warn all my countrymen against that most degrading of processes, the deification of mere intellectual acuteness, wholly unaccompanied by moral responsibility. . . ." His warning has not been heeded either by his countrymen or by the rest of the Western world; and the spiritual quality in man—in *every* man—which he called character has been relegated to the province of shimmering rhetoric.

Learning and intellect are not simply compatible with this spiritual wisdom—they can help to bring it into greater consciousness and give it greater expression. But when it comes to intellect and learning, this is *par excellence* the age of the philistine politician. G. M. Trevelyan summed up the decline: "In the seventeenth century, Members of Parliament quoted the Bible, in the eighteenth and nineteenth centuries, the classics, and in the twentieth century, nothing." (Perhaps because Harold Robbins, although at least as widely read, is not yet considered as eminently quotable.) Politicians have become exclusively committed to action: either the action that draws its inspiration from the uncouth vocabulary of sterile philosophical systems and controversies, with Marxism the most ensnaring and most sterile of all, or the action that springs from nothing other than expediency and abstruse economic calculations. At the one end of the spectrum we have Hitler expounding his philosophy in *Mein Kampf* and Nasser crowning a successful coup d'état with a *Philosophy of the Revolution;* and at the other, we have the obligatory conveyor-belt memoirs by our pragmatic leaders equating statesmanship with the ability to wade your way through a mountain of action-memos.

"Handsome editions of memoirs, Italian and French biographies, court histories, diaries of politicians—away with them! Have the politicians ever been right? Has not a single verse by Hölderlin not been of more value than all the wisdom of the potentates! Away with them."[14] Hermann Hesse wrote that when he was reorganizing his library in 1919. If he had been writing today and his library had included Harold Macmillan's *The Middle Way,* Harold Wilson's *The Labour Government, 1964-1970* (not to mention *Sir* Harold Wilson's *The Governance of Britain*), Jimmy Carter's *Why Not the Best?* and Lord Avon's *Full Circle,* his statement would be infinitely truer, though less dramatically arresting. In any case, the wisdom of the potentates, especially in pre-election campaigns when it is most readily on offer, is these days largely the product of their "lengthened shadows." John Kennedy's preconvention "lengthened shadow" in 1960 included, apart from his brother Robert as general manager of operations and Lawrence O'Brien as "commander" of the organizational base, Theodore Sorensen as "ideas" man and star draftsman—or as John Kennedy called him with unconscious candor "my intellectual blood bank."

But ideas are not produced by idea-specialists, nor are principles supplied by "intellectual blood banks." What these provide is the supreme reduction of life to a standard of so-called living, and the aura of technological omniscience with which our leaders invest themselves in their role of beneficent agents of the democratic consensus. "The central domestic problems of our time relate not to basic clashes of philosophy or ideology, but to ways and means of reaching common goals, to research for sophisticated solutions to complex and obstinate issues . . .they demand subtle challenges for which technical answers—not political answers—must be provided." No doubt the intellectual blood bank which supplied this passage from John Kennedy's Yale Commencement Speech in 1962 has come to fulfill the law expounded by Engels nearly a hundred years earlier, when he prophesied that authority will lose "its political character and be transformed into the simple administrative function of watching over the true interests of society." There was a time when the principal recognized function of political rulers, except at rare and short intervals, was to provide peace and the conditions in which justice could obtain. The transformation of political rulers to political leaders whose aim is—the words are Franklin Roosevelt's—"to solve for the individual the ever-rising problems of a complex civilization," is the single most significant change in the behavior of political figures. It cuts across the frontier between democracies and totalitarian regimes—which, considering that its intellectual provenance is distinctly undemocratic, is hardly surprising—and it calls for dash, initiative, campaigns, drives—in a word, for action.

The supreme irony is that in Britain, the exemplar of the "dynamic" transformation of Government to what *Punch* as early as the First World War called *govertisement*, or "government by advertisement," was a "faded, attitudinising Turf Club bummaree," [15] with Edwardian cricket boots, carefully darned undergraduate waistcoats, shooting gaiters *and* patches on his hacking jacket. The record of Macmillan's premiership reads today like a parody of all the liberal panaceas ever dreamt up in particularly unimaginative sociology departments. From his embracing of economic planning and an incomes policy to the setting up of seven new universities confidently expected to usher in the millennium, the same theme ran through Macmillan's burst of dynamic activity: the conviction that Supermac could somehow, through planning, exhorting and fresh advertising campaigns, after every fresh failure, *think* a new nation into being. So that by the end of his premiership, Supermac, the cartoon that Vicky had created from a conflation of Macmillan and Superman, looked quite sedate compared to the flamboyant postures of omniscience, ubiquity and supernatural power adopted by the Prime Minister himself.

Carlyle described Disraeli as a conjurer, leading the British people "by the nose, like helpless, mesmerised, somnambulant cattle." But at least Disraeli by a series of intuitive flashes had arrived at a coherent theory of Tory democracy and a clear vision of where he would like the country to go. There is not the slightest evidence that Macmillan's vision of Britain was anything other than of a society of illusions in which at regular intervals the Tory Party, newly transformed by him into a model social-engineering party, would convince the electorate that there is more and better politically contrived happiness the Tory way than any other way. As for his vaunted political virtuosity, it was the virtuosity of night club pianists, acrobats, and tightrope walkers, automatically practicing the mechanical part of an art.

The most unequivocal sign of the dwarfish state of modern political leadership is Macmillan's sudden transformation after a succession of TV performances into "the last of the giants." The race of giants has surely died out, if claimants for the status of giant have to be drawn from the conjurers' profession—because as a conjurer Macmillan was truly great. Not only did he succeed in completely obliterating the boundary between illusion and political reality, he also managed to convince the country—which admittedly was not adverse to being convinced—that there is a sort of Xanadu fountain that inexorably throws up riches and that this abundance is both unlimited, provided it is responsibly planned from the top, and endlessly fulfilling. "When a line of action is said to be supported 'by all responsible men,' it is nearly always dangerous and foolish," wrote "the last of the giants" in his recently published *Past Masters,* sublimely oblivious of how brilliantly he passes his own test.

"He was a statesman of the moment. Whatever was not wanted now, whatever was not practicable now, whatever would not take now, he quite drove out of his mind." It is hard to imagine that Bagehot said this of Palmerston, whose political preoccupations seem as philosophically general as McTaggart's bubbling on about the Absolute, compared to the relentlessly mundane preoccupations of our modern leaders. Yet nineteenth-century politicians were far from oblivious of the need to communicate and appeal to the people at the level of their own interests and concerns. Gladstone, after all, practically invented modern electioneering when he descended on Scotland to conduct his hugely successful Midlothian campaign. His speeches, with their high tone and a complete absence of materialistic appeal, illustrate to perfection the difference between demagogy that springs from conviction and ideas and demagogy that springs from the desire of cartoon-strip politicians for office, and from the thoughts and wit of PR men, experts and speechwriters.

Politicians and world-weary pundits have been telling us for years that in a mass democracy the exigencies of the image are so great that no real person and no "broad sweep" principles can survive. But this is to misunderstand the nature of the problem and assume that it is caused by the need in a democracy to project and communicate, rather than by the fact that modern leaders have nothing to communicate. The use and abuse of the "need to communicate" is exemplified in our own time by the contrast between Kennedy and De Gaulle. When James Reston asked Kennedy, after he was elected president, what his philosophy was, what vision did he have of the good life, he got a blank stare for an answer—hailed by Kennedy apologists as proof of their man's essentially pragmatic (the age's favorite euphemism for opportunist) nature. "Half the 'mick' politician, tough, earthy, bawdy, sentimental, and half the bright, graceful, intellectual Playboy of the Western World," was Benjamin Bradlee's description of the President. And the two halves added up to a PR dream of a presidential image—and very little else.

The contrast with De Gaulle could not be more complete. Fully aware of the central importance of communication in a mass democracy, De Gaulle, actually coached by a man from the Comedie Française, was a complete master of the art of TV politics; as for meeting the people, as Jacques Soustelle put it: "To say that he mixes with a crowd is an understatement, he plunges in it, wallows in it." But because he had a vision of France which did not stop at the Elysée, he could never have said what Harold Wilson did say: "A lot of politics is presentation and what isn't presentation is timing." And Wilson's opponents, although not nearly as skillful at either presentation or timing, began to talk incessantly of political "packages". Principles were reduced to a particularly stiff poster of Mr. Heath entitled: "Edward Heath, Man of Principle."

So political language became disembodied, an instrument to be seized and used by the strongest and the least scrupulous. But when issues are treated in terms of public relations and "image," politics becomes an annex of the advertising industry, and the ethics of politics the ethics of salesmanship. "When someone comes to you with an idea," as Michael Heseltine put it, "you ring up the marketing director and then sell, sell, sell": this is the political creed not just of Mr. Heseltine, but of a growing breed of politicians who can no more stop selling themselves than cease breathing. It is now considered the consummation of the politician's craft to be able to appear on television and convey a general impression of benevolence and determination, using the kind of speech that linguists call "phatic"—no meaning is communicated, but assurance is provided that the other party is on the line. But there is nothing reassuring, and a lot that is dangerous, about their staying on the line when they have nothing to communicate. When political leaders can offer no political truth and no political sense to the electorate, they debauch and pander to it instead. Their lies, however downright impudent, and however often and authoritatively they may be disproved, are repeated, copied, reproduced in the newspapers and reflected in the opinion polls—the same opinion polls that politicians consult in determining their subsequent lies and policies.

It is significant that the Kennedy Administration, which most boldly, cynically, successfully and with the utmost subtlety and imagination practiced the art of news management, was also the administration most obsessed with opinion polls. "We were not unlike the people who check their horoscope each day before venturing out," wrote Evelyn Lincoln, providing both a description of the twelve years she was secretary to John Kennedy and an appropriate epitaph for postwar reactive leadership. Government by PR men and meaningless opinion polls is the supreme perversion of the important democratic truth that public opinion is where criticism can enter the language of politics and where communication can take place in the opposite direction.

The question of whether political truth can be communicated to the electorate unadorned has preoccupied political theorists since Plato. Lord Melbourne is reported to have set his back to the door at a meeting of his Cabinet and said: "I don't care what damned lie we must tell; but not a man of you shall leave this room until we have all agreed to tell the same damned lie." And Shaw's commentary on the story was that "whether this tale be true or not, the most honest statesman has to govern the people by telling them what is good for them to believe, whether it is true of not."[16] This was also Caesar Borgia's policy. Our modern leaders have further refined the theory by defining what is good for the people to believe as that which will maintain them in power. So while legitimate political rhetoric is concerned with the potency of things and uses exaggeration only to the extent that it reflects real potentiality, the exaggerations of modern political speech would be more accurately described as irresponsible mendacity, rather than political rhetoric.

During the Second World War, at the depth of Britain's political disaster, Winston Churchill compared the future of Europe to "broad sunlit uplands." Now the reality of the moment was in fact a valley of humiliation. But the hope which transfigured this to broad sunlit uplands was not irresponsible; it was what could exist if human imagination and the latent human response could be awakened. Many have dismissed Churchill's "imaginative liveliness" as sentimentalism and romanticism. Churchill's rhetoric was, in fact, political rhetoric at its noblest; without it, it is doubtful whether Europe would have been able to resist Hitler and his brand of evil rhetoric which had persuaded multitudes that his order was "the new order" and the future. While the world must move, evil passion is more powerful than no passion and evil rhetoric of more force than no rhetoric. Without true passion and real rhetoric, the contest would have been lost by default. The passion of rhetoric, unlike the passion of poetry, has a practical end; but both with their own purpose are trying to advance the borders of the imaginative world. This is why we can unequivocally say that rhetoric is extinct in modern politics. What passes for impassioned language is in fact base rhetoric that keeps what could elevate out of sight; by focusing on the audience's prejudices and immediate desires, it works against their true understanding and brushes aside the restraint of truth.

But the old question is still asked today: if truth alone is not sufficient to persuade men, what can be legitimately added? In one of the exchanges with Phaedrus, Socrates puts the question in the mouth of a personified Rhetoric: "I do not compel anyone to learn to speak without knowing the truth, but if my advice is of any value he learns that first and then acquires me. So what I claim is this that without my help the knowledge of the truth does not give the art of persuasion." Today we have dispensed with truth and artful presentation alike, and are worshipping instead that most false of false idols, "objective" political speech dominated by vast political abstractions and decked out in glittering statistical measures. The result is that far from achieving objectivity in political language, we have lost all feeling of accountability in political utterance. Political beliefs today—and this at a time when the claims of politics are more tyrannically obtrusive than ever before—are as incidental to the man who expresses them as the little man on the top of the wedding cake is to the substance of the cake.

No man, for example, whose beliefs on communism and freedom are an integral part of himself, could *ever* "forget", "make a mistake", or "mumble" on television, as Gerald Ford did, that "there is no Soviet domination in Eastern Europe". And what meaning or conviction could one attribute to his subsequent "clarifying" statements to the effect that the peoples of Eastern Europe "yearn for freedom", and "their spirit has never been broken and never will be"—except that they were just so much mumbo-jumbo, and just as extraneous to Gerald Ford as his "mistake".

So the old preoccupation with educating political leaders, which is as old as Aristotle's dreaming of his young Alexander, springs today from the more modest need to instill some elementary—indeed remedial—education in them. There was a time when the ideal ruler was a very real conception, and endless attempts were made to compile the qualities regarded as essential and to influence the education which would ensure that virtue, and not vice, would win "the contention for the soul of the Young Prince." Even Cromwell, who did away with Young Princes, provided a detailed outline of a future leader's education: "I would have him mind and understand business, read a little history, study the Mathematics and Cosmography—these are good with subordination to the things of God . . . these fit for public service for which a man is born." In a democracy, where there is no means of prophesying who the future leaders will be, the old preoccupation with educating political leaders from a young age has been superseded by the modern preoccupation with selecting political leaders.

Whenever dissatisfaction with our chosen leaders turns into desperation, the cry goes up for reform of the selection procedures. But the selection method favored by a democracy cannot be judged in isolation from the prevalent conception of government. Those who favor, in the name of democracy, of course, an even more active and intrusive government, are against keeping leadership elections in Britain wholly within the closed Parliamentary circle and demand that the party conferences should be predominant in determining the result. Those who, on the contrary, wish to restrain the power exercised by small party caucuses in determining who will be the party's candidate in a particular constituency, demand primary elections to weaken the stronghold of the local party establishments.

Many detailed schemes and a large number of funny ideas are abroad in the name of democracy, and we shall do well to keep our political ears pricked. There is an infallible litmus test that can be applied to every scheme and idea: does it increase, or does it inhibit the individual politician's freedom of action and, even more important, his independence of judgment and thought? This is the chief advantage of the American system of primary elections; despite all the unattractive features of prolonged preconvention campaigning and political traveling circuses, the American system does make it possible for candidates outside the party establishments to gain national exposure and even to defeat the old machine politicians. And this *pari passu* is the principal disadvantage of the British selection system; the right of small party caucuses to select and endorse the candidate—which in safe seats is tantamount to determining who will be the MP—means that the traditional Burkean notion that Parliamentary responsiblity depends on an MP's being unfettered by the chains of the rigid mandate, is becoming increasingly difficult to maintain.

Also in Britain, a clearly defined ladder from the back benches through ministerial office to Downing Street makes it institutionally even more likely that those who finally grind through the system to the top jobs will be the ones least handicapped by any political vision—and least concerned about compromising their principles and accumulating political debts on the way. The fact that, however great its virtues in theory, in practice the American system of selection has neither enriched the democratic ideal nor improved the quality of political leadership relative to other selection systems, shows how ineffective institutional reforms alone would be in ensuring that our political leaders are not exclusively chosen among the men of passive conformity and easy security—the men who live for a ribbon and for applause by the lonely crowd.

Erasmus reserved his severest censure for those flatterers who corrupt a prince; indeed, he proposed that the only fit punishment for them was death. But he was being dangerously indulgent toward the princes. "It was a lonely road to be Lord Wellington," concludes Philip Guedalla; and it has always been, and will always be, a lonely road to be a great political leader. The chasm between De Gaulle and the majority of postwar leaders is summed up in his reply to Jacques Soustelle, who had just returned from a visit to Algeria and remarked that all his friends there were bitterly opposed to the General's policy: *"Changez vos amis."*

The only other Western European postwar leader who does not come into that thickly populated category of reactive leadership is Konrad Adenauer. Probably the least colorful of all the statesmen who shaped the destinies of Europe in the twentieth century, he was in his own way more effective than any other German leader since the founding of the Wilhelmine Empire—not excluding Bismarck himself. "My economic advisers tell me that your policies will lead to disaster," the American proconsul, General Clay, warned the German chancellor in 1949. "Don't worry," came back the De Gaulle-like reply, "mine tell me the same." Lonely opposition to prevalent illusions was in fact the *leitmotiv* of Adenauer's political career: In the winter of 1945–46, he succeeded in refashioning the Christian Democratic Party into a party of definite Western orientation against both the illusion of anti-Western "Christian socialism" and the illusion fostered by the founders of the Christian Democratic Movement themselves, that the CDU should be directed from the capital of the Reich and therefore remain opposed to any anti-Soviet alignments; in February 1949, he persuaded his reluctant colleagues to adopt Ludwig Erhardt's "social market economy" program, which was being attacked by the leader of the Social Democrats as "the fat propaganda balloon of private enterprise filled with putrid gases of decaying Liberalism," but which, as it turned out, became the foundation of the German "economic miracle"; later, he accepted German membership of the International Ruhr Authority, which was to administer Germany's most important industrial complex despite accusations of surrendering German rights, and so succeeded in gaining for Germany a voice in policies which affected the whole of Europe, and gradually in eliminating Germany's inferior status as an occupied country. All this was achieved by a man who in 1948 was not even listed in the German *Who's Who* for that year, and who, when on September 20, 1949, he mounted the rostrum in the Bundestag to outline his government's program, was 73 years old.

Adenauer and De Gaulle, that other amazing gerontocrat, are between them the most effective symbol of the premature senility of the remainder of postwar Western leaders. They also epitomize what Solomon wisely recognized and the Athenians widely practiced with their regular and arbitrary ostracism of prominent leaders: the dangers inherent in high position, and especially the danger that the leader will become a legend to himself and, Caesar-like, claim as a man the greatness and objective power of his political function. This is a danger to which Adenauer succumbed, even more than De Gaulle. Acutely responsive as he was to the romance of history in the making, and totally identified as he had become with his political office, he found it impossible to wrench himself from power. There is, nevertheless, something decidedly undignified in the way he held on to office until he was forced to retire on October 15, 1963, having done nothing to prepare any well-qualified successor.

Electorates this century have intuitively been remarkably sensitive to the dangers of long tenure in high positions. "We shall astonish them with our ingratitude," proclaimed Metternich, and there are definite Metternichean echoes in the way France repudiated Clemenceau, who had saved her during the First World War, and England rejected Churchill after the Second. The echoes are just as strong in the case of

De Gaulle: in 1944 he returned in triumph to liberate France and just over two years later he was retiring to Colombey-les-Deux Eglises, after the Constitution which he bitterly opposed had been accepted by a referendum; and in April 1969, when France again in a referendum denied him the support to which he believed himself entitled, Le Général took once more the road back to Colombey.

But the electorates were right, and those who castigate them for their ingratitude wrong. What is essential today is for the public to realize that the dangers they intuitively recognize in cases of outstanding leaders are just as real in the case of gray mediocrities, entrusted, as a result of the modern collectivist onslaught, with even more highly concentrated executive and administrative powers.

Today it is in institutional reforms and mechanical devices that those prophesying the collapse, demise, death or destruction of democracy seek salvation. By diverting attention from our real predicament and the need for a profound inner transformation, they are, in fact, hastening the collapse they are predicting. The contrast between the flimsiness of the cures offered and the extravagance of the hopes pinned on them is quite alarming: Lord Justice Scarman and Lord Hailsham believe that the British constitution is breaking down, and so call for a written constitution to save it; David Wood is worried about the collectivist onslaught, and so proclaims that "nothing except a Bill of Rights to protect the people's interests will stem the socialist state";[17] the Houghton Committee believes the survival of popular democracy to be in danger, and so calls for state subsidy of the bankrupt party political machines; the Liberal Party and the Conservative Action for Electoral Reform are unhappy with the mess of things politicians have made so far, and therefore want to unite through proportional representation all moderate politicians responsible for the mess; Mr. Peter Jay has noticed that the money supply has been growing far in excess of the productive potential of the economy, and so has called for the creation of a Currency Commission required by statute to regulate the growth of the money supply; Professor Claire Palley is worried about "the use of law as a social control," and so calls on lawyers to "devise governors and thermostats to prevent the law machine going out of control and to shock the controllers who pull the levers too far";[18] Robert Moss predicts, in a book of the same title, *The Collapse of Democracy*, and so calls for increased use of the referendum, or the "people's veto," as he describes it, to save it.

All these institutional reforms being put forward in Britain, and countless similar ones in America and elsewhere, can be divided into three categories: those such as the creation of a Currency Commission, which are excellent but unrealizable; those such as the introduction of a Bill of Rights, which are theoretically admirable and practically ineffectual; and those such as the subsidization of political parties, which are downright wrong. All demands for institutional change, not excluding the demand for devolution, are in themselves spurious outlets for real dissatisfactions. They can only be effective to the extent that they accompany fundamental changes in our dominant ideas and assumptions about the role of politics and of democratic government in our lives; they can neither effectively precede nor can they precipitate such changes in our political outlook.

In the absence of any real differences in philosophies or ideas among our political leaders, those striking fancy postures as political "thinkers" can only do so by espousing one or other institutional reform. But it is only a family game, and the public has remained stolidly unmoved. Instead, its fascination with authority in *déshabillé,* with the private lives, foibles and vices of political leaders, has steadily increased, expecially as there is little to differentiate politicians these days except style and sexual tastes. But by spotlighting the political leader's private weaknesses, we are in danger of being led by men who have no private weaknesses, or indeed private thoughts, private ideas or private values—in fact, by smiling, handshaking computers programmed with all the requisite answers and fed with all the requisite speeches.

"Is it to be the cherub or the tiger?" Churchill asked Graham Sutherland when he was about to sit for the portrait Lady Churchill later destroyed. In that short question he summed up a great truth: no man is hewn out of a single block, and no great man, whether a politician, a philosopher or an artist, has ever been of a piece; it is an inescapable truth of history that the greatest men have been enigmatic composites of the godlike and the demonic. The danger is that by focusing on the intimations of pettiness and the weaknesses of character and thought that are always there to be revealed—and this has been one of the techniques used to devalue Solzhenitsyn—we miss the man's essential greatness. Indeed, "show me a great man and I will dismantle him for you" has become one of our best-loved games: zealous Freudian dilettantes "demystify" the giants of the past—happily reassured that there are no giants of the present requiring their services. So our attention is sytematically, and with a definite kind of vindictiveness, diverted from the greatness of Tolstoy. Dostoevsky, Newton or Molière, and focused on the "discovery" that Tolstoy was schizoid, Dostoevsky an epileptic, Newton paranoid and Molière consumptive. After the errors of rationalizing and moralizing from biographical facts have been committed, and the giants assigned to this or that class of neurotic, the plucked contents of their work can be left behind on a heap of ruins.

When someone complained to Lincoln about Grant's drunkenness, he suggested that they find out what brand he drank and send a case to every one of his other generals. Grant won victories, and this was after all the essential qualification. Tolstoy translated the ordinary into a shining marvel, and no fault should be allowed to detract from the force of this miracle. In politics, the translation of the commonplace into greatness is never as unambiguous and the essential qualification is not as easy to define—but very easy to distinguish from the inessential ones, except by those long past making distinctions.

Today it is the political leader's secondary qualities, and especially his moral flexibility masquerading as political genius, that are venerated as invaluable assets in the art of government. And zealous publishers, editors, authors and authoresses are eagerly pulling aside the curtain to the inner sanctum of the inspired opportunists who have been leading us—to reveal to our consternation very little indeed, except Lyndon Johnson "crumpled, ragged and defenseless" [19] and John Kennedy out to improve on Casanova's record. Henry Kissinger, the man who proudly informed us that power is the greatest aphrodisiac, explained once that "in every democratic country so much energy is absorbed in getting into office that leaders are not always as well prepared as they could be." Apart from De Gaulle and Adenauer, the third and last postwar exception to this rule of Western political leadership is to be found in the Antipodes. "It was a terrible thing to be told that your services were no longer required, at a crucial time in the world's history," [20] wrote Robert Menzies, when his Government fell just after Australia entered the Second World War. But it turned out to be the best thing for Australia. Menzies used the time of Labour's rule, not planning Macmillanlike to recreate his party in the image of his opponents, but *rethinking* the philosophy of the Liberal Party and its role in Australian politics. The result was a series of clearly formulated proposals for "the revival of Liberal thought which would work for social justice and security, for national power and national progress and for the full development of the individual citizen though not through the dull and deadening process of socialism." [21] And in 1949, just after Ben Chifley, the Labour Prime Minister, had begun implementing his party's objective of "the democratic socialization of industry, production, distribution and exchange" by trying to nationalize all Australian banks, Menzies came to power. The *Washington Post* may have been exaggerating when it called him eighteen years later "probably the most completely successful public man of his time," but Menzies—serious though some of his mistakes were on the foreign front—did undoubtedly succeed where most Western democratic leaders failed: he refashioned the Liberal Party, halted the collectivist onslaught, and governed his people from 1949 till 1966 without promising to lead them into a wonderful world where figs grow upon thorns the instant they are nationalized and mountains are transformed into rock candy the minute they are democratically socialized.

Menzies retired on January 20, 1966, by casually winding up a Cabinet meeting: "Well, gentlemen, this is the last time I shall be with you." He was determined, as he explained later, not to repeat Churchill's example, and decline gradually before the public eye. Political leaders' attitudes to retirement have always been ambivalent. Lord Rosebery, who succeeded Gladstone as Prime Minister, wrote that "there are two supreme pleasures in life. One is ideal, the other real. The ideal is when a man receives the seals of office from his Sovereign. The real pleasure comes when he hands them back." Harold Wilson's pleasure from handing back the seals of office comes into an altogether different category: the desire, when the time came to pay for the damage he did to his country, not to be any longer at the helm. Otherwise, most politicians hate being parted from positions of power and eminence—whether through resignation or retirement—and this overwhelming reluctance is, in fact, one of the most powerful pressures toward mindless conformity in politics. The more political leaders resemble in reality the barren portraits of their campaign or hagiographic biographies, the more reluctant they will be to relinquish power and have to face their inner emptiness—and the more determined to cling to office at whatever cost.

"If you wanted to put the world to rights," asks Roitman of himself in the darkness of *The First Circle*, "who should you begin with: yourself or others? . . ." Our modern political leaders continue to peddle in great abundance policies and programs with an eye only on the discounts and the state of the market; they communicate facts and statistics and pass on nothing of the person communicating. "Any new line should come out of this proposition," ends a memorandum on the Nixon campaign by his advertising director. "Things aren't right and they are going to get worse because the programs and policies we have now aren't working. A change is urgently needed. There is only one candidate who stands for change: Richard M. Nixon." [22]

If you left a blank where the name of Richard M. Nixon is, to be filled by the name of any politician around at the moment, the proposition would reflect with grim exactitude the modern approach to political leadership. Yet—and paradoxically this puts us into even greater peril—most politicians today are not simple, straightforward hyprocrites; those few who are, may conceivably repent and mend, or they may be unmasked and made to reform. But who can unmask and who can reform those who attempt no deception, those deceived deceivers precipitating the end of Western democracy, unable to see that they could ever behave otherwise?

"It is an unhappy country that has no heroes," says Andrea Sarti in Brecht's *Galileo*. "It is an unhappy country that needs heroes," is Galileo's correction. And the West today is an unhappy country in need of "heroes," teachers and great men who will activate our awareness of where the unhappiness lies, of the one-sidedness of our lives and of the grave error our age is committing. The great men who will help to change the environment of opinion and loosen the stronghold of politics on the individual are unlikely to emerge from inside politics. For their greatness will not lie in providing the age with blueprints, let alone in oppressively implementing them, but in bearing witness with their lives to the integration of the rational with the long-neglected spiritual element in man, and in helping to awaken the divine gift that lies dormant within each of us. Their first commitment is to this unfolding of the still raw and amorphous spirituality in man and in the age, and therefore their first allegiance in practice is to man's individual freedom—for freedom is, and has always been, the first law of the spirit.

But the lives of those who have achieved truth are only a proof that the goal can be reached. Their greatness and wisdom are only reflections of the greatness and wisdom within and a spur towards acknowledging this truth and turning inward to the original image itself. Happy indeed is the country that needs no heroes—and no leaders. And the only legitimate aim of the new leaders will be to help us make them redundant.

6

"THE DAY CINDERELLA NEARLY WASN'T ALLOWED TO MARRY HER PRINCE"

The dominant characteristic of modern leadership—the lack of any moral or political commitment that goes beyond the merely expedient—is a reflection of the dominant characteristic of the age: the corrosive spiritual exhaustion that has made our world too prosaic for man's imagination, too unlovable for his affection, and just right for the managerial abilities of political mediocrities.

We are even flying away from a common popular mythology—how else can one explain the latest film of Cinderella? So total is the stifling of the imagination that not even fairy tales—our only remaining common myths and symbols—are safe. Embarrassed scriptwriters feel obliged to introduce the "real world" with intricate political complications, so that Cinderella nearly wasn't allowed to marry her prince. The royal advisers deemed the marriage inadvisable for "reasons of state," and if it were not for the executive producer deeming the climactic wedding drama advisable for "reasons of profit," Cinderella would probably not have married her prince.

The war against the imagination is complete. Yet imagination is man's most princely faculty—the one that most sharply distinguishes him from other creatures. It is imagination which gives meaning and value to our experience, which both discerns mystery and brings comprehension and order to our world. Without imagination there can be no affirmation. When nothing is affirmed, life loses its essential character and politics descends to the bedrock of administrative technology. And we are ready to embrace the first totalitarian solution that promises to end our cosmic sense of meaninglessness; or less dramatically, we seek to impose meaning through an increasingly totalitarian state.

Tearing politics away from its cultural context is one of the most dangerous fallacies. We regard references to the state of religion or the arts as irrelevant to our understanding of politics, and approach our political predicament exclusively through statistics, polls and think-tank reports. Culture is treated as a varnish, politics becomes tantamount to administration, and political theory is reduced to an isolated description of representative institutions. But human societies are representatives of a transcendent truth, and it is futile as well as misleading to seek to understand them without exploring the symbols by which they interpret themselves as representatives of this truth. It may seem absurd to "the modern mind," but a great part of political history is purely symbolic. The Bastille, when it was taken, was not a horrible prison—it was hardly a prison at all. (It was found to contain only seven old men who were annoyed at being disturbed.) But it was a symbol and its destruction was the breaking of a stone image. And Mrs. Thatcher does not wear hats with any regularity—indeed, she hardly seems to wear hats at all. But her hats are not merely a joke. They symbolize what the British public instinctively suspects to be wrong with her: the suburban truisms of the political morality she espouses and the frozen perfection she represents.

Yet we persist in looking at society in two-dimensional terms; we ignore the interaction between culture, politics and life and so remain oblivious to the dangers of the unifying spirit that informs them all—the "spirit that denies," and that views everything and everybody from the ground. "Pardon me," says Mephisto to God in the Prologue to Goethe's *Faust,* "I cannot utter fine phrases." So utterly unreal does he find any noble emotions, and like all his species—is he not, after all, the archetypal figure of our modern world?—so incapable is he of believing that others feel such emotions, that for him all nobility and grandeur of phrase is grandiloquence and untruth.

And the modern Mephistos, everywhere in the ascendant, continue unabated to destroy our few remaining religious symbols, and deflower our common Western myths. Films lend themselves ideally as a medium for "demythologization." In the course of a single year, it is not just Cinderella who has suffered at the hands of film-makers: Robin Hood returns home after twenty years, and when he is confronted with Will Scarlett thumbing his lute in the transformed Sherwood Forest, explaining that the people yearn to hear over and over again the deeds the heroes did, he casually ripostes: "But we didn't do them"; *The Little Prince,* Saint-Exupéry's masterful symbol of the sure wisdom of innocence, is produced with such contemporary self-consciousness and lack of conviction that even the moment when the Little Prince confides the great secret imparted to him by the shy fox—"It is only with the heart that one sees clearly. What is essential is invisible to the eyes"—is made to seem whimsical, rather than magical; and *Lancelot of the Lake* is turned into a ruthless valediction of the Arthurian legend and the quest for a spiritual idea, having in the process destroyed the greatness of the myth and left our imagination unstirred.

At the same time, Brigid Brophy has advocated that children should be told "in a *factual* way, the content of the myths and doctrines of as many religions and objections to all religions as the teacher's general knowledge will run to." [1] But myths factually recounted and religions demythologized become simple nonsense. What Brigid Brophy, the modern Mephistos of the film industry and, much more important, the millions who do not see the manifest absurdity of their proud matter-of-factness fail to understand, is that myths, whether in religion or in fairy tale, are not *our* inventions. They point to irrepresentable realities beyond themselves, and they correspond to psyclical realities within ourselves long before we have analyzed and understood them.

Just as we have begun in our century to investigate and understand the subliminal processes to which myths have for centuries given imaginative expression, the attempt to destroy their truth has grown increasingly frenetic. And we are asked to accept in their place the stock of commonplaces, prejudices, and follies piled up within the modern "educated" mind.

Our enlightened age has made "myth" practically a synonym for falsehood, a label to be applied to anything dismissed as illusion; and within the cerebral norms of our time, anything that affirms the existence of invisible and nonconceptual forms of reality *is* an illusion, a primitive remnant of primordial times. But the depths of the human soul are themselves "primordial times," that deep "Well of Time" where myth has its home, and where the source of the original norms and forms of life is to be found. "For Myth is the foundation of life; it is the timeless pattern, the religious formula to which life shapes itself, inasmuch as its characteristics are a reproduction of the unconscious. There is no doubt about it, the moment when the story teller acquires the mythical way of looking at things . . . that moment marks a beginning in his life. . . . This is usually reserved for the later years of life; for whereas in the life of mankind the mythical represents an earlier and primitive stage, in the life of the individual it represents a late and mature one." And what Thomas Mann wrote from his own experience about the storyteller applies with just as much force to each individual and to every culture: acquiring the mythical way of looking at things marks a beginning in our lives. In the past, there was no need to acquire it. The myth has, after all, been identified as a phenomenon of human society so universal and so critical in importance that it is difficult to imagine a culture having for long any coherence and life if it lacks the mythological bond.

Western culture has received its life force from the Christian myth—with Christ as the most complete living example of the realization of man's divine self. He has indeed been the most transfigurative symbol of illumination and renewal accessible to Western man, either directly or through the inspiration he provided to the greatest philosophical and artistic minds of our culture over hundreds of years. But the remorseless secularization of Western society is killing the Christian myth, and leaving us with stultifying doctrine at one end and an "ecumenical project" to demythologize Christianity and replace it with a vague philanthropic humanism at the other.

With Christianity demythologized, and our fables and fairy tales, that hid within them the doctrines of all the philosophers, deflowered and dead, what will be left to awaken in our soul the memory of who we are? Our age has, by snuffing out the spiritual mystery of man, denied God, and by denying God it has denied the truth that leavens the individual and the world, and so denied life. In place of movement and life, the modern spirit is, through politics and the state, seeking to impose rest, immobility and death. For whatever ceases to change and transform itself, halts the flux of life, decays and perishes.

"This place will sink," cries Medea in Thessaly, betrayed by Jason and the new "rational" order. "You do not mark the center. Grass, earth, stone, speak to me." Modern man has let the roots of life in the deepest parts of himself decay for the sake of a misplaced rationality, and all that remains now is to institutionalize this individual "death in life" by erecting everywhere totalitarian states, buttressed by our spiritual sterility and in turn reinforcing it. And then the bond that keeps society together will be the bond of fear and force. Because the only other bond, the bond that does not bind but frees, and does not restrain but bestows—the spiritual, mythological bond—will have been rejected.

The danger is instinctively apprehended by all. But it is not for reasons of divine economy alone that the ancient Chinese symbolic ideogram for *crisis* is the same as that for *opportunity*: the moment of crisis and supreme danger, whether in the life of an individual or in the life of a nation, is also the moment of the greatest opportunity for renewal. The crisis and danger is that religion, having been reduced to ethics, can no longer control the demonic in man, nor provide man's need for a futurist idealism; so its place is being everywhere usurped by political salvationism. The opportunity is that, for the first time in our history, we can dispense, once and for all, with the view of religion which asserts that "ordinary" man must be handed down by some corporate organization a system of doctrine and belief—his learning being considered too limited, and his occupations too pressing, for him to reach to the life-giving part of himself, and there discover his own divine truth.

Yet even those who, like Daniel Bell, have called for a revival of religion and a new place in our lives for the sacred as the only solution to the present predicament, feel impelled to conclude with a "practical, constructive" proposal. So it is that Professor Bell, unable to provide a dramatic climax to *The Cultural Contradictions of Capitalism* by promising that he will be crucified and rise within three days from the dead, thus founding a new religion himself, has concluded instead with a proposition, which though no less impractical is at least academically irreproachable, and has been hailed by critics as a "major practical" suggestion. He has called for "public households" to reconcile the kinship feeling of the home with the recognition of the problems and limitations posed by "families" that contain millions of members. This rather stretches even the broadest and most fashionable definition of an "extended family"; yet Professor Bell has put this monumentally meaningless proposal forward as a practical suggestion. And Anatole Broyard of *The New York Times* has commended him for "not washing his hands of us," and for eschewing "spiritual"—and by definition impracticable—exhortations.[2]

So we go on approaching the world with a cool curiosity, untouched by love or wonder, and trusting that behind the practical solutions, the economic graphs, the pills and the opinion polls there are experts who understand whatever else there is to understand. And the scientific experts proudly proclaim their own dispassionate approach and swear their objectivity.

One thing is certain: there was nothing dispassionate about all great scientists. They all shared a sense of wonder, which is the common source of religious mysticism, pure science and great art. "Men were first led to the study of natural philosophy," wrote Aristotle, "as indeed they are today, by wonder." Clerk Maxwell's earliest memory was "lying on the grass, looking at the sun and *wondering*." And Einstein effectively defined wonder as a precondition for life, when he wrote that whoever is devoid of the capacity to wonder, "whoever remains unmoved, whoever cannot contemplate or know the deep shudder of the soul in enchantment, might just as well be dead for he has already closed his eyes upon life." In fact, we can no more escape the pull of magic inside us than we can the pull of gravity. But today we have relegated magic to the province of the carnival and the occultist, and perversely deny ourselves entry into the world of wonder and belief where the great drama of life is taking place—dreamlike in fact, but terribly real in spirit.

"We shall take upon us the mystery of things and be God's spies," says the doomed Lear to Cordelia. Awareness of the mystery of things, though inexpressible and not reducible to any objectively demonstrable knowlege, is the only way for the human spirit to look beyond its workaday world into the unknown; it is the first step toward enlarging our capacity to experience. This is the first meaning of religion: wonder and reverence for the riddle that man is, and homage to his mystery, which includes the great as well as the demonic elements of his nature. But modern man, the man with the utterly prosaic mind, cannot stop shrugging his shoulders. Increasingly incapable of experiencing the power of the heroic, and lacking the will to believe, he grows obsessed with the comforts of civilization and denies, as a matter of course, the spiritual truth that gave it birth.

"A man who bows down to nothing," cried Dostoevsky in *The Possessed*, "can never bear the burden of himself." And paradoxically, only in bowing down to the miracle of life, and to those who have miraculously extended our conception of what is possible, only by accepting the existence of things not only unknown but unimaginable, can man find the strength to lever himself out of the dead weight of our withering culture. Otherwise, lacking an Archimedean fixed point and a spiritual center, he does indeed end by finding himself a burden. And impotent, unbalanced, restless and dissatisfied, he flocks to every new banner in the hope of finding something for once which will atone for his own supreme insufficiency. Destitute of faith, yet terrified of skepticism, like Goethe's Faust, and just as profoundly sad, he is prepared to enter into any compact, including the rejection of his own soul, to achieve an illusory happiness and cry "Stay, thou art fair" to the passing moment.

The sick children, instead of trying to establish what disease they, and their world, are dying from, have cried so loudly and for so long that an increasing number of them have cried themselves to sleep. Those who are still awake seem incapable of outgrowing their adolescent cynical misanthropy, and are treating their questioning estrangement from the prevailing culture not as a by-product of the pursuit of life's true and neglected values, but as a value in itself.

Having no sense whatsoever for what Ulysses called "the still and mental parts" of battle—and this is the level at which the battle will have to be fought—they put the blame for all our modern tragedies on someone else, something "alien," some special interest; and they are aiming at all the easy targets: dirt in the media, welfare scrounging, cheapening of sex, unemployment of school-leavers, Trotskyite infiltration and lack of playing fields. "How many wolves do we feel on our heels, while our real enemies go in sheepskin by." All that the ornamental preliminaries about our "dehumanized culture" have bred is a consciousness of righteousness which the dissenters' own excesses can never destroy, but only confirm.

"The slogans of yesterday," wrote Eldridge Cleaver, who after seven years' exile abandoned his sterile rage and hate in search of answers less simple and less untrue, "will not get us through the tests at hand. . . . I think that my generation has been more critical than most and for good reason. At the same time, at the end of the critical process, we should arrive at some conclusions." His own conclusion is unambiguous in the wisdom of its hard-earned *personal* understanding: "I had gone astray from being human. . . . I also learned that it is easier to do evil than it is to do good. . . ." The search for ways to ensure that man does not go astray from being human, has in fact preoccupied philosophers and political thinkers ever since their breed came into existence.

"Man is the Measure," asserted Protagoras; "God is the Measure," objected Plato. But the two measures are much less incompatible than men have hitherto assumed. God is undoubtedly the invisible measure and his invisible harmony greater and infinitely more powerful than the visible. But man himself can become the measure of things. Only to the extent, though, that his soul has been awakened to the invisible harmony, and he has manifested the divine truth he incarnates; for then he is truly born again "of water and the spirit," and has entered the Kingdom of God within. But the invisible harmony will never be found, and man will never achieve his second birth unless the soul is animated by an anticipating urge in that direction. Yet skepticism is *par excellence* the disease of our time. Its morbid symptoms are everywhere inescapable. The unrest is the unrest of the disease; and the cures on offer those of societies which, dead within, are merely seeking a regulating principle to postpone their impending disintegration.

Nothing seems more obscure and impenetrable, and yet nothing has fascinated humanity more intensely, than the nature of the power that moves our communal life—and the sense of the aim toward which the power moves it. But today the human mind has recoiled from the profound obscurity and from life's great, hidden, all-determining laws, and has instead invented sociology, to play with the foam of the surface. Yet our continuing fascination with fifth-century B.C. Athens or the Italian cities of the Renaissance has little to do with the sociological conditions under which communities survive, and still less with facile generalizations about the kaleidoscope of changing institutions. What distinguishes these periods is their unifying public spirit and their unified culture. We do not have to accept in its entirety the atmosphere conveyed in the political discussions recorded by Plato and Xenophon, with tradesmen and shopkeepers just as involved as the political elite; nor do we have to believe in the ubiquitousness of the noble proportion, the clarity, the high seriousness, and all the other exalted qualities commonly associated with the Renaissance, to feel even at this distance the deep longing for an eternal harmony in all things which characterized these periods; it was this that made them politically and culturally the most alive in history. The reason the glory of the Athenian city-states and the Italian Renaissance were only supreme *moments* of human history—although admittedly two of the three supreme moments on which our Western civilization is based—is to be found in the baneful effects on man's search for his true existence of a great culture once it has begun to regard itself as definitive. Then man has to be painfully reminded again that there are no definitive epochs, no civilizations crystalized for ever, no Romes Eternal; and that however great may be man's achievements, they are inferior to himself.

The moment an age begins to feel that it "has never had it so good," its decline has already begun. In the molds for the coinage of Hadrian, with the collapse of the Roman Empire imminent, we read about *Italia Felix, Saeculum aureum, Tellus stabilita, Temporum felicitas.* One of the most hopeful signs for the West today is that the period of self-satisfaction is over. Our age is no longer seen as "the plenitude of time"; we no longer feel that the end of the journey has been reached; nor do we actually believe that it is anywhere within sight. The danger is that the questing and the dissent are taking place in a cultural environment which, instead of treating doubt as a circumscribed tool, has turned it into the basis and condition of life. Skepticism has become a conviction, and this world, seen as an infinitely ambiguous and deceptive creation, has become the only recognized form of reality.

It is this lack of faith, which springs from our loss of all sense of the infinite significance of everything in the world, that permeates all dissent. It has turned social criticism into a series of feverish, fashionable reactions, and social critics into angry fugitives, with nothing except the cold and uncertain glimmer of intellectual theorizing to guide their flight from our spiritual wasteland. But after a while, even the narcissistic frisson of trivial dissent becomes difficult to sustain; after all, blasphemy is only daring against a background of belief. ("If you doubt that," said Chesterton, "try saying something blasphemous about Thor.") And we do not need to be able to call spirits from the vasty deep to predict that skeptical dissent from a hyperskeptical culture can only lead to a bottomless abyss—because there is nothing but frail rationality to hold either our culture or those mechanically revolting against it. So both the official culture and the official counterculture are, under the guise of trivial, frenetic change, defending the age against the infusion of spiritual truth which would, it is true, destroy many of its cherished aspects, but which alone could save it.

This act of cultural redemption can only take place through the individual. And this is our age's great departure from the past. Political and social theory have so far been principally concerned with what binds people to one another and what holds societies together. Today we have reached the stage where unless we shift the focus to what holds man together *inwardly*, we have scant chance of holding societies together—except, of course, by force and compulsion. When Saint Augustine constructed the tremendous edifice of his *De civitate Dei*, he assigned to the secular state both the function of an emergency institution without which no human society was possible, and that of serving and protecting through the Church man's spiritual truth. Today it is time to proclaim unambiguously that the state has no salvationist function whatsoever—whether of the Augustinian spiritual variety or of the contemporary collectivist one. Its only function is indeed as an emergency institution without which no human society is possible; and the only rightful protector of man's spiritual truth is man himself.

The discovery of this truth is the only vital power that can bring men together, and help create that community feeling for which politicians are now praying to dead gods. For what is all too easily referred to as the "breakdown of consensus" is much deeper, much less political and infinitely more elusive than those who bandy the phrase about imply. A social consensus involves all the indefinable and imponderable agreements—spiritual and moral first, and political much later—on which any community is based. And the contemporary breakdown of consensus has to be traced back to that point in our history when we took the question that Pilate asked as a bitter irony against a Roman, and turned it into our culture's principal article of faith. When "What is truth?" supplants our conviction that there is a truth to discover and to bear witness to, nihilism takes the place of a community of belief, the dam breaks, and societies become increasingly ungovernable.

"Britain is drifting slowly toward a condition of ungovernability," said Eric Sevareid on a CBS program on the state of Britain—and his remark had resonances beyond the program. But he was wrong, both in implying that Britain's slide toward ungovernability could be halted by a political leader who did not dodge the contest between Parliament and the unions, and in assuming that ungovernability was a specifically British problem, rather than a Western problem that had reached in

Britain a stage more advanced and more conspicuous. When all common certainties and beliefs have evaporated, nothing is affirmed and therefore nothing rejected. Pluralism becomes a jungle in which all but Mowgli and Tarzan lose their way. As Chesterton's celebrated phrase runs, "When men cease to believe in God, they will not believe in nothing, they will believe in anything." And anybody. The question is whether we will discern in time that the only language that can unite the Babel of tongues raised in high-pitched and highly trivial argument is the oldest of all languages, the language of the spirit, newly and individually discovered.

This does not mean a reversion to 1075 and Gregory VII announcing that the Papacy was the final authority in all temporal, as well as spiritual affairs; nor does it mean that Mr. Callaghan, Mr. Carter, M. Giscard D'Estaing and the rest should together take the road to Canossa to receive the papal blessing. The initiative that will turn the language of the spirit to the healing language of our time lies with each individual—*and with no one else.* It requires from every individual a moral step well within his power: the liberation of his soul from participation in the life-denying lie of our age. It is this lie that has denied man's spirit, has led to the putrefaction of his soul, and is leading gradually to his political enslavement. Once it is acknowleged, and our individual consent to it withdrawn, Western societies, now like magnets that have lost their charge, will be remagnetized by the vital energy of the liberating truth. At the moment politicians are desperately trying to infuse their nations with this energy by mechanically drawing from the word-hoard of "virile" political metaphors. But when words are cut off from the spirit that once gave them life, language becomes too sterile even to give us a mild flutter, let alone infuse us with fresh energy.

What our political leaders have forgotten is that the Western system of government, incongruous though it may seem today, is based on the conviction that there is a higher spiritual law, higher than laws and statutes, that binds a society, and indeed humanity, together. It springs from a dim understanding which mankind is forever perceiving, and then losing, and then seeking to rediscover and repossess. And it has an impeccable intellectual pedigree, from Aristotle through Aquinas and Grotius to the founders of English Constitutional government and the creators of the American Republic. When the conviction is reduced to the level of fanciful whimsy, no Constitution is worth the paper it is written or not written on—a country may have all the forms of freedom but will not for long enjoy its substance. Constitutional safeguards stop being a great affirmation of faith in the human spirit released from authoritarian arbitrariness, and become a series of arid negatives. But if there is no such higher spiritual law, then our belief in the value of the individual rests on a negative principle, and we are confronted with the terrible possibility—were it not an absurdity—that our civilization rests on a delusion.

With the cramping and impoverishment of values that have followed the loss of belief in an ultimate reality, "the greatest happiness of the greatest number" has been turned into the blind pursuit of the greatest *comfort* for the greatest number. Life has become journalistic—a day-to-day adaptation to the shifting surface of things. And politics has become equally journalistic—not a series of difficulties to be overcome, but a set of problems to be removed before the next edition.

The thought-power of society—almost its soul-power, for those still prepared to talk of so insubstantial a thing as a soul—is no longer in its literature and the arts, let alone in its religion, although the latter drags on a feeble existence and the former teems and spawns; it is in the buzzing, booming confusion of the daily press, and the incessant radio and television. The "sacred" media, like sacred immaterial and ultra-physical powers, have since the war, at different points, and by rival groups, been denounced for all the world's evils or praised for all the world's goods. It is impossible to make sense of the increasingly sepulchral tones in which the debate on the media is being conducted, unless we recognize their special role as the implement by which our culture seeks to account for its existence, at a time when man is with growing intensity questioning the existence of any reason for it. Every culture and every civilization has a need for images not only of its past but of its present. But when the focus of life becomes as narrow and as journalistic as ours has become, then there is no more room for the spaciousness of the myth, the saga, the legend, the chronicle, the *geste* or any of the other forms to which previous cultures have turned to account for "what really happened," and to give the individual reference points for what was happening in his time. Instead we are bombarded with monumentally unimportant information, with prewrapped commentary and predigested interpretation, and with accounts of what has happened, to the nearest dazzling minute, and sometimes nearer, at which it happened.

"It is like the beam of a searchlight," wrote Walter Lippman nearly fifty years ago, "that moves relentlessly about, bringing one episode and then another out of darkness into vision. Men cannot do their work by this light alone. They cannot govern society by episodes, incidents and eruptions." [3] But we go on believing that we can. Indeed, the further journalism and broadcasting drift from any kind of reality, and the more they concentrate on trends, fads, fashions in opinion and passing ephemera of a dramatic moment, the more spectacular become their claims about what their function is. Afraid of drowning in our own confusion, and terrified of seeking our own truth, we run instead the danger of suffocating in the airless void of the easily surveyable, two-dimensional world that the media project as reality. We are increasingly behaving as if people and events are waiting in some mysterious limbo for journalism and television to make them real; and as if there is no other truth except the electronic replicas spewed out by television.

The more inescapable becomes the conclusion that "insights," "probes," "in-depth" commentaries and "broad-sweep" interpretations have not advanced public understanding, and still less public solutions, for our problems, the more insistent become the demands for a different—indeed *radically* different—kind of probing, interpreting and commentating. A particularly stirring call along these lines was sounded in *The Times* by John Birt and Peter Jay.[4] They castigated "television's bias against understanding" and its "lack of painstaking and abstract analysis"; and they proclaimed the need for "a clearly defined *mission* to demonstrate the forces in play." The italics are mine—and in the italicized word lies the clue. In the view of Birt and Jay, television could save us—indeed, it has a mission to save us—if only we would "match manpower to task" and let the omniscient experts, as opposed to those they contemptuously call "personality interviewers," explain to us the "geopolitical ideas," and the "microcosms" and "macrocosms," in the course of a painstaking and abstract analysis. Unfortunately this recipe for boring yourself into salvation is unlikely ever to be put to the test: human beings, whatever else may be wrong with them, are still sufficiently sane to have switched to the late movie, long before they have been turned into mini-experts, expertly conversing about the difficulties of extracting oil from the North Sea or, for that matter, moonbeams from cucumbers.

Our world may be in short supply of a long list of commodities, but it will have been sunk by experts long before it runs out of expertise. As for the vaunted information explosion, it actually seems to have led to an atrophy of the mental nerves. Yet the more blunted our understanding becomes, the more frenetic grow the demands for more information. As those crying out for more facts tend to be the same people who believe that polls never lie, it would perhaps be instructive for them to look at the results of a Gallup Poll comparing levels of cultural information in the United States and Great Britain. Three Americans out of ten were unable to say what important event occurred in 1776, while 95 percent of those interviewed in Britain did not attribute any significance to the date. Less than one half of those interviewed could correctly identify Freud, Aristotle, Marx, Raphael, Tolstoy or Rubens, although in Britain the average score was admittedly a full 10 percent higher than in the United States. As for the large percentage scored by Beethoven, the likelihood is that it is due more to *Peanuts* than to the Pastoral. Or it may be that after many years' continuous practice, the public is actually getting better at answering silly questions.

Knowing who Tolstoy was, or what the problems of extracting oil from the North Sea are, has, in fact, as much relevance to the solution of the world's problems as a precise knowledge of the menu at the working lunch that preceded the final signing of the Helsinki Declaration—and only slightly more relevance than the Helsinki Declaration itself. Yet the myth persists that once we have mastered the statistics, the chronology, the personalities and the graphics, we will have mastered the solutions; and that the main—and, according to some, the best—medium for the mastering is television. So we have reached the stage where bystanders at campaign rallies during the American primaries could marvel at the sight of three TV crews lined up one behind another—the first crew filming the candidate, the second filming for a program on the way the media cover the primaries, and the third preparing a film report on the way the media cover the media.

There was an old Aristotelian and scholastic distinction between material, moving and final causes. It would not be a bad idea if the distinction were rehabilitated and popularized; if nothing else, it might stem the flood of irrelevant suggestions, solutions and recommendations, and might even provide an explanation—to those who need one—for all the disappointed expectations about the use of television as a medium of salvation, or indeed reform. When the BBC repeat of *Cathy Come Home*, Jeremy Sandford's account of a young homeless family moving toward disintegration, coincided with a well-timed announcement that homelessness had actually doubled since the film was first shown ten years ago, astounded social reformers sought to provide a reason by indulging in all sorts of contortionist explanations; one of the most ingenious ones was that *Cathy Come Home* had in fact kindled not a passion for reform but a mood of resignation among both homeless and bureaucrats. The simple truth that you cannot eradicate real problems by recourse to media fantasy, any more than you can resolve a crisis by concentrating on its manifestations, was deemed unworthy of consideration by reformers and commentators; with an incurable penchant for complexity, they seem firmly in the grip of the conviction that responsibility for all evils belongs to "the system" that makes human beings what they are.

"The world behind my brow, *that* makes me what I am and no one else." Peer Gynt's claim sounds whimsical rather than proud today—but it is no less true for that. Once it is admitted again, television, radio and newspapers will assume the modest role that alone belongs to them, and will rest content with informing people, instead of attempting to *form* them by forming their opinions. Much more important, we will recapture the truth which our age has lost: that our strength—and our happiness—lies not in our tortuous dealings with the outer world, but first in our dealings with the "world behind the brow." Until these are mastered, our dealings with the outer world are bound to remain tortuous.

Yet the doctrine of our world, "Forsake your inner truth and live this tortuous life ending in a meaningless death, and you shall receive nothing in this world or the other," is listened to and obeyed. It is the power of this prevailing error that welds men together, and that threatens to bind them into a tyrannized collectivity. And only truth, not proclaimed from pulpits but in action in each individual life, can dissolve the homogeneity of error, and detach men one by one from its bonds. The power of error and evil can never be shattered—as large sections of humanity persist in believing—by violence or revolution. The only force that can detach men from error, and put an end to all the modern martyrdom exacted by fidelity to the doctrine of the world, comes from within. "Men think that by hammering upon the mass they will be able to break it in fragments, but they only make it more dense and impermeable than it was before. . . . The disruptive movement must come from within when molecule releases its hold upon molecule and the whole mass falls into disintegration." [5] But Tolstoy's warning goes unheeded, and it looks at times as though our souls dread to be cured.

The wounds grow deeper every day. It is, of course, inadequate, and ultimately absurd, to seek to prove the existence and progressive deepening of these wounds by statistics and reports. But the fact that mental illness is America's number-one health problem; the fact that in Britain, one woman in six and one man in nine will spend part of their lives in an asylum; the fact that violence is everywhere in the ascendant, and, even more alarmingly, that a growing percentage of these violent crimes are committed by teenagers and children (35 percent of violent thefts and 48 percent of burglaries in Britain are committed by children aged ten to sixteen); the fact that the number of suicides and attempted suicides is going up so that in Britain they now account for 20 percent of all emergencies brought to general hospitals, and, what is more disturbing still, the increase is even greater among the young; [6] the fact that Alcoholics Anonymous, only one of a proliferating number of groups dealing with the problem in America, reports a membership of more than 900,000; and the fact that the orgies of violence directed against buildings, especially those provided out of idealism, public spirit and public money, are spreading on both sides of the Atlantic—all these facts cannot be dismissed as yet more manifestations of human folly, with the worldly wise shaking their heads and passing on.

The human casualties proliferating at such a spectacular rate in the world today, and ranging from violent criminals to harmless alcoholics, cannot be explained away as an aberration. Nor can we look censoriously upon the abnormalities in asylums and clinics, secure in our vaunted normality. In the major battle of our age, the battle of the individual for the meaning of his life, these abnormalities and aberrations are magnifications of the suffering in ourselves, pleading for recognition as a reflection of a tragic neglect. This does not dispense with individual responsibility. But it should have made it impossible to go on cherishing all our threadbare illusions, and to go on refusing to recognize that, when there is as profound a division between spirit and life as there is today, sentence is passed upon life. And we are all afflicted, to a lesser, or greater—or overwhelming—extent with the sickness of an entire age and culture. We have got hold of our sprig of truth, or our straw of an ideal, have treble-locked it in a hermetic construction, and neither the suffering in our souls, nor all the evidence of the suffering everywhere around us, can make us abandon the half-lies we have built into certainties.

We imagine ourselves content with inadequate or wrong answers to the questions of life, we seek its meaning in position, reputation, money or outward success, and we consider ourselves civilized because we remember on appropriate occasions to mouth the clichés about the infinite worth of the individual and to talk solemnly about the "quality of life." But the quality of our life depends on the quality of our aim, and to talk indignantly about the quality of life while leaving its aim unexamined is sheer moralizing. Many, with their soul safely imprisoned, regard the fact that suffocation has for them become a normal state, as a sign of healthy maturity; and their claim is fully endorsed by our dominant culture. But a growing number end up on the psychiatrist's couch, seeking the meaning to their lives from psychiatrists most of whom are in no less need of healing than their patients—and who, worse still, seem ignorant of where healing is to be sought and found.

"Among all my patients in the second half of life, that is to say, over thirty-five," wrote Jung, "there has not been one whose problem was not that of finding a religious outlook on life. It is safe to say that every one of them fell ill because he had lost that which the living religions of every age have given to their followers, and none of them has been really healed who did not regain his religious outlook." [7] There could not be a more unequivocal conclusion. And yet the heirs of the man who was the first to integrate the soul into psychiatry, and who sought to reintegrate the spirit in man, have relegated this, the most salient aspect of Jung, to the level of Jungianism, to be eruditely assessed against Freudianism, Adlerianism and Skinnerism. "I do not want anybody to be a Jungian," Jung had said, "I want people above all to be themselves. As for 'isms,' they are the viruses of our day, and responsible for greater disasters than any medieval plague or pest has ever been. Should I be found one day to have created another 'ism' then I will have failed in all I tried to do." The failure is hardly his. He explored and charted a new world within, greater and infinitely more significant for our lives than the world Columbus discovered without; it is not his fault if his importance not only in healing the abnormal, but in healing the so-called normal man and his societies, has been missed. We refuse to follow the only path that can lead to the renewal and reintegration of our wounded, fragmented selves, and prefer instead to run around and around in our cage driven by a mounting sense of insufficiency and dissatisfaction.

The aim of modern psychiatry seems to be to make us socially adaptable to our cage: human suffering is reduced to mental illness, human problems to psychiatric symptoms and human beings to malfunctioning machines—the causes for the malfunctioning being sought in everything except the purpose which the human "machine" is made to serve. It is as if reasonable psychiatrists, practical men and moderate politicians have taken a vow to dismiss all purposes of life that do not confirm the superficiality of our existence.

Freud's great contribution was to burst open the dam holding back the flow of the unconscious; he exposed the mud behind our social counterfeit virtue, but offered nothing on which we could stand to lift ourselves out of it. He was blind enough to believe that it is possible for "enlightened" patients to achieve a totally rational approach to life. All experience has shown that it is not, and that unless we discover that space within where all is forever known, we will never be able to climb up out of the mud of the commonplace—whether it is our commonplace conventions or our commonplace repressions. Nor are modern man and modern culture likely to be healed so long as we continue to look at human beings as creatures of ephemeral desires, who, like horses, dogs or giraffes, enjoy life while experiencing an agreeable sensation or when stimulated by an agreeable activity. Especially as the modern Epicureans have perverted even Epicureanism: the philosophy of desire of the ancient pioneers included the most profound distrust of desire, and their policy of maximum satisfaction led them to advocate the most strenuous minimization of desires. Today the satisfaction of proliferating desires has become the aim of life, with a growing number of our desires being turned into politically imperative needs.

But as Goethe put it, "This life, gentlemen, is much too short for our souls." And when our spiritual hunger is not nourished, it is not only individuals who go mad; whole societies, cultures and civilizations become demented. Yet even though two world wars should have amply demonstrated just how demented our civilization could become, we go on—and here contemporary psychology is the supreme culprit—conveniently confining the problem to the abnormal and psychologically sick. We ignore the unlived meaning in derangement and suffering, crying out to be allowed to live, not only in the life of the sick, but in the life of the "normal" and their withering societies. We are discovering with growing urgency every day that our culture, having decreed that commitment to anything except a higher standard of living is meaningless, has not succeeded in eliminating the impulse towards a higher commitment in our souls.

Just as material rewards have become our principal preoccupation, the materialism of the capitalist system is singled out as the main culprit for the ills of society—for all the horrors that Western social organization is supposed to create, and bourgeois complacency to ignore. Treating materialism as an exclusive characteristic of the capitalist system is pure fantasy. The Greeks, that people of artists and philosophers, were at the same time traders and imperialists who built the Acropolis with money stolen from their allies. In groups and individuals, the love of money has been denounced since biblical times, and even brought about the downfall of the mendicant orders dedicated to holy poverty. The average man, middling and sensual, is not a modern invention. And yet ambition, greed, sloth, vanity—in fact, all appetites apart from the sexual which is glorified—are deemed the product of capitalist society.

The loss of belief in some ultimate good is bound to be accompanied by a loss of the sense of evil, and "the system" has become the most accessible scapegoat for all shortfalls from the ideal. Radical reform through political action is the catechism of this particular creed, an expansionist creed that has the alternative secular creed, from which springs the liberal tradition, on the run, abandoning one strategic position after another.

These two dominant political ideologies cannot be understood, nor the ascendancy of the one and the retreat of the other explained, if we strip their political solutions from the general solution they are offering to the problem of existence and the ancient desire to grasp all life as unity.

Liberal individualism saw man, liberated from the arbitrariness of state despotism and emancipated from religion, leading an earthly life satisfying within its own dimensions and on its own terms. Tolerance—putting up with people and being able to stand things—was the keynote of the creed, and subtle, intelligent, witty, *civilized* men were its evangelists. But a purely rational human life, satisfying within its own dimensions alone, is a life balked and deprived of its most powerful dynamic source, and is therefore untenable except briefly and artificially. So—and this is the linchpin of enlightened liberalism—art was to be the redeemer, the carrier of truth and the minister of the individual spirit. It was to act as the receptacle for the shreds of atavistic cosmic feelings, and to become a spiritual addiction rescuing man from the horrors of the physical world. Baudelaire invited all good liberals on this particular trip, promising:

> Nothing but Order, Beauty,
> Luxury, Peace, and Sensuous delight.

And Schopenhauer produced the theory to accompany the lyrical exhortations: the world was to be seen as an illusion projected by the will, which could only be detached from actuality by being attached to art.

In our century, having lost the sense of the "starry vault above and the moral law within," on which liberal individualism was initially based, we have reduced liberal philosophy to a series of vacuous negatives, proudly summed up by E. M. Forster in 1941: "What the world will most need is the negative virtues: not being huffy, touchy, irritable, revengeful. I have lost all faith in positive militant ideals; they can so seldom be carried out without thousands of human beings getting maimed or imprisoned." [8] But man needs to live at least partially in the world of timeless values. It is true that his search for the absolute is often expressed in perverted positive ideals; but through all its errors and perversions it obeys an inner law which pushes man toward the absolute at the center of his being without which he would crumble to dust.

It should have been obvious by now that all our humanist rosewater moralities, all our cherished beliefs in tolerance, geniality and personal relations are doomed to destruction by the hidden powers within us, unless we recognize our spiritual force: the only force that is greater than all other powers, and so the only force that can transform them. Our century has shown the animal grimace behind the mask, and should have taught us that all the evil and violence that we secretly harbor can recoil on us again—and that we cannot cure the world's evil unless we cure what is at its roots in men. The truth about our nature may be painful, but where illusion is the disease, truth is the only healing thing. And yet earnest liberals persist in plastering the facade or, with just as much naïveté, they urge us to deploy against evil our own—the words are Bernard Crick's—"open and honest condemnation."

There were at the beginning two parts to the liberal ideology: an ethical and political system which establishes how men should live as individuals and in relation to each other; and a metaphysical theory which explains why men should live in a given manner and not otherwise. One necessitates the other. But the Age of Reason politely dismissed the metaphysical part as Christian superstition or poetic imagination; and the center of gravity of our liberal ideology was permanently displaced with only the practical portion left in view. So that man's first business, his physical needs and economic activities, became also his chief business—and life itself the only object of living. For the Greeks, life was an occasion for the development of the rational, the ethical and the aesthetic being. Christ's message, before it was falsified and perverted by centuries of official Christianity, identified the seeking for man's highest self—which was the main philosophical preoccupation of the ancients—with man's spiritual consummation.

Today all this is a little shadowy for our practical liberal ideology. Even the aesthetic ideal becomes increasingly difficult to attain. At a time of unbelief, artists have tended to become technicians and specialists, more and more remote from contact with the public as opposed to the refined elect. Culture is put between quotation marks and becomes the preserve of the few. Tolstoy may have gone too far when he said that the test of any art is its being intelligible to the least instructed peasant, but when art becomes private, isolated and quirky, it loses all vital power to bring men together. And it can no longer fulfill the two tasks that Albert Camus isolated, in his Nobel Prize speech, as the main constituents of the artist's greatness: "the service of truth and the service of liberty. Because his task is to unite the greatest possible number of his people, his art must not compromise with lies and servitude. . . . The nobility of our craft will always be rooted in two commitments, difficult to maintain: the refusal to lie about what one knows and the resistance to oppression." Fifteen years later Alexander Solzhenitsyn, in his own Nobel Prize speech, described how far short of this ideal modern artists have fallen: withdrawn "into self-created worlds" and "realms of subjective whim," having surrendered the real world to others, they are complaining in unison about "how hopelessly warped mankind is, how shallow people have become, and how burdensome it is for a lone, refined and beautiful soul to dwell among them."

In the artistic history of the West from Homer onward, there has never been a time when art has been as arcane and remote from the new audiences it professes to want so badly to reach, as it is today. It seems incapable of achieving universality except through emptiness and nullity. The result is that we are almost entirely bereft of artists who are both great and popular—indeed, even artists who are great and *un*popular. Art, as a bridge between the transitory individual life and timeless truth, has become the specialized preserve of the few—with its circles but with no public. As the liberal ideology's solution to man's need for harmony and order, art suffers from a weakness which, in terms of the ideology's political appeal, is insurmountable: it is fundamentally undemocratic. Even if the ideology had not been suffering from other fatal weaknesses, this would have been enough to account for its actual or emotional displacement by state Caesarism.

The craving for what Dostoevsky called "a community of worship . . . and for a universal unity" persists. And the modern collectivists with their promise of a political Kingdom of Heaven on earth are there to satisfy it. They offer man redemption from selfishness and the commonplace, the same satisfaction of man's transcendental need that the elect get from worshiping Mozart or Wagner, and in the same kind of language that they use to describe their artistic ecstasies: "From the museum orchestra down below," wrote Neville Cardus from Bayreuth, "was wafted the incense, the enchanting fumes from the old magician's cauldron. Weak to the point of servitude, I succumbed, or rather relapsed, to faiths supposedly outmoded. . . . I am back in the thrall, actually glorying in the renewal of bondage." In the same religious vein, the politically aware today rush to identify with China, Tanzania or Allende's Chile, moved by the ethic of human brotherhood against what they see as a hostile, selfish, inhuman capitalist world.

What people need shapes what they see. And people need to create a world more real than daily existence, a world eternal and indestructible. Such a world belongs to man's spirit. But in the absence of belief in man's spiritual reality, the dream of creating it through state action has taken moral hold, and is shaping people's reactions to political events. This is what explains the double standard of those protesting against injustice. Unless we grasp the emotional need behind the political reactions, we will not be able to understand why a wave of anger sweeps the world at the reluctance of the United States to grant full independence to the people of the Virgin Islands while a wave of silence greets the turning of an entire country, Cambodia, into a concentration camp.

The humanist liberal solution has never been as tragically inadequate as it is today. A redeeming faith is needed more urgently than ever to save man's reason, if not his soul. The news of stories about starvation, massacres and torture is being piped incessantly and deadeningly through every available medium. And even if we are capable of insulating ourselves against atrocities that do not immediately touch us, wherever we turn we are unremittingly confronted with the seven modern deadly sins: utilitarianism, functionalism, triviality, quantification, mediocrity, fetishism and fragmentation.

Mankind has been suffering from utilitarianism for over a century, but today so widespread are its effects that nothing has any value unless it is useful; and increasingly nothing is useful unless it serves to bring, to acquire or to produce money. Utility is the real god of our life, the stuff of which it is made; all the rest belongs to its parts of ornament, embellishment, amusement and dispensable improvement. Culture and ethics, religion and aesthetics, are assigned their place as adjuncts to life, but they are not part of its very substance. What is important is that the production line of terrestrial happiness—that is, of uninterrupted affluence—should proceed without friction.

Functionalism reduces everything to its so-called *essential* function in a forlorn attempt to satisfy our impulse to abandon culture, by taking refuge in technological lyricism and austere purposefulness. The modern sculptures that look like cranes or engineering structures could act as the symbol of this modern sin; political philosophy should be marked out as the representative victim, completely under the sway of the functionalist notion that ideals and values are *essentially* ideals and values, and can therefore safely be relegated to the fantasy world of the desirable; and "spiritual technology" would have to be singled out as functionalism's *reductio ad absurdum,* with religious exhortations to "plug into the Power House where the greatest of Engineers . . . is your silent partner," to "learn to pray correctly and scientifically," to "employ tested and proven methods," and to "avoid slipshod praying," [9] preserved for future ages to marvel at.

Triviality is as old as Jonah, but today it has become the very stuff of our lives. Jonah was condemned to the Night Journey in the belly of the whale for his complacency and thick-skinned triviality. Condemning an entire civilization to the belly of a whale might strain even divine ingenuity. Yet for so long has modern man been confined to the trivial plane, in the grip of shallow conventions and trifling vanities, that we remain for most of our lives unaware of our bondage, reduced to the status of skilled automata, which Behaviorism proclaims to be our only condition. Indeed, were we not drowning in it, the triviality which surrounds us would have been unimaginable. And, far from achieving freedom through the realization of our nothingness, as Sartre had promised us, we are selling ourselves into collective enslavement. Even freedom has become too trivial to be worth defending. By quantifying our trivial concerns, and computerizing our trivial conclusions, we are desperately trying to convince ourselves of our fundamental seriousness. The modern Inquisitors are all quantifiers: whether they are asking us to "assess the candidate's emotional stability on a scale of 1 to 5," or to answer for purposes of some US Customs statistical inquiry whether we would or would not assassinate the President of the United States, they are faithfully obeying the Commandments of Quantification. So are the academics undertaking, for example, the computerization of 516 urban riots and disturbances in France for the period 1815 to 1914, and establishing beyond all reasonable doubt that market riots occur on market days, in or near the market. And so are the historians who announced triumphantly the decline of faith in the city of Marseilles between 1700 and 1789 on the strength of the size and number of church candles used at funerals, baptisms and weddings.[10] What makes this modern obsession dangerous, rather than merely ridiculous, is that it stands in the way of clear judgment not only on peripheral academic issues but on central political questions. Jeremy Bentham singled out self-interest rather than sympathy among the moral concepts of the eighteenth century because it is conceivably measurable. Today, true to the Benthamite tradition, our political leaders allow only interests that can be measured—that is, economic interests—to dominate our political calculations. So the myth persists that although we are dealing with trivialities, at least they are objective and quantified trivialities. And our mediocrats are satisfied.

Mediocrity is not, of course, a specifically modern sin; what is specifically modern is its overwhelming acceptance as the normal condition of humanity. Our political leaders are undoubtedly the most visibly successful mediocrats, but the two main ingredients of mediocracy—suffocating matter-of-factness and cowardly inertia—have infected every area of our lives. Here again, the state of the churches—demythologized, eviscerated, paying homage to creeds that failed—can stand as a symbol of modern mediocrity; and fashionable churchmen can stand as symbol of modern mediocrity in arms, against which the gods themselves are powerless.

Our sophisticated civilization has come back full circle to the direct worship of individual earthly objects. Except that modern fetishism is infinitely more humdrum. After all, fetishism had once given life to the worship of the sun; today it gives life to the yearning to join the ranks of the two-car family. But our pursuit of material objects is invested with the same, far from materialist, passion: it has become a spiritual endeavor to which all else is subsumed. We have made fetishism the axis about which revolves the life of an entire civilization.

There is nothing that we need more today than to have disproportion restored to proportion. Yet the fragmentation that besets our culture makes such restoration seem at times impossible. Fragmentation has nothing to do with variety: pluralism and the most prodigious variety can coexist with harmony and coherence. The great altarpieces of the Flemish painters contain just such a prodigious variety of detail, and yet the central theme of the picture is unmistakable: there they all are, the shepherds and the angels, the kings and the philosophers, the fools and the burghers, the maidens and the clerics, with every feature, even the most insignificant, painstakingly executed—but in no way detracting from the central focus, the Lamb of God. But the variety of our culture, lacking such a central focus, has turned into fastidious immersion in single small ideas and all their trivial ramifications. And it is our compulsive, fumbling attempt to make marginal fragments stand for the whole, rather than the divorce statistics, the sales of pornography or the plans to film the sex life of Jesus, that has made our culture decadent.

But the danger is even greater and more general: "Physics, as taught in the classroom," wrote Einstein, "was split into special fields each of which could engulf a short life's work without ever satisfying the hunger for deeper knowledge." Einstein escaped, but no culture can long survive if it is possible only for the occasional Einstein to escape its stultifying fragmentation. Yet the trend toward greater, and still greater, fragmentation seems unstoppable. It was only in the mid-thirties that sociology, psychology, anthropology and the rest were certified by the philosophy of science to be separate departments, leaving philosophy with the fever-swamp of linguistics. So man, dissected, his world split up into a thousand specialities and arbitrarily selected snippets, lacks any meaning to hold him together. Like a slide prepared for the microscope, he can dissolve into a world of fleeting and broken picture sequences; except that he will probably go on to the end claiming that the fragmented pictures, objective and quantified, are the only way to the complete "scientific understanding" of man. And when we attempt to integrate the fragments, without first establishing a central focus, we end up with the Open University humanities course—a nibble at Vasari, a chunk of Descartes, a bite of Saint Mark's Gospel—the ultimate combination of two of the seven modern sins, fragmentation and triviality.

There can be no integration of our split culture unless we have first healed the painful fragmentation within ourselves. For it is the split within that has blurred our vision, so that everywhere we find and perpetuate the reflection of our own "sins," and the echo of our own tumult. We feel that something in life has been missed, something that *ought* to be there; the chasm between what we are and what we need to be is deep, and growing deeper, but as this same incompleteness is obvious in the lives of others, we accept it as "natural," as our share in the common lot.

The all-devouring entities of Political Man, Religious Man, Aesthetic Man and Economic Man that have dominated our century are only projections of the fanatics who invented them; but they manifest the same denial of man's complex humanity and drive toward wholeness that is at the source of collectivist solutions which seek to reduce all life to politics. The classical Greek conception of the whole, balanced man does indeed remain a Western ideal. But today the conception has a new urgency and a new, greater meaning. Our century has established evil as a determinant reality that can no longer be dismissed from the world by circumlocution—it can only be combatted at its source in ourselves. Eve ate the apple lured by the promise of increased conscious knowledge. And today only such an expansion of our consciousness can save us. Yet we persist in dealing with a two-dimensional conceptual world in which the reality of life is well covered up by so-called clear concepts. But no one has any obligations to a concept, and so names are substituted for reality.

Confucius was once asked what would be the first thing he would do if it were left to him to administer a country: "It would certainly be to correct the language," he replied. "If language is not correct, then what is said is not what is meant; if what is said is not what is meant, then what ought to be done remains undone; if it remains undone, morals and art will deteriorate; if morals and art deteriorate, justice will go astray; if justice goes astray, the people will stand about in helpless confusion. Hence there must be no arbitrariness in what is said. This matters above everything."

The people *are* standing about in helpless confusion. But it is impossible to correct language, just as it is impossible to "correct" political leadership, without transforming the cultural context from which they both spring. And the crisis of our culture, like the crisis of the state, can only be approached elliptically through the crisis of individual man. Only when this is recognized, and the climate of opinion transformed as a result, will there be an end to the isolation of our culture from our politics and from the rest of our life.

There is, it is true, a more straightforward way, a truly instant solution, but freedom is its first victim and humanity its final one. It is the solution of state collectivism, which by offering salvation through state action puts an end to the split between culture, politics and life. Art becomes propaganda, the artist a slave to the political ends of the regime, and *Pravda* exposes formalistic "mistakes" in Shostakovich's operas. The First Congress of Soviet Writers in 1934 clearly defined what the theory of Socialist Realism demands of an artist: "a truthful, historically concrete, portrayal of reality in its revolutionary development." And in China today, sound painting is painting that serves the people by furthering the campaign against "the right-deviationist attempt of Teng Hsiao-p'ing to reverse the correct verdicts" [11] —in other words, sound painting serves the current campaign of the party. The artist must not only portray the "reality" which does not contradict ideological orthodoxy, but must also portray the assumed certainty of the perfected "reality" of the future. "Our writers must march in serried ranks, and he who stands off the road to pick flowers is like a deserter." [12] Konstantin Simonov's words signal the end of art; but other ends will have to take priority in the mourning.

In any case, the subterranean messianic ramblings of Marxism and its collectivist progeny are expected to cater, without the need of either art or religion, for all passionate emotion and individual "oceanic feeling." It is Western humanism that, unashamedly geared as it is to material prosperity, has assigned to art the role of mopping up the populace's excess passion.

Shakespeare classed persons insensitive to aesthetic impressions as dangerous defectives. And Plato regarded music—using the term in the largest aesthetic sense—as an essential branch of republican education. But today art is not enough to save the republics. For a start—and this is a personal tragedy for civilized humanists, as well as a political weakness of the liberal ideology—art is not a complete redemption. The material world remains only partially displaced, and disgust with it deepens as the cultivation of art refines sensibility. "As for living, our servants will do that for us," de Lisle Adam was driven to say. And in this century, they have done so with a vengeance.

Even more dangerous for democracy and for our freedom is the fact that Western liberalism, based as it is today on a fatally incomplete view of man, has misunderstood both the supreme function of art and its inescapable limitations. By disregarding man's spiritual dimension, it treats man's life as entirely rational, and man's mind as the destined archangel of life's transformation. It is indeed an old fallacy with an impeccable pedigree going back to Erasmus, who devoted himself for a time—admittedly not a *very* long time—to the pleasant idea that *bonae litterae,* cultivated and sustained by the concord of ruling princes, were about to usher in an era of happiness, culture and peace. Rabelais was just as devoted to a restoration of *bonnes lettres* as a means to a general rebirth and renewal. And a large number of pious souls since, sharing Erasmus's spirit but lacking the Erasmian and Rabelaisian chuckle—Schopenhauer and Nietzsche being the extreme cases—have tried to live on a purely aesthetic diet. And many are, with growing difficulty and dissatisfaction, doing so today. With an almost pathetic desperation they overestimate the emotional content of everything artistic they touch; and at the same time they pour scorn on those other modern "pious souls" who, equally oblivious of the true channel for their piety, are glutting themselves instead on poorly understood, and poorly understandable, "isms."

"But tell me," Hesse's Narcissus asks Goldmund, "besides this desperate coming and going between lust and horror, besides this seesaw between lust for life and sadness of death—have you tried no other road?"

"Oh, yes, of course I have. I've tried art."

And our modern liberals have indeed tried art. But the renewal, both personal and cultural, that they have sought in art is simply not attainable through art. Or rather, it may be attainable through it, but not in it. The supreme function of art is to cleanse the doors of perception, to change our vision of the world, and, since to see falsely means to live falsely, to change the world. This connection between the aesthetic and the ethical is undoubtedly the connection that gives art its dignity, its meaning and its power. But it is a connection which, when made explicitly and socio-realistically by the artist, turns art into pretentious journalism and ineffectual propaganda. The connection can only be made within ourselves. By piercing through all the crusts of our life, the exclusive ideas, narrow interests and padlocked moralities in which we have barricaded ourselves, art liberates the truth we carry imprisoned within us.

The trap is that we will confuse the revelation of our soul—which, however momentary, overwhelms and glorifies everything it touches—with the circumstances of the revelation. So that if we have been listening to Mozart, nothing except music will be true and divine for us; and if we felt the stirrings of our soul in front of Rembrandt's self-portraits, we will make a religion of painting and turn Rembrandt into our Gospel. Then our self-transcending emotions, unintegrated into life, will be nothing more than euphoric flickers of romantic enthusiasm, destined to atrophy and shrivel away. This is a trap into which millions have fallen. The trap has by no means always been art. Indeed, it has much more often been a particular creed or religion. And this is where error and superstition begin. The trap is to take an intermediate stage for the end. And the danger is that, satisfied with the occasional life-giving artistic or religious ecstasy, we will forget that the end we seek is the state of integral mastery that in *full consciousness* will put an end to the gulf between life and the spirit. Beethoven, Shakespeare or Shelley are not evolutionary ends: they give us access to the highest truth, they raise the curtain of smoke, and reveal a new world with new values, new reliefs and new correspondences; then it is up to us to integrate these insights into our life, and make the new world manifest. "Sacrifice," wrote Hermann Hesse, "is no longer a matter of doing specifically sacred things only on particular occasions, but of sacrificing (making sacred) all we do and all we are."

The primary requisite of art is indeed that it shall move us, not that it shall instruct us. But after we have been moved, our conscience entrapped by the play within the play, the living meaning is lost unless we use this intermediary experience to gain real understanding and real transformation. "Formation, Transformation, Eternal Mind's Eternal Re-creation," cries Faust. It is this living effect of art on man that makes art at its highest what Goethe believed it to be: a sister of religion, by whose aid the great world scheme is wrought into reality; no mere amusement to charm the idle or relax the careworn, but a mighty influence, serious in its aims and joyful in its means.

Art, as the mediator that brings the sublime within the ken of earthly mortals, can make us recognize the extraordinary in the ordinary, the great in the commonplace. "After all," wrote Whitman, "the great lesson is that no special natural sight—not Alps, Niagara, Yosemite or anything else—is more grand or more beautiful than the ordinary sunrise and sunset, earth and sky, the common trees and grass." Art, like religion, can awaken this certain vision, insight and instinctive response in the soul, which removes the vagueness and dullness of habitual perceptions. And by protecting all that which can be experienced but not explained, it helps man to satisfy the need—a need that uniquely distinguishes him from all other creatures—to render his experiences harmonious.

The clue in terms of our individual transformation—and only through such transformations can we transform the world—is neither the frequency nor the intensity of our artistic experiences, but the use we make of them to integrate our truth into our lives. For in the same way that all bodies at a certain degree of heat become luminous, all men have experienced moments in their lives when they have felt the exaltation of this truth; but reduced to normal temperatures, that which was luminous becomes again opaque, and man, momentarily integrated, becomes again split.

Ever since the mystery plays of the Achaeans, the cave paintings of Altamura and the first mythological epics, art has spontaneously encouraged the unfolding of man's participatory emotions, neutralized his most disruptive self-asserting tendencies, and so helped to keep a community together. But the enthusiasm of the Renaissance, the self-assurance of the eighteenth century, the high hopes of the nineteenth, have given way to universal doubt among artists, and to isolated private worlds of art. So much so that we tend to forget that the pictures we see in our museums once formed part of the natural decoration of churches and palaces, or that Bach's cantatas were written for the practical needs of the daily Lutheran service. We are in danger of confining art to museums. And Kenneth Hudson, author of the *Directory of Museums*, foresees a great future for "museums verging on the exhibition, with a large temporary element," and for "eco-museums": "You take an area," he explains, "maybe a piece of countryside or a chunk of city, and everything in that area is in the museum. Every cow, person or coal mine is an exhibit." [13] So it is not only art that is to be confined to museums, but life, too.

But art does not merely reflect, let alone report as though it were the latest by-election result, the mind of an age. It does indeed draw its sustenance from the experiences of its time, but it gives back much more than it receives. It transcribes the experiences of the age and raises its mind to a much higher power. It may do this with or without "poppycock," but what is certain is that it cannot do it by facts and information alone. Even Milton had to abandon pamphlet writing and the "sea of noises and hoarse disputes" before he could produce *Paradise Lost*. And Napoleon, who wrote to the Commissioner of Police to inquire why there was no flourishing literature in Europe, and to ask whether he could please see to it that there was, had in the end to come to terms with reality. Ultimately only the artist who expresses personal experience can reach universal experience. And this is why practical men of revolution have always found artists intensely uncomfortable. Except that increasingly today, "practical" artists seem to be finding *themselves* intensely uncomfortable. "If I were in charge of a revolution," wrote Genevieve Taggard, clearly thirsting for accusation, "I'd get rid of every single artist immediately; and trust to luck that the fecundity of the earth would produce another crop when I had got some of the hard work done."

Once you accept—as our officially anti-Marxist culture undoubtedly does—the fundamental tenet of Marxist epistemology, that truth is the final result of long investigation, the direct relevance of art to truth, and to life, is lost. "But don't we perceive a sort of twilight truth before any investigation has begun?" asks Kondrashev Ivanov in *The First Circle.* At the moment we obviously don't. And art, instead of helping us to recognize this truth, is reduced—and this at its most elegant—to a Beckettian monologue by a disembodied mouth. "I have nothing to say," explains the man who once said that he would like to see *Waiting for Godot* play to empty houses, "but I can only say to what extent I have nothing to say." Those less concerned about having nothing to say are turning aside to write lullabies for their cats—art as escape and soporific. Except that, gradually, even our escapism becomes the world lost rather than the world saved: *Earthquake*s, and *Towering Inferno*s, and jumbo-jet holocausts.

In the last Karamazov dream, there is, as a road sign at nightfall warning of a dangerous incline on a steep pass ahead, the appearance of a desperately frail young woman, standing with empty breasts and a famished baby in her arms, against a wintry setting of ice and snow, pleading to a dead world for nourishment for the child. Dostoevsky's nightmare vision of the starving soul of man has never been equaled in intensity; and his bloodcurdling scream, so accurately anticipating the explosion of unexplored forces in man, shows up the fashionable pessimism of today's art for the bad-tempered whining that it is. And yet his art, like all great art, by revealing something of the harmony and promise of joy that are at the foundation of existence, is ultimately optimistic. This is the optimism not of ignorance but of supreme understanding. It is the optimism that Solzhenitsyn embodies today, and that makes him believe that true art, as a reflection of beauty, has the capacity to reveal to man truth and goodness—and through this trinity of Truth, Goodness and Beauty to awaken in him the knowledge of the divine unity which is the source of all existence: "If the all too obvious and the overly straight sprouts of Truth and Goodness have been crushed, cut down, or not permitted to grow, then perhaps the whimsical, unpredictable and ever-surprising shoots of Beauty will force their way through and soar up to that very spot, thereby fulfilling the task of all three." [14]

The task of all three is the inward renewal of men; and through this, the renewal and the longed-for transformation of our world. The idea of renewal, rebirth, revival and restoration has obsessed humanity for centuries. But it has always been restricted to a shadow of the truth, to a narrow hope of specific renewal—whether the aesthetic renewal of the Renaissance, the renewal of the Christian faith at the Reformation, or the political renewal of our own times. In fact, the hopes and ideals animating the exponents of all great historical movements spring from the age-old longing to be born again in our own lifetime, but this time in the full glory of our true nature.

"At the Renaissance," wrote Burckhardt, "religion was really alive only in the form of art." It is only those who cannot conceive of religion except in terms of churches and creeds who will find this statement paradoxical. At every historical period, religion is most alive in whatever form most successfully awakens the slumbering souls of men. Once religion is alive not outside but inside man, then the renewal we long for will have been achieved, and the expectation of salvation fulfilled. The tragedy of our modern period is that with religion asleep in our souls, and dead both in our churches and in art, political salvationism has stepped forth to fill the gap. Except that the theory of salvation through politics presupposes not human beings but automata—on those occasions, that is, when it does not presuppose corpses.

Dante was the first to broaden in the *Commedia* the concept of rebirth to encompass spiritual, aesthetic and political renewal; and he looked to the aesthetic renewal he clearly detected in his day as a symbol and catalyst of the great renewal he so fervently longed for. Today our inward, spiritual renewal has to precede all other renewals. But art, now as always, and now more urgently than ever, has the supreme prophetic mission to expose the lie of our age and warn humanity of its tragic path. "One word of truth shall outweigh the whole world," said Solzhenitsyn in his Nobel Prize lecture, quoting a Russian proverb. "It is on such a seemingly fantastic violation of the law of conservation of mass and energy . . . that my own activity is based, and my appeal to the writers of the world." The writers and other artists of the world seem to prefer escapism or propaganda. But the truth is there, imprisoned in eternal works of art by all the great inspirers of our civilization—if only we would free it by letting it act on our souls, and liberate us. Then art will help to bring about the miracle of our inner transformation and win the battle against evil.

7

FROM IMAGINATION TO CONSCIOUS KNOWLEDGE

"Imagination is more important than knowledge." What is extraordinary about this remark is not that it was made by Albert Einstein—although this would appear not so much extraordinary as incredible, to hard-headed modern man—but the fact that all our naïve notions about our scientific mastery over our destiny have managed to survive this, and many equally unequivocal, statements about the limitations of mental knowledge by the men who did, after all, create our proud, scientific age.

Man's reason moves naturally between two limits: the abstractions of the analytical intellect and the practicalities of everyday reality. The function of imagination is totally different. It is not, as is often supposed, to give us access to cosmic reveries, nor is it to make spiritual romancing more phantasmagoric. It is to sow the seed of aspiration toward the unfolding of the unique truth we embody. Imagination acknowledges something in us before we know, sees before we see, and sends its vision to the surface in the form of a need, a seeking, a faith, which is at first inexplicable, but is neither illusion nor elusive. Indeed, it is the most important and the most solid entity that exists in the world today. It begins as an imaginative intuition, but it is only waiting for experience, first individual and then collective, to verify and justify it. In fact, it is not merely waiting; it is leading toward experience, and precipitating confirmation.

The need to go beyond the intellect, and its pondering and measuring reason, is inescapable. We have to recognize the disease of overintellectuality from which our age is suffering before we can pass from our mechanistic existence to the realization of our larger self—from the scrutiny of the things that explain to the experience of the things that reveal.

Our proud Age of Reason is sick unto death; but it seems unable to die. We go on believing that the rainbow has been reduced to mathematics, and that all that is left is for reasonable men to get together to put the mathematical equations into effect and so transform our lives. "Men have become like gods," writes Dr. Edmund Leach, Provost of King's College, Cambridge. "Isn't it about time that we understood our divinity? Science offers us total mastery over our environment and our own destiny, yet instead of rejoicing we feel deeply afraid. Why should this be?" [1]

Belief in the ultimate mastery of science and in the ultimate power of reason are less and less confidently asserted; they do, however, continue to dominate our century. When Bishop Berkeley, turning the tables on the early materialists, maintained that matter itself very possibly did not exist, Dr. Johnson, who did not like such bottomless fancies, kicked a stone with his boot, saying "I refute him thus!" Today our avenging pragmatists can spare their boots: the century belongs to them, and so do the bishops.

This is why the first task in any program of renewal is to try to rescue from the rubble the main casualty of our time—the human imagination. It is only imagination that fuses all the other powers of man, misused in everyday life. And it is only by salvaging the human imagination that we shall be able to understand the nature of the political threat.

In an age overflowing with facts and documents, we go on regarding as an illusion the only thing that can save us from our "objective" illusions and feed our starving souls. We go on clinging to our "objective" and "subjective" categories and forget that the way humanity has progressed so far is by a series of imaginations which human will has turned into accomplished facts. By contrast, the train of illusions which have created the horrors of our age and bedeviled our century have been the result of that most deceptive organ of knowledge, the human intellect; it is man's intellect that weaves a veil of arbitrary fixations of time and place over the truth of a perfected humanity, toward which we are driven by our imagination. Then (and this is the supreme illusion and ultimate hubris) man seeks to bring it about through political action.

We go on being duped by our concern for "objectivity," oblivious of the fact that if we made the so-called objective the sole criterion of truth, our entire world—as the science, let alone the poetry, literature and music of our century, have not ceased proclaiming—would be in danger of slipping through our fingers. There is, of course, a sense in which a T-bone steak is more objective, and its reality more universally verifiable, than Beethoven's last Quartets; but we have denuded the world, not enriched it. And our critical rationalism, uninformed by any deeper knowledge, has been busy purifying the world through emptiness for a very long time. It has eliminated as futile speculations things that it regards as incomprehensible, and it gives short shrift to anything that it rules out as impossible—however many times our science has discovered that the impossible is actually the true.

"The world of imagination," wrote Blake, "is the world of eternity." And our task is to actualize eternity, and turn imagination into conscious knowledge. Yet we persist in looking at our intellect as the only source of knowledge and attributing to it a final omnipotence which both our disordered history and our present reality patently disprove. For far too long, and with the full scientific panoply of the Freudian school, we have made a dangerous monster out of unconsciousness—as if the horrors and perversions perpetuated by man's conscious mind this century were not enough to cure us of our belief that all that is good, beautiful and true dwells in consciousness.

When Jung was asked once which people he had found most difficult to heal, he instantly replied, "Habitual liars and intellectuals." [2] Jung, with his supreme understanding of man's intellectual achievement, was hardly likely to despise the intellect. What he did despise was the intellect's neglect of other aspects of man, at least as valid and important. By being untrue to themselves through these constant deeds of omission, many modern intellectuals have indeed become habitual liars—mass-producers of concepts with which they continue to shield themselves from reality. And the concepts, however hollow and weak they may be, expand and become intellectual forces that dominate our minds and conquer territory at the expense of other, non-rational sources of awareness. So man's existence has become fatally compartmentalized.

"I would rather be governed by the first two thousand names in the Boston telephone directory, than by the entire Harvard Faculty," [3]

William Buckley has said more than once. But Western culture is still in the grip of the modern version of that old Pelagian heresy that education would save us all. And it is here that our second major task lies; for although education, properly understood, could indeed bring man out of the darkness of ancient and new superstitions, and help him draw out and perfect that which is greatest in him, education as it is today mutilates man's growth and defaces his latent perfection. We go on confusing education with the acquisition of knowledge, and interpreting knowledge as the storage of facts, figures and information. And educational progress has come to signify numbers going up, class sizes coming down and more money spent. Indeed many have come to talk about university expansion in terms of "an increase in productivity" and "a more intensive use of university plant." [4]

What modern educationists have forgotten is that they are not sculptors dealing with dead material and shaping educational masterpieces out of human wood or stone. What they are dealing with is the elusive substance of the human mind; by ignoring the subtlety of the human mind and the reality of the human soul, they are educating children out of the natural spirit that first prompts question and answer, and are equating the instrumentalities of man's mind with the whole of man. It is, of course, a very old fallacy, and one to which those who ascribe to the state the function of shaping man are particularly prone.

The aim of all totalitarian systems of education was unambiguously summarized by Olof Palme, who before he became Prime Minister of Sweden was Minister of Education. "You don't go to school," he said addressing Swedish schoolchildren, "to achieve anything personally, but to learn how to function as members of a group." [5] Or as a departmental chief at the Swedish Directorate of Schools put it: "Everything in our school system is practical. History has been cut down, because subjects of practical application are more important. Classical studies have been abolished, because they are impractical and, therefore, unnecessary." [6] And what stands between Sweden and the rest of Western democracies is a protective shell of the values on which our civilization is based. But the shell is becoming increasingly fragile; and the values are being reduced to obligatory remarks on "choice," "freedom," and "our Western heritage."

The rationalist, constructivist hoof of our culture is clearly showing—and nowhere more clearly than in the official approach to education. Lord Crowther-Hunt has politely told the vice-chancellors of British universities that they must conform to the government's manpower needs or go to the financial wall. What will happen when they discover that the planners had, after all, got their targets wrong? Will they, like disgruntled farmers who have heeded other fictional official production targets, clamor for compensation? And if so, do you compensate for the glut of mechanical engineers on the same principle that you compensate for a glut of potatoes? The answer depends on the answer to a larger question: is the role of universities to educate the whole man or to express the values of society, to meet the economy's manpower needs or to investigate the purpose of life? We will only be able to resolve this age-old debate when we have really listened to and understood the message of the sages—"Know thyself." Only then will we recognize the fallacy of reducing it to the message of the thinker—"Educate yourself"; and what is worse, reducing the message of the thinker to the message of the technocrat, and education to technical training.

The educational ideal has always involved the division of education into two parts: the one dealing with the acquisition of knowledge, and the other concerned with the ordering of experience. But modern education has lost sight of this second function. Yet this is the function which, instead of limiting itself to ascertained knowledge, uses it as a stimulus and a point of departure from which to seek to grasp the elusive and unascertained that alone can give meaning and order to experience. Humanity has advanced to its present stage only because of these still rare and imperfectly developed faculties, so much distrusted by critical reason. But instead of seeking to develop them further and reduce the element of error, caprice and fancifulness that they often contain, modern education simply ignores them.

And on the few occasions that it takes them into account, it does so with the kind of clumsiness and lack of understanding that has led the Cognitive Research Trust in Cambridge to suggest "thinking" as a curriculum subject; and that has led Edward de Bono to talk portentously about the different sets of skills which go to make up the "operating idiom" as opposed to the "academic idiom," and to announce that "pupils who have been regarded as academically backward can turn out to be effective thinkers. . . . It seems that they are poor on the input side but nevertheless strong on the output side." [7] Hardly a new discovery, once you turn it into English. All that Mr. de Bono is grudgingly acknowledging is that there are other sources of knowledge apart from those that proceed from absorbing information. As if the entire history of intellectual degeneration in gifted races were not sufficient proof, not only of the existence of other, more creative sources of knowledge, but of what happens when these are neglected. And today they are being neglected with a vengeance. Indeed, much of the shallowness, conformity and futile mutability of the average modern mind can be attributed to this neglect, and to the vicious principle of teaching by snippets and a smattering of facts. So it has come to pass that we have a grandiose specialism at the top, founded on nothing except these snippets at the bottom, and a vast and comprehensive ignorance in the middle.

In the eighteenth century, that period of supreme and supremely misplaced optimism, a succession of popular writers from Pierre Bayle and de Fontenelle to Diderot and his fellow contributors to the *Encyclopédie,* which appeared in France from 1751 to 1777, aimed to interpret the whole of knowledge and bring it within the reach of any educated person; it was an attempt to recapture and extend, three centuries later, the Renaissance ideal epitomized in the Academy of Florence, dedicated to the study of all aspects of knowledge and of art. But it became increasingly difficult to entertain such illusions of mental omniscience, not so much because of the vastly widened range of knowledge, but mainly because men began to realize that a whole life of study would scarcely suffice to still the craving hunger for knowledge.

There are in our century tendencies, as yet infant and subordinate, which carry within them the first glimmering of the realization that each human being is a self-developing soul, and that, therefore, the right object of education and indeed of the whole of life is to deepen man's inner experience and evoke his hidden truth. Then we will begin for the first time to make universal the isolated achievement of a few outstanding individuals in human history—to live according to the true and deepest law of our being. The discovery that education must be a bringing out of a child's own capacities, and not a mechanical forcing of his nature into arbitrary grooves of training and knowledge, seemed at the beginning to be the seed of a collective recognition that the secret, whether with child or man, is to help him find his deeper self, the real psychic entity within. But it soon degenerated into an attack on the values of culture and reflective life, a monotonous harping on the notions of spontaneity and practicality, and a naïve application to education of Rousseau's doctrine of a state of nature.

John Dewey, who crystalized the beginnings of the new trend with his *Cardinal Principles* in 1918, placed the child at the center of the educational system, with the child's developing interests and impulses displacing the rigid authority of the teacher and the traditional weight of the curriculum. But the very strength of the element of truth in Dewey's thought and in the new educational theories on both sides of the Atlantic increased the strength of the element of error they contained. What is worse, the nature of the error is being almost invariably misconstrued. It does not lie in the rejection of rigid authority, as so many of the most vociferous critics of the new theories have assumed; it lies in the purpose for which modern educationalists sought to liberate the child from a mechanical forcing into molds fixed by conventional ideas.

The purpose at the core of the new education was to form a type of character and mind suitable to the work of social reform. So the individual child was put at the center of the educational stage, not because it needed freedom and help to discover and manifest the truth it embodies, but so that it could become a major force in social reconstruction. And the element of truth from which the new theories imbibed their strength has been so abused and perverted, that it now seems impossible to extirpate the counterfeit without destroying the very fact of truth. Especially as, under the panoply of scientific findings, modern educators have taken an increasingly sterile anti-intellectual line, until it seems at times that they will propose and do anything in the name of science except encourage children to study it.

"There is no use in education. I hold it to be wrong. It is the great sin."[8] Blake's jeremiads against education have an even greater poignancy now than they had in his own day. Ultimately the value of all efforts at reform depends on the value of the human ideal that inspires them. If the ideal is wrong, no attempt to transform reality will be of any use. And our ideal today is both wrong and ridiculous. When Erasmus described how ridiculous he thought it was that a person should acquire a reputation of being clever for knowing what was happening in the world, what the market situation was like and what were the plans of the rulers,[9] he could not have imagined that a time would come when what he thought ridiculous would be regarded as ideal.

Truth has to be lived; it cannot be learned. This is why the whole controversy about religious education at school is so profoundly irrelevant. Religion has also to be lived, and cannot be learned as a creed. But modern educated man has become like Chesterton's character in *The Man Who Was Thursday,* who knew all about Christianity because he had read about it in *Religion the Vampire* and *Priests of Prey.* He has been turned into the modern democratic town version of the village cobbler, incapable of believing in anything save what he can touch and see.

This is the last rescue operation we will have to carry out: the rescue of man's religious sense. Only when men stop blinding themselves to their own religious promptings because of their childish passion for narrow mental enlightenment will we be able to understand that the peril which threatens us all comes not from nature, but from man himself. And only then will we be able to redefine the role of politics.

Politics will seem at first an extremely strange starting point from which to approach the ultimate truth. But this is a starting point chosen for us by a century which has ascribed to politics the role of molding, not only the whole character of a society and a civilization, but the character of man. The hubris of our age has been to expect the actions of politicians and the methodologies of social scientists to create a universal culture, globally managed and kept alive by the technocrats of politics and administration. And when the political vision is so dramatically superimposed on our private vision that our private truth is being increasingly questioned, sentient beings have very little alternative but to address themselves to politics in order to salvage from it life's ultimate secret and meaning. Yet wherever one looks and listens in politics, one sees nothing but walking definitions of political cowardice and hears nothing but their silence.

"Politics, amidst the interests of the imagination, are a pistol shot in the middle of a concert. This noise is ear-rending without being forceful. It clashes with every instrument." But what Stendhal and the confirmed apolitical fail to realize is that unless we take time off from the concert and relate the ultimate truths and absolute realities to the burning questions that we have been trying to solve with reference to everyday, mundane realities alone, politics will not merely clash with every instrument; it will ultimately silence the concert. And human beings devoid of the spiritual truth to which alone their uniqueness and their greatness can be traced, will be reduced to supernumeraries on the stage of the world theater.

Yet there is nothing more difficult than seeking to express in the terms of a three-dimensional world the truth of four-dimensional reality. In a world which has sold its soul for a mess of disconnected facts and impossible promises, and where so many are casually using words to work off on themselves and on others feelings that they do not really have, when these same words are used to bear witness to real spiritual feeling, they sound flatulent, bombastic, self-righteous—a shade absurd. We need a new, another language to express what these higher planes of consciousness bring to man and how they change our vision of ourselves and of the world when we begin to rise to them. But more important, we need to understand what we mean by rescuing the religious sense in man, especially when such a rescue operation is discussed in relation to its political effects—because in no other area are misunderstanding and confusion as likely, or as dangerous.

We do not mean that, as Ernest Van den Haag put it, "Religious sanction is required—just as the police force is—for any society which wishes to be stable without being totalitarian"; we do not mean, as he concluded, that "religion is a useful, even a necessary opiate—a sedative protecting us from excessive anxiety and agitation and from those, who, like Marx, thrive on agitation and, therefore, hate the sedative and would replace it by the murderer's hashish";[10] we do not mean the kind of "religious revival" that President Eisenhower had in mind when he opened his inaugural address with a prayer, thus setting a precedent for future presidents to follow; nor do we mean that, as William Henry Chamberlin put it, "religion, patriotism, the integrity of the family and respect for private property" are "the four pillars of a sound and healthy society."[11]

In all these modern defenses of religious belief, there is the same fallacy: that religion is faith in a creed or a set of fundamental beliefs, an outward observation of rules and an individual participation in religious ceremonies. This is to mistake the oyster for the pearl. The oyster is certainly valuable, but only to the extent that it promotes the growth of the pearl. Once the highest truth, the God within, is discovered, faith is gradually transformed to conscious knowledge and the use of the oyster of ceremonies and rites is exhausted. No man can reach, manifest and live the reality of the spirit unless he has gone beyond orthodoxies and conventions, beyond the keeping of commandments, however strictly, and the observing of ceremonies, however faithfully. For this is to subject the higher to the lower principle, and to bind down the self-disclosing spirit to a provisional compromise with the mind and with social realities. From this, it is but a short step to explaining what is higher by what is lower, and perpetuating the reductive attitude of dismissing every truth as a case of "nothing but"—nothing but something else of an inferior sort.

Most of the modern, conservative exhortations to a religious revival are textbook cases of the "nothing but" philosophy; they are treating the social function of religion, not merely as supremely important at a time when the totalitarian temptation is becoming irresistible, but as an end in itself. This is hardly a new conservative position. Perhaps its most emphatic formulation was made in 1795, when Edmund Burke in his *Letter to William Smith, Esq.,* described Christianity as "the grand prejudice . . . which holds all the other prejudices." But this is to treat Christian beliefs in particular, and religious belief in general, on the same level as the Roman auguries which Cicero regarded as essential "on account of popular opinion and of the great public utility." [12]

We are trapped between two official approaches to religion. The first and most fashionable is simply one more version of the secular redemption theory with political rhetoric dressed up as Christian concern; it ranges from the identification of religious truth with social problem-solving to the World Council of Churches and its consecration of international Marxist aggression. The other official approach, which springs from the Conservative, civic attitude to religion, is detached from our common experience and is based on very little other than the Christian doctrine of original sin and the pessimism deduced from it; it looks at religion not as a new window opening on this world, but as a skylight giving on the next—a "theological religion," with which you can do very little except believe it without hope.

The one approach has secularized the divine; the other has relegated it to outer space. Our purpose is to make the divine manifest on earth, so that religion, instead of being a gloss on social reform, or an expression of dogmas and metaphysical speculations, will be a continuous living experience. And the nearness of man to God will reflect the extent of the nearness to his sense of his own greatest meaning. This is why it is in the descent of the Son of God to earth that lies the supreme importance of the Christian message for modern man. It is the manifestation of Christ on earth that should make clear in the West—if, that is, we succeed in ridding the truth of the clutter of nearly twenty centuries of Churchianity—the possibilities of the manifestation on earth of the Christ within every man. And it is this manifestation of our divine reality that will be the resurrection not of the dead but of the living who are dead to their own truth.

"It is the soul that is moved and awakened," wrote Saint John of the Cross, "it is as if God drew back some of the many veils and coverings that are before it, so that it might see what he is." And then our soul, now a stranger to our superficial pilgrimage in the world, will give substance and reality both to our everyday lives and to the shadowy phantoms which churchmen call our creeds, and metaphysicians our philosophy of the absolute. The earth will remain just as positive and real as it ever was—but it will have been transformed by the reality of the soul made manifest. At the moment our store of alive, collective wisdom concerning the inner life, on which we could draw for a deepened self-knowledge, is a mere nothing. But the knowledge, enriched by our century's scientific findings on the objectivity of the soul, is there; and so is the longing, great and growing every day, as the evidence, both psychic and external, of the tragic failure of our technocratic solutions becomes inescapable.

Many a modern Ulysses has set off for his native land—the real country, the world of unseen truth within. But never has the perennial problem of communicating the experiences of the soul been as great as it is today, in a world which vulture-like is feeding off dead principles. Truth has been reduced to something for men to play with to stop them from being bored, to sharpen their minds or to demonstrate their intellectual superiority. In our democratic age, all debate has been reduced to an aristocratic duel of words. And we respond at the intellectual or the emotional level to speech and argument that grips us because it can imitate the truth, and even appear more convincing than truth itself. Truth in its completeness is literally beyond words, and so lacks all the angles which make ideas and doctrines easily understandable.

This is why spiritual knowledge ultimately cannot be communicated from one intellect to another. Wisdom is of the soul and has to be worked out by the recipient within himself—to be recreated before it can be experienced. All mythology, all great poetry, all spiritual teaching, is studded with symbols and veiled in allegory precisely for this reason; not in order to obscure the message, but on the contrary, because direct definitions at this level obscure by limiting. This is what makes the New English Bible and other such attempts to make spiritual truth journalistic and "easy" so misguided. An enigma or two, it is true, do not add up to depth, and ambiguity may be merely concealing emptiness and even conscious or half-conscious deception. But against this, one's ability to make critical distinctions and, ultimately, one's inward judgment, so deeply buried under all the modern clutter, are the only protection. How little protection our vaunted reason, anchored as it is in nothing higher than itself, has been, we have the whole preposterous commercial fantasy of the current art scene and the worship of Pinter and other elliptical *artistes* to prove. So it has come about that without a theory and an erudite interpretation to go with it, we cannot see a painting, nor can we watch a play.

An infinitely greater modern failing is our response to the spiritual statements of the great poetry and great literature of the past. All words which speak from a higher plane of consciousness sound inevitably in vain to those who do not dwell on the same plane. And yet because, at the same time, we cannot fail to be moved by their beauty and grandeur, we have resolved the dilemma not by seeking to expand our consciousness to integrate their reality in our lives, but by treating them as "poetic truths"—and, therefore, in terms of their impact on our lives and beliefs, as untrue.

So we admire Wordsworth and are moved by his

> . . . with an eye made quiet by the power
> Of harmony, and the deep power of joy,
> We see into the life of things.

or by

> . . . A motion and a spirit that impels
> All thinking things, all objects of all thought,
> And rolls through all things.

But when it comes to any compulsion to examine our own lives and our own values—which is, after all, the only valid response to the communication of truth—we might as well have been admiring an exotic flower arrangement.

While our world remains the world of newspapers and "common sense," spiritual truth will continue to be treated either as poetic ornament or as mischievous imposture—the product of Mysticism, Romanticism or, in the case of Walt Whitman, "Yankee bluster." But despite all the reductionism, the misunderstandings and the confusion, something passes from these men to us, of more importance than all that we could learn from the ordinary scientists and philosophers. And it is this that leavens the world—and that makes us remember, however briefly, who we are. To turn that brief instant of remembering into a glorious, continuous reality is the purpose of a living religion.

At a moment like the present when the intellect of mankind is, after a long wandering, turning again toward the search for our spiritual truth, reason has indeed a pertinent role to play in expounding to the intellectual part of man the truths, the experiences and the effects of a spiritual existence. It can draw inferences and analogies from the data given by rational experience and from our knowledge of the facts of physical existence, and it can appeal both to the conclusions of science and to the greatest individual manifestations of the human spirit in poetry and in music. But reason can convince only when the imagination is already awake and the intellect predisposed to belief. And even if it convinces, it cannot by itself turn belief into conscious inner knowledge. Because ultimately the soul is the only means of *knowing* anything about the soul. Indeed, the danger is that reason alone will harden the spiritual truth into an intellectual system and present the form as if it were the essence. This has, after all, been the case with all churches in the West that have indulged in the semantics of definitions of the indefinable, as remorseless as they are vain and misleading.

Science designates all experiences, including dreams and inspiration, that cannot be traced to the conscious personality part of "the unconscious"—and by classifying them it can give the comforting illusion that it has comprehended them. Of course the reality does not change, whatever name we may give it. What is affected is our response to the reality. But the divine element in the world, as Plato held, is not coercive but persuasive; so it is on our own response to it that its effective working on earth depends. In the divine plan, man is indeed God's co-worker, and this is why naming the unknowable by a positive name such as God is important. It evokes the emotional quality of numinosity, and promotes a positive attitude to a positive reality. At the same time it brings the reality closer to the possibility of being experienced, and being not merely believed but consciously known—provided it is clearly understood that God is not a remote truth far beyond our power, but that part of ourselves which is preexistent to consciousness and which we call our soul.

Verbal expression can influence both our attitude to the truth and our actions. This is why freedom of expression is in every society one of the most important and, at the same time, most abused rights; by giving utterance to our view of the world we are remaking it, if only a little, and are handing it over to others in a shape which may influence their actions. The Greeks described the man clever at speech as *thinos,* meaning, in addition to clever, fearful and terrible, and so explicitly acknowledged the power for evil of articulateness empty of truth. Against this power, operating with a vengeance today, our only protection is experience of the truth. Because until a reality is experienced, it can be suspected of non-existence—all the more easily when in modern, clever attacks on the spiritual truth, linguistic dexterity masquerades as profundity, and narrow logic is mistaken for incontrovertible reality.

The eager longing of our time, born as it is of misery, thwarted hopes and a growing will to explore and experience the truth, can lead into strange paths—and this is the danger which accompanies the beginnings of everything great—but it can no longer be stifled. Our age is still profoundly atheistic; but religious doubt is spreading. And the more inescapably obvious it becomes that the trivial preoccupations of our daily life cannot satisfy our deepest needs, nor fulfill our native hunger for wisdom, the more the doubt is transformed into a positive yearning for a new philosophy of life, for new symbols and for new attributions of significance.

The single most important characteristic of this new longing is that it is individualistic. The whole movement of religious freedom in Europe took its stand first on a limited and then on an absolute right of individual experience and illumined reason to determine the truth of inspired Scripture and the true Christian ritual and order of the Church. The vehemence of its claim was measured by the vehemence of its revolt against the usurpations, pretensions and brutalities of ecclesiastical power, which claimed to withhold the Scriptures from general knowledge and impose by moral authority—or indeed by physical violence—its own interpretation of Sacred Writ. The results ranged from tepid compromises such as the Episcopalian churches to a proliferation of earnest sects—the Anabaptist, the Independent, the Socianian, and countless others. But each Protestantism, however great its venture beyond the bounds of a monolithic faith, adhered unreservedly to doctrinal authority, shunned worldly civilization on principle just as defiantly as medieval Catholicism had done, and placed the Church squarely in the foreground. So the modern spirit was to find its first, full expression not in Protestantism, but in the Enlightenment with its ideals of tolerance and self-determination in matters of conscience. This spirit had indeed been in preparation in the Renaissance, with the opening of the eyes and soul to all the greatness of the world of the individual personality. As a result, the liberation of the individual from a binding authority and authoritative norms, instead of ending by individualizing religion, ended in the questioning of all religious belief and suprarational truth, no less than of all outward creed and institutions. The spiritual momentum spent, the social and political motive that had at first followed behind the religious as a useful ally assumed the lead and became gradually all-devouring.

"Without the intervention of the civil authority, what would our precepts become?—Platonic laws,"[13] Melanchthon, one of Luther's lieutenants, had said. And on the eve of the French Revolution many religious sects, as well as strange fraternities and secret societies—the Martinists, the Freemasons, the Illuminati, the Rosicrucians, the disciples of Strict Abstinence, the Mannerists—that had been at the time of their birth purely religious and philosophical, turned to politics and sought to achieve through political means the regeneration of society. "We found," said Perthes at the time, "that by becoming highly enlightened, one might become perfect." And the enlightened, having achieved what they regarded as perfection in their intellectual schemes, sought with growing fanaticism to impose them through politics on our imperfect societies.

So our modern age, which began with the individual conquering his rights vis-à-vis the religious collectivity, is now in danger of ending with the individual becoming a slave of another collectivity—political and more brutal and more totalitarian. We sought to escape from the prison of self-ignorance built by religious conventions no longer alive to the truths from which they sprang. Having succeeded, we forgot that our escape was a step toward self-knowledge—and rested increasingly discontented in the apparent which we proceeded to accept for the real. This has been, and remains, our one major error, root of all others and cause of our stumbling and suffering, individual and collective.

"He who looks outwardly, dreams. But he who looks within, awakes." And once we discover the tiny light within, and awake, our first task is to keep our hands cupped around it to protect it from the gales of the world that threaten to put it out at any moment. This is the first step on the road to fulfilling the much talked about, and so little understood, need for a "religious revival." And this is why Archbishop Lefèbre's "fearless stance" against the Catholic Church is so misguided: his insistence on a dignified ritual and on a dignified priesthood mediating between Christ and the faithful; his lamentably superficial analysis of church history which traces the breakdown of the Catholic Church to the Second Vatican Council; his breathtaking statement that "so far as the Catholic is concerned the only thing to do with a Protestant or an Anglican is to try to convert them";[14] and, perhaps most important, his large following, and the praise lavished on him by those who equate a religious revival with "someone taking a stand" against fashionable, liturgical aberrations, are all evidence of such a spectacular misreading of the spiritual needs of the age that one cannot help hoping that the church traditionalists would go back to sleep.

Yet the voices that demand a return to doctrinal orthodoxy and church ritual, in order to save religion, are growing in number and intensity. If this trend continues and spreads, perhaps we shall be hearing next from political traditionalists demanding that MPs who, before they take leave of public life, have to become Stewards of the Chiltern Hundreds, revive the traditional duties of the steward to hunt wild robbers near Chiltern—in the cause of saving Parliament. Those who seriously believe that by providing men with a festive calendar and a doctrinally impeccable creed, and the church with saved souls measurable in conversions, they are promoting religious belief, do a lot to strengthen the conviction that, as was said in Goethe's "In Memoriam," "there lives more faith in honest doubt, believe me, than in half the creeds."

> He fought his doubts and gathered strength;
> He would not make his judgment blind;
> He faced the specters of the mind,
> And laid them: thus he came at length
> To find a stronger faith his own.

Relentless traditionalism has through the ages been a very popular method for obscuring doubt; men have always insisted most vehemently on their orthodoxies and their heavily barnacled creeds when their hold on them has been most gravely shaken. But religion will only be restored to the world when meaning is restored to religion. The truth is that official Christianity is influenced by the spirit of any given age much more than it is influenced by the spirit of Christ. It is the spirit of the age that has historically molded the representative types of Christian piety: one century saw the finest pattern of Christianity in the monk, another in the Crusader, a third in the social philanthropist; and ours, Archbishop Lefèbre notwithstanding, sees it in the sociologist—when, that is, it does not see it in the theologist of revolution.

"I make no apology as a Churchman," writes Bishop Montefiore with all the easy assurance of someone in tune with the times, "for intruding into such technological fields as energy, transport and supersonic flight, for all too often vital ethical issues are obscured by a mass of economical details." [15] The ethical issues that the bishop turns out to regard as vital are whether the community should pay for the maintenance of roads and whether commercial flights are justified. When he expounds on "Changing Directions," in a report produced by a committee he chaired, he is referring to changing directions in inter-urban and long-distance travel; and when he talks of the long-term future, he means, of course, the long-term future of the automobile. Yet the bishop is the embodiment of the spiritual *zeitgeist*, both among bishops (the Bishop of Worcester announced in a speech to the Church of England in General Synod that the churches would not be credible unless they could agree on certain general economic principles; and the archbishop, not to be outdone, pronounced on the major spiritual issue of golden handshakes and rewards for boxers), and among lesser folk (the National Conference of Priests of England and Wales seemed primarily preoccupied with using church investments to exert shareholder pressure on companies with overseas interests; and the Warden of Keble College, in an essay in *Christian Believing,* was expounding "reverent agnosticism").

This is not the first time that churchmen have betrayed religion. On numerous occasions throughout its history, in different countries and different times, the church, provided it could retain its rank and its wealth, had been prepared to renounce its faith; today it is prepared to renounce its faith provided it can retain the respect of the Welfare State. We could hardly have had a more explicit admission of the attempts of modern churches to derive their moral authority from their identification with the ephemeral enthusiasms of contemporary politics, than the Bishop of Worcester's list of suitable church objectives: more equitable modes of reward, incomes policies, wages and differentials, conservation of resources and responsibilities of unions and management. What is extraordinary is not so much that a list of objectives drawn up by a rather unimaginative atheist politician seeking reelection should not differ in the slightest from a list of objectives drawn by a bishop, but that churchmen can seriously believe that by making the church more secular, society would become more religious—more moral, more just and more equal. The church has surrendered to the state and simply follows in the train of its victor. And if it is permitted a formal existence, it is only because men dread to shatter the chalice that once—a very, very long time ago—contained the water of life.

At the roots of our secular age is the fatal error that has led us to regard organized religion and the spiritual truth that man embodies as one and the same thing—and so to deny the reality of the one because we have rejected the absurdities of the other. But spiritual truth cannot be pinned down to one final dogmatic interpretation. The Book of Revelation is proof that, as Laurens van der Post has pointed out, the Bible itself ends "with the drawbridge of the Christian citadel let down and the road open once more for the spirit of man to travel to the end of time with a renewing and infinitely renewable capacity for fresh religious experience and revelation." [16] Although the inner spirit is indeed one, the spiritual life insists on freedom and variation in its self-expression and means of development.

" 'I *believe* in God,' " wrote Goethe, "is a beautiful and praise-worthy phrase; but to recognize God in all his manifestations, that is true holiness on earth." [17] And to live out the god within, that is true perfection on earth. That is the real new birth for which man has longed, and for which humanity has been waiting as the coming perfection of its long and tortuous course.

The West has for centuries hidden behind the sacrifice of Christ instead of treating the meaning he manifested as a new point of departure for every man. Our civilization did indeed derive its vital force from the truth of Christ and his teaching. But the truth unconsciously absorbed, and consciously increasingly negated, has now withered, and can only be revived if it is *consciously* accepted, this time not through institutions and codifications, but in the lives of individual men. Renan said once that you should never believe a German when he tells you he is an atheist. In fact, you should never believe any human being whether German, Chinese or Peruvian. No man is an atheist in those hidden depths of his soul which modern science has uncomprehendingly called his unconscious. But what remains unrecognized in the unconscious is all too easily rejected as untrue.

It is in these depths which, when neglected, cast up the forces of destruction—as our century has already tragically shown—that man must seek the powers that will rescue him. They will substitute the guidance of the spirit for the guidance of the inadequate ego with its futile willing and striving. Then we will recognize that God is not a wishful, remote and unapproachable reality somewhere out in the blue of heavens, but present in the soul of each one of us. His creation is not an arrested reality that can be captured and handed down in mental creeds, but a continuous and continuing process that can only be completed by our own full participation. Man is no longer alone at an almost intolerably supplicant receiving end, but is also at a giving end, living in his life the answer to the problem of creation that theologians have sought to provide by using their razor-sharp logical minds to slash the air. Meister Eckhardt scornfully proclaimed in the fourteenth century that if God were good, He could be better. And he was right. Not, of course, in the sense that the God principle as it exists inside and outside us is not already perfect, but in the sense that for this perfection to become manifest, man's consciousness has to be expanded to include God's reality now unconscious within us. God's great intermediary, the Son of Man, and Western man's greatest realization of his ultimate truth, was not just a single, never-to-be-repeated historical event. "Jesus Christ," said Blake, talking to Mr. Robinson, "is the only God, and so am I, and so are you."

This was the truth from which the Reformation drew its strength in its struggle for the recognition of the absolute primacy of individual conscience against the absolute prescriptions of the Church. But, like every subsequent attempt to salvage the truth from an established church, it ended by wrapping up the rights of individual liberty of conscience in new exclusive doctrines and profundities.

We should by now have recognized that the truth, when directed into a canal, ceases to flow in a sparkling stream; what were intended as aids enabling men to recognize and manifest it, become instead powerful barriers making it increasingly difficult to extirpate it from all the counterfeit doctrines weighing it down. And liberating oneself from half-truths often turns out to be even more difficult than liberating oneself from lies. The enduring corruptibility of church power is no less real today than it has been throughout our history—not any longer of course because our enlightened clergymen are likely to be suddenly transformed into latter-day Torquemadas, but because of the much subtler, and so infinitely more pernicious, corruption of the truth that the churches are theoretically meant to embody, and which they are in practice betraying.

At the same time we should stop daydreaming about founding a new religion with its own churches, dogmas and institutionalized beliefs. Propagating any organized religion, new or purified old, will merely make us share in one more idea among the millions of idea-forces that are abroad at the moment. What is important is to help open for everyone a way that is still blocked, and only then transform these personal, permanent realizations into a collective reality. This individual search and finding of God is the deepest heart, the inmost essence of religion. It is not a theoretical search, nor is it an abstract finding; it seeks to bring truth into existence and turn the intellectual love of God into an actuality. It is this longing for the hidden truth of things that has motivated and fueled man's revolt against traditions, conventional forms, and all stereotyped images obliterating his own experience. But he believed that the search could be carried out and completed by his critical and analytic reason alone.

"Thus, the native hue of resolution is sicklied o'er with the pale cast of thought." [18] Already in the nineteenth century the sicklied cast of rationalism and naïve materialism began to give way to a subjective search for the truth, to Nietzsche's will-to-live and Bergson's exaltation of intuition. Nietzsche called himself in a letter "a man who wishes nothing more than daily to lose some reassuring belief, who seeks and finds his happiness in this daily greater liberation of the mind." [19] But the freedom he was seeking was not of the mind, but of the soul. He mistook his ego for his true self, and in following a false light on the right road to self-knowledge, he reached his tragic ruin.

The perils are as profound for society as for the individual. Traditions and conventions are at least protective moral practices that save the individual from becoming a jumble of responses. They are cohesive common ties that prevent the disintegration of society into individual, isolated bundles of wants and satisfactions. The dangers are indeed great, and the warnings to abandon that path and go back to the older and safer ways are growing in intensity. But to go back is always impossible, the attempt to do so a tragic illusion. The warnings should be not against the misuse of the great powers within us, but against the temptation, in the long search for our soul, to rest content with discovering our force. The dangers of the emancipation of the imagination from any allegiance to standards have obsessed culture-doom-watchers from Matthew Arnold to Lionel Trilling, F. R. Leavis, and beyond. The dangers are just as real if the search for our spiritual truth is reduced to mystery-mongering, with obscure mysteries being substituted for the great ultimate Mystery.

Mystical escapades that lead to the loss of consciousness in cosmic beatitudes and a barren bliss are the direct negation of man's supreme aim to extend his consciousness without gaps or ecstatic breaks, from matter through reason to a permanent supramental reality. The modern obsession with the occult is only an aberration, a pursuit of garish mirages instead of an ever higher truth. Christianity itself, with its insistence on Christ's miracles, is partly to blame for this aberration—as if the truth Christ manifested would be in any way diminished if someone proved that he never cured a leper! All that we in fact call miracles are only phenomena of whose processes we are ignorant—a sort of jugglery for adults. It is the whole of our lives that is a deeper mystery than we have ever dreamt. To the eyes that see, all is strange and deep. But those who lack the imagination and the will to commit themselves to the spiritual venture that would transform their vision of the world, satisfy their appetite for the marvelous and give themselves a *frisson* by dabbling in the silly side of transcendentalism. As Ramakrishna put it: "I do not wish to be sugar, I want to eat sugar!"

The pattern of extreme action and extreme reaction is a constant in human affairs. In the Middle Ages, when the dominant culture lay dreaming, the rational intellect turned to a primitive sophism and to the syllogisms and dogmatic formulas of Scholasticism. Just before the French Revolution, those who claimed that now in all things reason reigned supreme, were described by Toqueville as running "to and fro, like a benighted traveler who has lost his way, and who, instead of getting onward, doubles back up his own footsteps." [20] They seemed prepared to believe in any extravagances, and to put their faith in every invisible and supernatural influence, except in that of God. And today, when the technocratic bend of mind dominates our culture, the approach to the supernatural is weighed down with occult absurdities, trivial miracle-jugglery and every manner of mystery, fakery, ritual and rite.

Of course, those who cling—and let us not forget that they are the dominant majority—to the triumphs of reason are all too ready to level the indiscriminate accusation of mysticism against anyone who stresses the need to rediscover the life of the spirit. But this is a fundamental misunderstanding of what is mysticism and of who are the mystics: "Mystics" says one of Hermann Hesse's characters, "are, to express it briefly and somewhat crudely, speakers who cannot detach themselves from images, therefore not thinkers at all. They are secret artists: poets without verse, painters without brushes, musicians without sound." [21] There are highly gifted, noble minds among them, but they have fallen victim to the eternal disposition among men to deny one thing before they feel able to affirm another, and so to mistake an intermediary stage for the final end. The religious-mystical stage, to the extent that it is fixed on the beyond, can never be an ultimate goal; unless, of course, we are prepared to accept, as so many mystics have done, that the world is only a mask and an illusion, and our life and body only means to help us escape from life and the body—which would make creation redundant and the world's suffering a cruel game. In fact, over however many and however deep abysses the mystic's soul may stretch, his body is here to perform its own duties; and, however great the supreme peace and the intensities of the spirit that we may achieve as individuals, they are not enough if we do not bring the amplitude of the spirit down to our chaotic, suffering world. Only then can we pass from a religious existence inviting us to seek completeness in another world, to a spiritual existence that seeks totality here, in the transformation of our prosaic earth to the place of victory and fulfillment of man's highest law.

"If the flesh has come into existence because of the spirit, it is a marvel; but if the spirit has come into existence because of the body it is a marvel of marvels." [22] Yet contrary to the teaching of Jesus, official Christianity has put the transcendent Father outside the whole messy human affair. And at the same time that materialists are treating everything except matter as a hallucination, spiritualists are glorifying mystical monstrosities at the expense of spiritual reality. But life, in its inexhaustible variety and vitality, was not created to be humiliated. It is the church that chose Christ's crucifixion, instead of his life-affirming resurrection, as its symbol, so that even if we believe in a suffering Christ we can no longer believe in a laughing Christ; and though we understand sadness, suffering and death, we seem incapable of understanding life. Instead of the waves of universal renewal and joy emanating from the believers and taking a hold on the unbelievers as well by making man's victory real and actual, and not somewhere beyond the frontiers of time and space, the darkness and the sorrowful pessimism have driven away by the million even the natural believers. "Unfortunately this Christian Church has become the Church where you must not laugh," wrote Shaw in the Preface to *The Devil's Disciple,* "and so it is giving way to that older and greater Church to which I belong: the Church where the oftener you laugh the better, because by laughter only can you destroy evil without malice." And today, whether in its betrayal of spirituality or in its denial of life, official religion has become formal, soulless and antagonistic to that expansion of consciousness that lifts the actual into the ideal, includes the simple and the commonplace in the spiritual, and, far from being dead to the world, opens man's eyes to it for the first time.

"There is in the Four Gospels," wrote Goethe, "a reflection of the greatness which emanated from the person of Jesus, and which was of as divine a kind as was ever seen upon earth. If I am asked whether it is in my nature to pay Him devout reverence, I say—certainly! I bow before Him as the divine manifestation of the highest morality. If I am asked whether it is in my nature to reverence the sun, I again say—certainly! For he is likewise a manifestation of the highest Being. I adore in him the light and the productive power of God; by which we all live, move, and have our being." [23] And if this is dismissed as pantheism, then Christ was a pantheist: "Cleave a piece of wood and I am there; lift up the stone and you will find me there."

It is only arid theological distinctions between pantheism, monism, and transcendentalism that have led to equally meaningless controversies as to whether Goethe was a Christian or Beethoven a pantheist. The thirty-eight notes of the trumpet call in *Fidelio* which announce that at the moment when all is lost, all is saved, and that when Florestan is about to die, he is about to live, provide a statement of Christ's message of renunciation, redemption and resurrection infinitely more powerful and more true than all the millions of words written by Christian theologians. Those who can read Goethe's words and not perceive in them Christ's spirit and Goethe's deeply religious feeling, must limit Christ's truth to official Christianity, and the word *religion* to the designation of their own doctrines.

As for the message of renunciation, it is hard to think of a greater perversion of a great truth than its reduction to a pseudo-ascetic indifference to this life and a burning desire for deliverance from this world. The message does indeed have a profound relevance for modern man, but in the sense of the denial not of life but of the false identifications that dominate our life and reduce us to marionettes identifying our external puppet self with our whole self. We do not renounce so that, like the ascetics, we can become attached to our renunciations instead of remaining attached to our possessions, but in order to reevaluate the lesser with regard to the greater; so that we can go beyond, always beyond, not seeking to leave life but to widen it. This is the mystery of growth, continuous growth and regrowth. And if Christianity is failing, and deserves to fail, it is because it sought to arrest the evolution of the human spirit in one moment of divine revelation of the Son of God nailed to the Cross.

So the church preached the merit of blind faith, while the dominant culture inculcated a narrow intellectual rationalism, with the result that today we plead in vain whether for faith or reason. "*Credo quia absurdum est*" is only the first step on the road to a higher principle of knowledge, when what seems impossible or absurd to the unaided reason becomes real and true to the reason lifted beyond itself by the power of the spirit. Then you need no witnesses, no theological proofs, no higher authorities; if a blind man has started seeing, he does not require anybody as a witness to say that now he can see. This does not, of course, preclude doubt, or its supreme value in the search for truth, and in the impulse it provides for the continuous transformation of belief into ever more conscious knowledge. But this is doubt in the context of belief, motivated by the conviction that "seek and ye shall find," and culminating in the *salvitur ambulando* of the discoverer. "Your difficulty is solved by its moving" was George Stephenson's reply to those who argued by strict scientific logic that his engine on rails would not, and should not, move. And as the expansion of our consciousness begins to bring about the regeneration of our life, we too will be able to reply to the skeptics that their difficulty is solved by its working.

But, as Edward Carpenter put it, "there is no sudden leap out of the back parlour onto Olympus, and the routes when found, from one to the other, are long and bewildering in their variety." [24] What is certain is that once the seed of aspiration is sown, and the shoot breaks ground, it is forever growing, strengthening and changing all the scenery of the life of the individual, and of the collectivity. This process of interaction between the personal and the general is inevitable; but it has been fully understood in all its closeness and inevitability only by the greatest of spiritual teachers, although it has also been documented by the greatest of modern scientists. We have been autohypnotized, by centuries of repeating it to ourselves, into believing that change can only be brought about by external revolution or gradual external reform. We start from the world, and through our prescriptions of universal cures, we arrive at new diseases that were not there before. Scared of self-knowledge, we continue to support each other's fictions, and escape from ourselves by looking out, and selflessly seeking to change the world. But the only thing we can really change *is* ourselves, and the moment we begin to change, the world starts changing because we are all a vital part in it: the moment our consciousness, which is what makes us part of an interconnectedhumanity, begins to rise, all other consciousnesses are affected.

The soul that believes that the Kingdom of God is within is indeed blessed; but the soul that *knows* that God is in it, the soul in which God wakes, begins to feel the identification with the universe which is the supreme blessing that distinguishes all great spiritual teachers and, however momentarily, all great artists. So far, we have accepted the theory that the many are destined to remain always on the lower ranges of life, with society used as a kind of shadowy background for a few luminous spiritual figures—as if spiritual development were a question of erudition or aristocratic provenance that cannot be extended to the majority of humanity. Spiritual evolution is, in fact, the destiny of all mankind, but it is not brought about by outward institutions, and still less by social machinery. It has to be lived out by each man; the living out begins with self-knowledge, which is also conscious knowledge of God, and ends with "the union of the soul with God." This was for Spinoza the soul's second birth: "... and therein consists man's immortality and freedom." [25]

It is modern man's contempt for his immortality, which is equivalent to contempt for his spiritual nature, that leads directly to spiritual death—which is, after all, the desired and inescapable end of materialism. And this denial of man's immortality, this denial of his soul, is the fundamental metaphysical lie on which all other modern lies are based. It is at the source of the reduction of human beings into exclusively material creatures controlled through their material nature by an all powerful state.

At the end of *The First Circle,* several political prisoners are loaded into a van marked *"Meat"* in four languages, and carried away to a hard-labor camp; as the van moves through the city, a French journalist from *Liberation* notices it, takes out his notebook and with his dark-red fountain pen, writes: "Now and again on the streets of Moscow you meet food delivery vans, clean, well-designed and hygienic. One must admit that the city's food supplies are admirably well organized." In that one episode, which could turn out to be a suitable epitaph for our age, is summed up both the Great Lie and its inevitable effect—both the transformation of man to meat and the inability of meat-man to make any distinctions between manufactured symbols and reality. The same Great Lie is today at the center of our own assumptions and prescriptions. We may indeed be spared the culmination of the lie in political prisons and hard-labor camps, but this will be only if we have by then so unreservedly accepted our meat-condition as to make them redundant. The denial of man's spiritual nature inevitably leads to the denial of consciousness, and—since it is assumed that individuals and their reactions are materially determined—to the denial of free will. So it may yet prove to be much more foolproof and efficient than political prisons and camps: once a living death is accepted as normality, only the few certified abnormal are left to register their unconscious revolt.

"We were intellectually intoxicated," wrote Shaw, summing up the "infidel half-century" that followed Darwin, "with the idea that the world could make itself without design, purpose, skill or intelligence: in short, without life. . . . We took a perverse pleasure in arguing, without the least suspicion that we were reducing ourselves to absurdity, that all the books in the British Museum Library might have been written word for word as they stand on the shelves if no human being had ever been conscious, just as the trees stand in the forest doing wonderful things without consciousness. The first effect was exhilarating: we had the runaway child's sense of freedom before it gets hungry and lonely and frightened. In this phase, we did not desire our God back." [26] By the time the next phase came, and the children had gotten, if not hungry, then certainly lonely and frightened, their God had disappeared. It had been explained away by psychoanalysis as a replica of the protective childhood game; it had been analyzed away by the ingenious perversions of the comparative science of religion; and it had been investigated away by sociologists who accounted for everything which did not meet their criteria of veracity as fraud. So belief became the most difficult of all the arts. And with regard to questions of immortality, the soul and suchlike, modern man seems quite content with the erudite thought that there are many contradictory opinions—which he may even recite for you, if you do not stop him in time—and no convincing proofs. We have lost sight of truth, and have sacrificed to our gambling intellect both belief and moral certainty. But the atrophy of belief is rarely accompanied by an atrophy of the longing for what is timeless, or at least what can provide a regulating principle for life. And the state has emerged as the principle that will regulate and sustain life—except that in practice it does at the same time suffocate it to death.

"Belief," T. S. Eliot thought, "is something detached from temporal weakness or the corruption of an institution." But history has proved him wrong. The vehemence of recoil from the absurdist strife of creeds, the moral hypocrisy of the clergy, and the fanatical aberrations of those clutching at the shadow of faith, promoted a destruction of belief itself. And the record of massacres would have gone a long way, even without the emerging rationalist tendencies, toward the disintegration of belief. Especially as in the eighteenth century, individual clerical crimes such as the hanging of La Rochette, the execution of Calas, or the beheading of La Barre for blasphemy, became, particularly through Voltaire's passionate denunciations under 130 pseudonyms, part of popular history, evoking the horror that leads to outright rejection—not merely of the churches and their corrupted conventions, but of the truth entombed in them.

Of course, whenever crimes, nose rings, perversions, and gorilla hides are discarded, soul is at work. And it was soul that was seeking to escape from the spiritual carapace over it. This is why so many of the rejecting and disintegrating tendencies were, however circuitously, taking man nearer his own truth: they were preparing him for the next stage in his evolution, away from a religiosity centered on another world and towards a spirituality centred on this.

There are still millions who are at the stage of regarding religion as a matter of abstract dogmas and infallible dicta—although happily very few who would echo Wolfrid Ward's wish, and long to have "an infallible papal pronouncement delivered at their breakfast table every morning with *The Times.*"[27] The officially religious and those openly professing religious beliefs are often those most bound by dogma, and least ready to accept the psychic reality of religion and seek to experience it. So religion appears increasingly to modern man as something to be classed with the outside world. Despite its theoretical two-thousand-year old concern for the "inner man," Christianity today—the words of Christ learnedly or ignorantly repeated—no longer appears to modern man to come from within. It bears little relation to man's psychic life and so, even at its most profound, it opens the soul toward a transcendent reality and a source of supernatural order, but not toward the realization that this source is to be found within. So the light that is in us has become darkness; and the darkness is full of horrors. The most tormented are those in whom the soul is most awake—those least able to find truth in dogma or meaning in materialism, and yet still shying away from taking that single inward step with which begins the journey of a thousand miles toward conscious knowledge of the God within.

"Ask your soul!" pleads Hermann Hesse in *My Belief:*

> Ask her who means freedom, whose name is love! Do not inquire of your intellect, do not search backwards through world history! Your soul will not blame you for having cared too little about politics, for having exerted yourself too little, hated your enemies too little, or too little fortified your frontiers. But she will perhaps blame you for so often having feared and fled from her demands, for never having had time to give her, your youngest and fairest child, no time to play with her, no time to listen to her song, for often having sold her for money, betrayed her for advancement. . . . You will be neurotic and a foe to life—so says your soul—if you neglect me, and you will be destroyed if you do not turn to me with a wholly new love and concern.[28]

There are innumerable pathways but they all lead to the same goal: what is latent in us we must evoke and educate; what is asleep we have to arouse and allow to unfold; and what is awake we have to make fully conscious. All the pathways are based on the same great incontrovertible truth: "What a man thinketh, he becometh." And where a man places his consciousness determines what he becomes. This is why a religion of faith, good conduct and good works is not enough: our consciousness has to be lifted and expanded, first to recognize, and then to include, the divine truth we embody.

The reason why the life has been drained from religion, has very little to do with Galileo, man's biological evolution, urbanization, industrialization, or indeed, pornography, television, the automobile and the permissive society. But it has a lot to do with the attempts of churches, theologians and professed believers to arrest our evolution at the stage of faith. "Religion," wrote John Henry Newman, "has never been a deduction from what we know; it has ever been an assertion of what we ought to believe." [29] So the officially religious, both Catholics and those Protestants who gave up long ago protesting against mere assertion, have become like bats in the twilight, happiest when there is least light to see by.

"Dazzling and tremendous, how quick the sunrise would kill me, if I could not now and always, send sunrise out of me." But Whitman's insight is not shared by a religion left at the stage of supernatural assertion. And the light of truth is correspondingly dimmed under religious half-truths and the culture's savage intellectualism. We have dogma for the theologian; good conduct and church bazaars for what remains of the middle classes; religious sociology for the committed; and skepticism for the civilized.

There is nothing more certainly fatal to the pursuit of truth than pure skepticism. Montaigne did not merely question all religious belief; he doubted equally strongly the new cosmology of Copernicus. And it was not only the clergy that pointed to the story of Joshua stopping the sun and moon in refutation of Galileo's discovery: the schoolmen too refused to look through the telescope on the grounds that there was no authority in Aristotle for the new assertions. And, as our century has shown, the learned skeptic's shrug turns with disconcerting ease into resolute propaganda and political master plans, with freedom as the main victim. Obsessed, as William James put it, with "shunning error," the skeptics ignore the other major moral duty of veracity—"believing truth." As a result, far from shunning error, they display a credulity and a readiness to suspend the operation of reason on a scale unequaled since the dancing manias of the Middle Ages, or the witch hunts of a later era.

And this at a time when, having abolished God to their complete satisfaction, the skeptically enlightened proceeded to claim for their reason such divine attributes as omniscience and infallibility. So that when, for example, the sequences in Pavlov's famous experiments occurred in the reverse order to the expected one, Pavlov would proclaim to tumultuous scientific applause the discovery of a new phenomenon—the Paradoxical Phase; and when the paradoxical phase would fail to materialize, the failure would be celebrated as the discovery of an ultra-paradoxical phase. It is through such impeccably positivist methods that reason is meant to work in its mysterious way to produce the truth. And when life and reality elude, as they constantly do, this sort of rigid rationality or the other sort of dialectic, they are dismissed as somehow unreal, epiphenomenal or a manifestation of "false consciousness." Or they are consigned to that catch-all category of the "unconscious," the "mystical," the "irrational" or the "purely subjective;" and they are grappled with only so that they can be tamed, exorcised or caricatured.

This applies not only to second-rate, pseudo-scientific contemporary minds, but even to the acknowledged great minds of our culture, so long as they refuse to recognize that existence is too large, profound and mysterious a thing to be entirely seized by the power of the intellect. So it came about, for example, that Gibbon dismissed the attainments of the spiritual tradition of the East as "the production of a distempered fancy, the creature of an empty stomach and an empty brain . . . adored by the Quietists as the pure and perfect essence of God himself." [30] The same kind of presumptuous ignorance is displayed today by our own sub-Gibbonian pundits toward any knowledge that goes beyond man's intellect; indeed such knowledge was recently dismissed by James Cameron, that one-man opinion poll on fashionable culture, as a "belief that Great Pan is after all alive and the oracles back in business," a belief which, as he informs us, he finds "most horrid and debilitating." [31]

Such self-satisfied dismissals of what could at the very least be regarded as pointers toward increased knowledge and new areas of investigation are all the product of a momentous "blind spot" in our culture, which, like the fatal blind spot in the character of a Greek or a Shakespearean hero, is what leads to tragedy. Bertrand Russell called it "the religion of thought" and celebrated it, driven by a death wish so overwhelming that he actually gave expression to it: "Better the world should perish than that I or any other human being should believe a lie . . . that is the religion of thought, in whose scorching flames the dross of the world is being burnt away." [32] Yet as he himself accepted in another context, the dualism of subject and object, on which not only his religion of thought, but most of Western philosophy is based, can no longer be accepted. "The distinction of mind and matter, the contemplative ideal and the traditional notion of "truth" all need to be radically reconsidered if the distinction of subject and object is not accepted as fundamental." [33] Quite so; and when they *are* radically reconsidered, there will be no more proud talk about ultimate beliefs being lies, simply because they cannot be established as truths by the traditional means of "knowing," when one entity, the knower or subject, is aware of another, the known or object.

"Knowledge," wrote Plotinus some 1700 years ago, "has three degrees: opinion, science, illumination. The means or instrument of the first is sense; of the second, dialectic; of the third, intuition. To the last I subordinate reason. It is absolute knowledge founded on the identity of the mind knowing with the object known."[34] Or as Francis Bacon, less explicitly but more poetically, put it, "The first creature of God in the works of the days, was the light of the sense; the last, the light of reason; and his Sabbath work ever since is the illumination of his Spirit."[35] This Sabbath work, far from taking away from reason its aspiration to perfection, gives it the means of its perfectibility.

From the Pythagoreans to the Renaissance and the Renaissance to our own times, scientists no less than mystics have felt what Einstein called "cosmic religiousness . . . the strongest and most noble driving force of scientific research. . . . What a deep belief in the intelligence of Creation and what longing for understanding even if only of a meager reflection in the revealed intelligence of this world, must have flourished in Kepler and Newton, enabling them as lonely men to unravel over years' work the mechanism of celestial mechanics. . . . It is cosmic religiousness that bestoweth such strength."[36] Whether one talks of belief in God, of cosmic religiousness, or of the more philosophical notion of the search for truth, these are only beginnings toward discovering the God within, attaining cosmic consciousness and manifesting truth. As our consciousness expands, the experience will sweep away the mental debris and carry its own reality and force apart from any theory that may precede, accompany or follow it.

Our search, however outward bound it may be at the beginning, can only lead us to the truth when we return from across the seven oceans, and take the inward way to where we started—to see the place for the first time. Which teacher will help our revealing, and which of the great will promote our unfolding, is a matter for us to determine. It is only our Western megalomania that has led us to suppose that Christianity is the only truth and Christ the only Redeemer. The Christ consciousness, it is true, came in Jesus into such fullness and plainness of manifestation that in his teaching we may find the greatest guide for the unfolding of our own truth. But those for whom, through the perverse teaching of the church, Christ is too closely and irrevocably associated with sorrow, suffering and submission, may be more profoundly stirred and guided to a deepened self-knowledge by the Upanishads, the Sutras, or Buddha's speeches than by the New Testament; not in order to take an emergency exit out of our own culture, but only so that we can be helped on the way toward the realization of our own divine truth.

Nor is it only the great religious spirits that can inspire us in our inward journey. All the great geniuses whom we admire and revere without really understanding, are speaking from a higher plane of consciousness and can guide our own climb, if only we stopped interpreting them with our reason and began to listen with our souls. Then we would realize that the gratuitous benefit of incoherence and poetic vagueness that we grant to them is the result entirely of our own mind. Having pierced through the misunderstandings and distortions of centuries of commentary and interpretation, we will discover the unity of the teachings of these men, and the remarkable harmony in their meaning.

Whether as art, religion or science, it is the same truth of man's divinity and of his soul's immortality that the great inspirers of our civilization have variously revealed; and it is the same truth to which they have given the rest of us access. When Dante says of himself that he was transhumanized into a God, it is no poetic metaphor; when Paul talks of men as "heirs of God and joint heirs with Christ," he is not indulging in mystical flights of the imagination; when Benjamin Franklin composes an epitaph to himself to the effect that his soul "Will Appear Once More In A New And More Elegant Edition Revised And Corrected," he is merely giving idiosyncratic verbal expression to his belief in the "conservation of souls," which preceded and indeed gave birth to his famous law of the "conservation of matter."

Carlyle once silenced with one question all the pietist cant about Goethe's lack of Christian belief; and what he said then could just as effectively be used today to silence all attempts to claim as irreligious all the sages who have refused to subscribe to religious dogmas. He had sat grim during a dinner party in Berlin, listening to devout Christians throwing up their eyes and regretting that so great a genius! so godlike a genius! should not have more purely devoted himself to the service of Christian doctrine, until at last he broke his silence and asked one of them, in his slow emphatic way: "*Meine Herren,* did you never hear the story of that man who vilified the sun because it would not light his cigar?"

Much more prevalent today is the tendency to relegate the poets' spiritual visions to the status of metaphorical license or lyrical exaggeration employed to lend color to their speech. So instead of opening ourselves to the visionary imagination on its own demanding terms, thus disturbing our conception of workaday reality, we applaud the dexterity with which the poet has created the illusion; we display toward his words the civilized tolerance of someone who does not mind leaving for a while the "real," practical world to be entertained by poetic statements. We can therefore safely admire Tennyson, having coined his spiritual visions into the legal tender of elegant verse. But Tennyson, unlike other poets, did not confine his spiritual beliefs to his poetry but gave them unambiguous expression in prose: "Depend upon it, the spiritual *is* the real; it belongs to one more than the hand and the foot. You may tell me that my hand and my foot are only imaginary symbols of my existence. I could believe you, but you never can convince me that the *I* is not an eternal reality, and that the spiritual is not the true and real part of me." [37]

The best objective scholarship on the subject can sensibly discount such notions as the product of an overexcited, though greatly gifted, imagination. So our technocratic order of life can roll on unchecked; and there need be no appeal from our reductive rationality. Anyone who finds it too disturbing to have to reconcile the man of the world with the stormer of heaven can easily discount Blake's metaphysical conceptions as madness or—more indulgently but no less dismissively—as divine madness or the madness of genius. But then, if we are going to regard Blake as insane we ought, for the sake of consistency if nothing else, to include Socrates in the list. After all, some of the things he said, let alone did, give him an infinitely better claim to the title, when judged against our workaday reason and conventions: "One morning he was thinking about something which he could not resolve; he would not give it up, but continued thinking from early dawn until noon. There he stood, fixed in thought. . . . At last, in the evening, after supper, some Ionians, out of curiosity, brought out their mats and slept in the open air that they might watch him and see whether he would stand all night. There he stood all night until the following morning; and with the return of light he offered up a prayer to the sun and went his way." [38] It is this incident that made Lelut date Socrates's insanity from the siege of Potidea in 429 B.C. And when Blake fixes his eye on the sun and sees "an Innumerable company of the Heavenly Host crying 'Holy, Holy, is the Lord God Almighty,' " our reason-mongers have no difficulty in rattling on very learnedly about the poet's disturbed psychic disposition. But eyes that see the world not as the commonplace object of the technocrat, but transformed through their visionary experience, see it as it really is. Only by sharing their sense of wonder will we escape from our suffocating workaday reality, and begin to feel the uplifting power of another reality immanent in nature and within ourselves.

The magic reverberating through all inspired art, the sense of a living force beyond our everyday conceptions, far from being antagonistic to science, is the magic of the highest science. It is completely in tune, both with the largely intuitive working methods of the great scientific pioneers and with the increasingly surrealistic discoveries of our century which pass through the very den of the metaphysician, and have completely supplanted crude materialism.

"If we had seen God in the flesh, we would not have known him any better, perhaps not as well," wrote James Clerk-Maxwell to his wife during his scientific investigations that inaugurated the post-Newtonian era in physics. And he has been echoed by all great scientists. In the same way that Franklin, starting from a mystical conviction about the conservation of souls, gave birth by analogy to a scientific theory about the conservation of matter, Kepler, starting from the concept of the Holy Trinity, proceeded to develop his theory of the trinity of Sun-Force-Planets. And even Darwin, whose evolutionary theory was naïvely supposed to have dealt a deathblow to Christianity, ends his two great books with the same transcendental sense of awe and wonder that we find in the most deeply spiritual of men: "There is grandeur in this view of life, with its several powers, having been originally breathed by the creator into a few forms or into one; and that, while this planet has gone cycling on according to the fixed law of gravity, from so simple a beginning endless forms most beautiful and most wonderful have been, and are being, evolved." [39]

And the greatest evolution of all that began symbolically when man came out of the state of animal happiness by eating of the fruit of knowledge is the evolution of consciousness. Today, having reached the curve of the intellect, and exhausted its smallness, we continue to evolve into the higher regions of our nature, until we achieve consciously the harmony we possessed unconsciously at the beginning of time. The whole process of evolution is a gradual transformation of what springs from the unconscious as faith and intuition into expanded awareness and conscious knowledge. The greatest danger for our future lies in the fact that our science and our mechanical ability to exterminate or, less dramatically, control and enslave each other, have gone ahead of the development of our consciousness.

Einstein's great discovery was to demonstrate that matter and energy are convertible—that matter is condensed energy. In the same way that we talk of mass and energy, particle and wave, being merely two aspects of one and the same process, we can speak of the latent spirit in matter—just as Ernst Haeckel spoke of the will in the atom. So the physical world becomes spirit seen from without; and the spirit, the world viewed from within. "There is not," wrote Frederick Pollock, "a world of thought opposed to or interfering with a world of things; we have everywhere the same reality under different aspects." [40] And this is why spirit is not a firework display shooting up into the void only to perish in midair, but a great—indeed the greatest—transforming power here on earth.

The conflict between matter and spirit is our own creation. "This is my body, this is my blood," said Christ, choosing the two most earthly and matter-of-fact symbols of bread and wine to signify that matter too is of spirit, and to stress the oneness between the two. But ever since

Descartes, the dualism between matter and spirit has dominated our thinking and has led to the shallow rationalism of our age. Yet the only gap between matter and spirit is the gap in our consciousness—our own incomplete awareness of ourselves.

It is this lack of awareness, this ignorance, that Christianity has so misleadingly called original sin. It is indeed the cause of all our imperfections, and all our suffering; but if it is a sin, it is a *felix culpa,* a fortunate crime, that marks our departure from a state of nature, and an unconscious state of innocence. "When our first parents were driven out of Paradise," Dean Inge said once, "Adam is believed to have remarked to Eve: 'My dear, we live in an age of transition.' "

What the dean said in jest is, in fact, a great truth: humanity has lived and is still living in a stage of transition between the natural and the ideal or spiritual life, when we will once again reach our source, and the circle will become complete. We needed the separation from the universal harmony to become conscious, to grow as individuals under the shell of our ego; but this separation from the world, from others and from ourselves has been the cause of our suffering. This is why Rousseau's Golden Age of nature has held such sway over men ever since he formulated it: it feeds our dangerous illusion of escaping from the responsibility of consciousness, back into an Eden of blissful irresponsibility where Mother Nature will enfold us in her arms again and instinct will carry us as unthinkingly and effortlessly as an animal. But there is no going back. Only by completing our journey into consciousness can we put an end to strife and suffering.

Once we recognize this spiritual meaning of our evolution—a spirituality which eliminates nothing and takes up everything—we begin to see why optimism has been the *leitmotiv* of all great thinkers. Through the cruelty, injustice and imperfections of our world, they could see perfection in the making; and they could also see that the key of perfect change was hidden within ourselves. Once we accept this truth we have two ready-made litmus tests we can apply to the proliferating exhortations, programs and plans for a religious or a political regeneration: the first is the test of freedom; the second of optimism. Any force or idea that seeks to achieve the transformation of life by restricting the freedom of the individual, substitutes suppression for man's need to grow into self-knowledge and freely overcome his limitations. So it goes against the law of the living spirit which continuously grows and outgrows its earlier expressions, and can therefore never be captured for long in our mental forms and inescapably imperfect institutions.

The second test, the test of optimism and joy, would rule out all religious exhortations that demand the sacrifice of the present to a beyond-this-world future, and regard damnation as the price of present enjoyment. It would therefore rule out that part of Christianity that has perverted Christ's message by seeking to console man's fears instead of confirming his hopes, or still worse, by warning of the torments of Hell, the Day of Judgment, the sinner's lost condition, and the anger of an avenging God. The gospel of sorrow, suffering and the vanity of things can only become a force for the discouragement of life, and so can never be the true law and guide of life. All pessimism is a denial of the reality and power of the spirit, an impatience which condemns or despairs of life, and seeks man's hope either in the end of the world or in political panaceas.

"There will never be any more heaven and hell than there is now." Both heaven and hell are within our soul, and which of the two will prevail depends on us. It depends on whether we have realized that flooding of our lives with a meaning and light independent of all outward things, or remain ignorant of our true selves, seeking some higher satisfaction for our souls by blindly embracing political salvationism, whether of the Chinese or of the milder Western variety.

"We are all under the same mental calamity," wrote Chesterton. "We have forgotten what we really are. All that we call commonsense and rationality and practicality and positivism only means that for certain dead levels we forget that we have forgotten. All that we call spirit and art and ecstasy only means that for one awful instant we remember that we forget." [41] Imagination is a sort of incantation that can call up the memory of our divine reality. Belief can make the memory linger for longer than one awful instant—and may even succeed in making it part of our lives. But only when belief is transformed to conscious knowledge, can our lives be lifted out of their imperfection and groping ignorance; and then the outward revolution will actually endure because for the first time it will be based on inner realities.

8

FOR THEY DID NOT DESPAIR OF THE REPUBLIC

"There ends the year . . . with great trouble to mind in reference to the public, there being little hopes left but that the whole nation must in a very little time be lost." [1] That was Samuel Pepys's last diary entry for 1667.

Despair over the future is nothing new. Nor is sorrow over the present: "Everywhere I see the affairs of men so corrupted I believe that in no age has so much been permitted to impudence, stupidity, and crime." [2] That was Erasmus writing to a friend in 1520. What is new today is that both the pessimism about the future and the sorrow about the present are based not on the value of something, but on the value of nothing. We are force-fed with horrors, and the disgust with the actual world has never been so deep. The Trojan Horses are within the walls, and even artists and court jesters have been turned into Cassandras and are confronting us with their celestial sneer. Sociologists and computer scientists have become the unchallenged high priests of the new despair, forgetting that trend is not destiny and that except on their graphs, growth curves never—not even in the case of rabbits—remain exponential for ever. The poets are following suit; by leaving behind sweetness and light they feel that they are at last working in the right groove of the artist-enemy.

We are all voyeurs now, and voyeuristically we watch, we anticipate, we wait. We have succumbed to the celebration, the culture of nothingness, to the banality, the illness of self-pity. In the fourteenth century, revulsion against the world gave birth to the shrill phantasmagoria of death and the gruesomely popular Dance of Death; in the fifteenth century, it led to rendezvous and parties held by fashionable Parisians at the Churchyard of the Innocents, with skulls and bones heaped in charnel houses along the cloister walls for all to see; today when life has lost its meaning and promise and we are enclosed by nothingness, it is as though a panic has broken loose and we heard the exhortation: "Let us eat and drink, for tomorrow we die!" And we obey—with all the profound sadness implicit in Faust's compact with Mephistopheles that if ever he shall say to the passing moment, "Stay, thou art fair," he is willing to perish eternally. But Mephistopheles is finding it increasingly difficult to produce such moments for us.

One of the leading authorities on the social insects has established that "while an ant is feeding on nectar or syrup her abdomen may be snipped off with a pair of scissors, without interrupting her repast." [3] And we have come to believe that what is true for an ant's abdomen is equally true for a man's soul, and that if only there are plentiful supplies of nectar and syrup around, we will not notice the detaching of our souls. But we do, however unconsciously, and so we oscillate between despair and increasingly desperate play. Culture has been turned into a leisure activity. And the more difficult it is to maintain the growth of material goods and services, the more compulsive becomes the growth of the economy's cultural counterpart—increasingly reduced to a sterile, self-generating hedonism.

Many have taken to gloom as others take to drink, and, the apocalyptic gleam in their eyes, they loudly and cheerfully proclaim that all efforts are futile and that we are doomed to perish; previous collapsed civilizations, from the Roman to the Maya and the Khmer, are indiscriminately offered as conclusive proof. Falls and catastrophes have always fascinated mankind—from Thucydides' fall of Athens to the stricken battlefields of Goya. There were Roman intellectuals who, when their empire was invaded, welcomed the triumph of the Huns and the Vandals as importing a higher primitivism to replace their guilt-ridden civilization. And a similar secession of the intellectuals is taking place today.

But continuous denunciation is hard to bear, and our sense of the condemned real world demands a heavy price. The immediate danger is that when all affirmation and belief are banished, so is hope. The result is that routine indignation gives place to a high complacency; terrors roar at us but can no longer frighten us. And that is not all. The sense of a condemned world does not do away with the need for a refuge, for some kind of futurist idealism, for a dream to reconcile us to life; what it does is intensify our longing for a refuge, and our impatience to turn the dream into reality. And whenever the life-starved inhabitants of the ivory towers invade the real world, their ideals of disembodied beauty are transformed into monstrous political solutions. The Muses of aestheticism are turned into the Furies of annihilation, and the swans and herons and albatrosses and flamingos and peacocks and all the rest of the aristocratic symbolist poultry give way to more "real" raw material of the creative imagination: destroy the cities of men so that, perhaps, they might be rebuilt after the image of pure aesthetic delight.

This aesthetic vitalism began as a reaction against rationalist smugness, a defense of life against utilitarianism, and of instinct and action against positivist science. But the revolt against the complacently shallow bourgeois conventions and the naïvely optimistic classical faith in reason can only end in an excess of aesthetic drunkenness and the glorification of barbarism—unless, that is, it goes beyond revolt, and leads to the reconstruction of human reason on a new and profounder basis. It was barbarism that Antonin Artaud glorified in his fiery manifestos and sought to embody in his plays of rapacity, blasphemy and revenge; and it is barbarism that the public unconsciously glorifies in its growing fascination with stories of Satanism, films of violent, avenging anarchy and, even more ominously, its barely disguised admiration for adventurous criminals and retired train robbers.

A life governed by mechanistic science is much less alive, said the aesthetes, than one governed by instincts and powerful illusions. But it was a false antithesis. Indeed, denunciations of morality and reason in the name of an all-consuming aestheticism are, just as much as the technocratic assumptions of our age, impediments we will have to overcome if we are to discover the spirit that lies behind the imperfections of life, and live by it. Most of modern art and literature has merely documented the reverse side of our surface emotions and actions; it has described the malady of life, the riot of its cravings and dissatisfactions, and so exaggerated life in the direction of decay rather than rebirth. There was a time in the last century when to lay bare the dubious foundations of our belauded virtues, and even to romanticize the evil behind them, was exhilarating. But our century has fully acquainted itself with evil in all its nauseating forms; and Freud has thrown a glaring light on the darkness and evil in our psychic hinterland, and has documented with scrupulous care all that is most repellent in our inner life. What we need now is to acknowledge the lower and demonic elements of man's nature, not as pathological aspects of life to be dissected and tamed, but as parts of ourselves that have to be brought into consciousness. Only in wholeness lies healing, and only in reintegration with our stubbornly neglected spirit lies renewal.

Socrates, whom Nietzsche from the aesthetic peaks of his grotesque error condemned as a "theoretical man," taught that only that which is conscious can be good. And only by going beyond the facile realism that brings into exaggerated prominence the ugly and the morbid can we open our souls to the beauty and the secret significances which are hidden from our reason and our senses. When Dostoevsky called himself a "realist in a higher sense" precisely because he described the depths of the human soul, he was defining the kind of realism that our world most desperately lacks today: not the realism that springs from the urge to descriptive imitation and ends in caricature, but the realism that is directed toward the meaning of things and ends in evocation.

This does not mean that we should ignore the political evil in which most of the world lies, and "write only about joyful things,"[4] as the Soviet Writers' Union called on Solzhenitsyn to do shortly before they expelled him; indeed, to do so today would be not constructive optimism but criminal complacency. Solzhenitsyn's polemical writings as well as his novels are almost entirely about ugliness, suffering and evil—about the nightmare reality of labor camps, political persecution and political cancer wards. Yet nowhere, not once, do we find the anonymous merciless darkness that permeates modern political tirades—especially those aimed at destroying the few remaining values that preserve freedom in the West—and that distinguishes most of contemporary art with its Beckettian lyricism of extinction and its gleeful visions of suspended apocalypse. We cannot combat evil merely by exposing it, let alone by reveling in its exposition and surrendering to an ontological pessimism that rejects not merely evil but life. We can only defeat it by breaking out of our narrow bounds, by communing with that which is behind the visible, external and transient, and by sensing the hidden essence of things which alone can give meaning to the meaninglessness that surrounds us. And then the horror we feel when confronted with evil will be the horror that has the power to heal. Because evil will no longer be seen as the product of impersonal systems and structures, and still less, as so many are poisonously whispering today, as the product of the dark forces of creation to which we must stoically resign ourselves; it will be seen as harrowingly real precisely because it is inescapably personal, and because however institutionalized it may appear, it is always to be found in man, caused by man and perpetuated by man. It is implemented by men's words and actions, and allowed by other men's silences; and this is why it can be overcome by men's actions and defeated by their words. Nothing is closed, condemned or damned. When we grow to realize this, we will understand why through all the writings of Solzhenitsyn, through all the remorseless suffering and absurd cruelty, there shines the same "morning of creation" feeling that is reflected down the ages in the words of the truly wise.

"I have found," said Gandhi, "that life persists in the midst of destruction. Therefore there must be a higher law than that of destruction. Only under that law would well-ordered society be intelligible and life worth living." And as our century has shown, when the intimation of that law is lost, jungle logic takes the place of human reason, and our world is gradually restored to the jungle.

"I once swore to renounce all repugnance." This was by far the most noble of Zarathustra's vows; but he failed to keep it. Modern man finds it unthinkable even to contemplate such a vow. So the symposium of dissolution goes grimly and fruitlessly on, while our spiritual sterility, from which start both the repugnance and the despair, remains unacknowledged.

While the cultured unbelievers are withdrawing to their catacombs, and the uncultured sophisticated are seeking new and emptier thrills to make the unbearable bearable, the politically committed are busy precipitating the day when Aldous Huxley's nightmare vision of a *Brave New World* would come true, and thrill-pills would be freely, or indeed compulsorily, supplied by the state: to produce "sane men, obedient men, stable in their contentment."

The political dreamers are growing more doctrinaire by the day. The voices exhorting us to destroy the cities of men so that they may be rebuilt after the image of pure aesthetic delight have grown weak; but the voices urging us to destroy the cities of men so that inevitably—and indeed historically, dialectically and materially—they *will* be rebuilt after the image of state collectivism are deafening us. The nature of these two terrible dreams is different but their source is the same: total condemnation of the real world unaccompanied by any spiritual warrant or the optimism of spiritual redemption. The aesthetic masochism of aesthetic absolutism is turned into the historical masochism of state absolutism: "History is the cruellest of all goddesses, and she drives her triumphal car over heaps of corpses, not only in the war, but also in 'peaceful' economic development." Right to the end, Engels kept to this Promethean myth: "There is no great historical evil without a compensating historical progress. . . . Let fate be accomplished."

The New Leftist, like the Old Marxist, displaced in a world he despises, becomes impatient with the slowness of social evolution, and looks to the violence of the state to hasten the process. It is not a new dream. Earlier doctrinaires had dreamt it before. And when reality broke into their abstract world, they turned its cruelty undeterred into cause for more celebration: "What scenes are passing in France! I know there are excesses, but the cost of a free Constitution is not too great. Is not a storm which purifies the air better than an atmosphere tainted as with the plague, even though here and there it should strike a few heads!" [5] It was again in the name of a freer constitution and a higher freedom that the Marxist intellectual elite, when it became obvious that the working classes would refuse to march under their leadership, turned from passionate exhortation to force—the force of fitting free individuals into the machine-made Procrustean mold of their social dream.

In politics, dreams, visions and wild hopes are mighty weapons and dangerous tools. And the vision of achieving happiness and perfection on earth through political transformation is just as mighty and dangerous when it is embodied in practical workaday schemes as when it takes the form of bloodcurdling slogans. It gives to its defenders the conviction that they are fighting in league with eternity, and to its opponents the feeling that they are defying inexorable fate. It is indeed the case that as long as our destiny is in the hands of moderate politicians of the middle way, sagely practicing the art of the possible, we will go on bowing with increasing frequency and promptitude to the household god of the inevitable. But anything that is treated as inevitable inexorably becomes actual. Today it is the growing power of the state which is in practice, if not in theory, treated as inevitable; and an increasingly totalitarian state will go on sucking out the marrow of society unless an opposite force interposes and puts an end to the full stultifying development of the state principle now everywhere in the ascendant. Unless such a force emerges, "All for the State; nothing outside the State; nothing against the State" [6] will be the order of the future—until, that is, the state, having stifled the individual and destroyed the vital life that now supports it, is left bloodless, a skeleton dead with that rusty, gruesome death of machinery.

The only opposite force that can defeat the coercive power of the state is the force of the spirit: it is the only force that is not, and can never be, its puppet. And it is our chief defense against totalitarianism because it is impossible to cure the world's evil until we cure first what is at its roots in man—in the same way that it is impossible to cure anything outside, if we do not first cure it within. The conditions under which we live on earth are the result of our state of consciousness, and this is why any revolution which seeks to change external conditions without a change in man's consciousness seeks in vain.

It is this evolution of consciousness that lies behind the evolution of the species and is reflected in the evolution of societies. The idea that consciousness is at the root of the material universe is not new: it can in fact be traced back to Parmenides. In our own century, Einstein, Jeans and Wheeler, all in their different ways, have provided scientific confirmation of what was until recently only a visionary insight. The implications are dramatic and, as yet, completely unexplored. They point inescapably to the truth that we have ignored in all our scrupulous social and political plans and calculations: that life does not unwind from outside inward, but from inside outward. This expansion of man's consciousness is a task performed for its own sake; as this is man's supreme task, it could hardly be otherwise. But the social and political fallout is incalculable, and the result of a greater revolution of life—but an evolutionary one—than man has yet imagined.

Throughout the history of European thought, there have been two major and conflicting approaches to man's evolution: the "descending" approach, epitomized in the fundamentalist trend in Christianity, and postulating an absolute act of Creation followed by a Fall and a marking of time until the Last Judgment; and the "ascending," or truly evolutionary approach, which had flourished during the heroic age of Greek science and awoke with renewed vigor during the scientific revolution. This view of man's evolution not as a fall from perfection, but as a gradual ascent, has come to dominate Western culture, and has imposed itself firmly on the modern mind. It is a view which owes a lot to Darwin; but it is an infinitely greater concept than the desperate struggle for survival and the merciless selection that shapes and perfects the machinery of life. In fact, the two most powerful expressions of universal evolutionism—Keats' *Hyperion* and Wagner's *Ring*—are pre-Darwinian; and so is its first expression in the *Oresteia.* As Paul Kammerer put it: "Evolution is not just a fair dream of the last century, the century of Lamarck, Goethe and Darwin; evolution is truth—sober, delightful reality . . . out of its own strength everything that has been created strives upward toward light and the joy of life, burying only that which is useless in the graveyard of selection." [7]

Until recently, men were content with the full-statured animal, the perfected art, the completed society; the phases of development and the laws of growth were disregarded or merely touched on in a vague, uncertain manner. Present law and form were mistaken for the eternal law of our nature and existence, and any change regarded as a deviation. The triumph of the evolutionary approach was to give man the courage to rid himself of many of the prejudices and lifeless knowledge of the past in an attempt to perceive not only the rule of what is, but the rule of what may, or ought to be. The tragic error was that modern man—as much blinded as enlightened by the victories of physical science, the naïve evolutionism of Voltaire, Turgot and Condorcet, and the loudly applauded pageants of world history unfolding on deterministic principles—came to believe that the destinies of mankind can be turned out to order in state factories. Fascinated by process, commodity and production, the modern, technological mind ignored the spirit in man and forgot that if the spirit of the things we profess is absent or falsified, no method or machinery can turn them out for us.

No single incident better symbolizes this slavishly mechanistic approach to evolution than the strange procession of Arabs, Prussians, Swiss, Swedes, Indians, Syrians, Barabanters, Liègeois, and so forth, that appeared, each in his national costume, in the National Assembly in Paris on June 19, 1790: in that idyllic year of the Revolution, when the evolution of humanity seemed to progress according to plan, and its salvation was fancied close at hand, they had all come as delegates of "the human species" to take part in the festival of liberty and fraternity, so that they could afterward announce the coming liberation of their peoples. The perverse reduction of the concept of evolution to that of progress had been completed: "progress" can by definition never go wrong; but evolution, including the evolution of ideas and even of "exact science," constantly does. So a tale of ever-repeated differentiation, specialization, and reintegration on a higher level came to be regarded as a straight, continuous process with men's lives treated as preliminary studies for a coming transfiguration brought about by economic changes, political developments, technological revolutions and other similar forces likewise presumed irresistible.

"Evolution is far more important than living," was Ernst Junger's summing up of this fallacy. But evolution can only take place when men live the answer for which life was created. It is man's failure to live out the expansion of his consciousness that has been the main obstacle in the path of his evolution. It is not so much his limitations that are responsible for the vulnerability of all his grandiose plans, as his failure to live up to the possibilities he embodies. Our wretched cleverness and our equally wretched notion of progress have made it impossible to give any name to man's unconscious motivations except that of madness; but it is these denied aspects of ourselves that can alone direct life to another effort at greater consciousness—and so save us from the abyss.

"The very first official thing I did, in my administration, and it was on the very first day of it too," says Mark Twain's Connecticut Yankee "was to start a patent office; for I knew that a country without a patent office and good patent laws was just a crab, and couldn't travel any way but sideways or backways." [8] The days full of hope, when our patent laws and our mechanical progress were expected to lead us forward to the Promised Land of milk and honey are over, and recognition of the inherent vulnerability of our efficient civilization is long overdue. "Progress to what and where? ... The European talks of progress, because by an ingenious application of some scientific acquirements he has established a society which has mistaken comfort for civilisation." [9] That was Disraeli over a hundred years ago. And yet like optimistic tadpoles, we go on basking in a puddle in the sun, in the shallowest of waters, crowding together and amiably wiggling our tails, oblivious of the fact that the puddle is about to dry up and leave us stranded.

But the human spirit has always responded creatively in times of crisis and decline—if only we allow it to surface again from the debris of arid intellectuality and mechanical solutions. So far we have had a multitude of theoreticians of evolution—from Spengler and Toynbee to all those who have sought to emulate them on however Lilliputian a scale. What we most urgently need now is *practitioners* of evolution. We have looked at the world as if it were a theoretical truth to be explored rather than a pragmatic secret to be lived and to be unraveled as it is lived; we have been taught by some that we are in Act I of our human tragicomedy, and by others, that we have reached Act V, as if the principle of physical determinism applied with equally irresistible force to human affairs; and we have had our various disorders traced to a series of picturesque social causes, as if sociologically established causal relationships could explain the mystery of man. All this at the same time that Einstein was prounouncing the Newtonian world of determinism obsolete, and physicists were expressing in the language of particles and self-generation the ancient Sufi belief that "every cause is the effect of its own effect." So we go on elegantly and eruditely debating the problem of freedom versus determinism, and have in the meantime denied ourselves the greatest freedom: the freedom to move on to a higher plane of consciousness, and so modify or annul the determinisms to which we are subjected at lower planes.

"Nothing ever is, everything is becoming," Heraclitus taught us twenty-five centuries ago. But religion has declared God a static infinite excluded from the world; and technocratic politics has established the state as the center of our expectations and has indeed ascribed to it God's autonomous powers to make mountains without valleys as the mood strikes him. As political events are, by definition, all events that are perceived politically, there are hardly any events left that do not enter the political consciousness of the community. This is the supreme danger. But danger itself fosters the rescuing power, and can lead us to the next winding of the evolutionary spiral. It was Paul Kammerer who compared the progression of reality not to circular or to pendular motion, but to motion along a three-dimensional spiral: "Its turns repeat themselves and move always in the same direction, but always at some distance along their axis: returning, yet advancing." [10] And now we are poised, if only we would rise to the challenge, for the greatest return, which will simultaneously be our greatest advance: away from a progressive differentiation of our surface consciousness toward the periphery, and the start of the inward spiral toward our center.

This rebirth can only be brought about by men consciously participating in mankind's evolution; leading others to recognize the seeds of the same spiritual evolution within themselves; and hastening the day when it becomes the recognized aim of society. Life, it is true, is not changed by miracles, but by instruments; but a society that lives not by its men but by its institutions ceases to be a collective soul and becomes a machine, its life a mechanical product rather than a living growth. Fascinated by the great but limited achievements of human reason, we have proclaimed modern man the triumph of humanity after many failures, and have forgotten to ask ourselves of what other triumphs may he not be the failure. We go on seeking refuge in escapist fantasies, both at the political and at the personal level, in a doomed attempt to postpone the inner confrontation. Yet even the man who seeks to live by reason is governed by irrational elements within himself that he does not recognize and indeed often denies. Acknowledging these elements, and consciously integrating them within ourselves, is the only way to renounce escapist fantasies; and renouncing escapist fantasies is the first step toward the truth. For where illusion is the disease, it is always the truth, however painful, that is the healing thing. "One must try to temper, to cut, to polish one's soul so as to become a *human being,*" says Nerzhin in *The First Circle.* And it is this apprenticeship of one's soul, this crystalization of that essence all men share but so seldom manifest, or even acknowledge, that is our aim. Otherwise, like Beckett's tramps, we will go on forever waiting under the wilted tree for our lives to begin; and perhaps for some imaginary political Messiah to give life, if not reality, to our lofty illusions.

Men have struggled for centuries after shadows. Only today, instead of being drugged with retrospective dreams of life and non-existent Golden Ages, we are lulled to sleep by futurist political illusions; and those who remain awake but daydreaming, seek to turn the illusions into reality by sacrificing man's freedom. One of the great strengths of man's intellectual faith was that it acted as an unsparing assailant of that which merely exists, and an unflinching champion of that which is to be. But it arrogated to man's intellect a function which belongs to man's spirit. It is man's spirit, rather than his intellect, that is faithful always to the future, continually building and rebuilding, calling to itself all the elements it needs and rejecting all those that no longer serve its purpose.

Even the backward-looking illusion which still persists today, in however attenuated a form, springs from man's spirit, as a projection of his sense of something pure and perfect within him. But it is a false projection, placed by legend, not inwardly in man's spiritual being, but outwardly in some obscure time in the past—in some Golden Age when man was freely social without society. In a sense, this is our highest aim; not that we should regress to an instinctive animal spontaneity, but that by a tortuous process of evolution, we shall move from an automatic harmony which reflects nature to a conscious unity which reflects the divine within us. This has persisted as man's dimly glimpsed concept of perfection, but it is history rather than man's inner truth that has been called upon as a justification for these aspirations of the present. The basis of the image has always been the thought that a return to a particular period in the past would bring happiness and salvation. The periods range from the Age of Pericles, through that of Caesar and Augustus, to the Renaissance, and even include the age of Louis XIV, "that age which," according to Voltaire, "was the most enlightened of all ages." [11] This last choice shows the complete arbitrariness of the selection. As for the attempt to emulate the greatness of any particular period by imitating what are regarded as its central characteristics, it is manifestly absurd—and inevitably doomed. The spirit of a culture, which after all is its chief motive power, can never be imitated; and this is why a copying of antiquity, or of any other period, can only lead to falsity, salon shepherds and marvelous material for the satirists. The past can only act as our foundation; it is the present that is our material and the future our aim and summit. The need of a developing humanity is not to return to its old ideals, but to progress to a larger fulfillment in which, when the old is taken up, it is transformed and exceeded.

Official Christianity ascribed meaning and direction only to transcendental history, including the earthly pilgrimage of the Church, and distinguished it sharply from profane history, which, according to St. Augustine, is simply awaiting the end with no direction except that of an age that grows old. This was the supreme abdication of Christianity from any attempt to establish the meaning of history apart from the supernatural destiny of man and his perfection through grace in the beyond. This Christian defeatism about earthly existence must share a large part of the blame for the onslaught of politically "progressive" notions which have treated history as an exclusively mundane phenomenon without any transcendental meaning. This is why Joachim stands apart as the greatest of Christian prophets: his was the first attempt to establish the possibility of fulfillment within history, not through revolutions and political reform but through a new eruption of man's spirit. Instead of fruitlessly castigating the vanity of human life, of its ardor and enthusiasms and of the ideals it pursues, he had the spiritual insight to see the necessity of a wiser and larger search after life's true law and aim, and the poetic vision to describe the greatness to which it would lead.

Modern man's error has been that he has sought to attach this new power not to his soul but to the collective egoism of the state; and the consequences are even more catastrophic than if he had sought to attach it to his ego, thereby creating a breed of Nietzschean Supermen. The consequences are everywhere unmistakable, and our time stands under the sign of chaos.

The stream of literature on the decline of Western civilization began in the eighteenth century, at the same time that the Western world was experiencing its most exuberant vitality in the sciences, in technology, in the material control of the environment, in the standards of living, of health and comfort, of social criticism and responsibility. The sun begins to set at noon, and a civilization advances and declines at the same time. The spiritual strength of the soul was diverted into the more tempting and more tangible creation of the terrestrial paradise. Pascal called it a *divertissement* from man's true nature and his eternal destiny. And to the extent that our civilization depended on this *divertissement,* its very success carried in it the seeds of its decline. The "decline of the West" *is* taking place, though not in as theatrical a fashion as many would like. But in the decline there are elements, if only we would acknowledge them, of the beginning of rebirth: the weariness of overspecialized functions of the soul, both in the individual and in the nations, the abandonment of what has already died and the first, often unconscious, stirrings towards a greater truth.

The imagery of death and renewal is of course very old: in myth, death is always transformation, and in Goethe's theory of colors, darkness is celebrated not as nullity but as the creative antipole of light. But those who do not see that our world is incomplete and in the making fail to recognize the elements of renewal in what is dying, and so persist in defending their age with all its familiar fixtures, including the moribund and dead ones, against anything unknown and immeasurable.

In the whole of human history there have never been so many avenues to inner consciousness being explored as there are today, nor anything remotely approaching the proportion of people seeking some such avenue for themselves. If our decline continues to be viewed today from the wrong—the political—end, it is only because of a disastrous emphasis in our culture on what we do, as opposed to what we are. This distorting emphasis dominates even our approach to religion, despite Christ's unambiguous warning: "If you fast you will beget sin for yourselves; and if you pray, you will be condemned; and if you give alms, you will do evil to your spirit." This, one of the strangest and most meaningful of Christ's sayings, will be incomprehensible to all those who profess themselves Christian but who regard religion as a question of what to do, rather than what to *be.*

The call of the spirit, more than any other, demands that we shall follow it always to the end; and the end is neither a divorce and departure from life as the East has claimed, nor a superimposition of a few spiritual ideas and motives on our physical and mental existence as the West has practiced. Asia, it is true, was the first to see further, and make the rational, the ethical and the aesthetic, the three supreme ideals of Greece and Rome, subordinate to a spiritual consummation. But she made a gulf between life and the spirit, explained away matter as *maya,* as mere illusion to be discarded, and continued to dream in Asiatic misery and squalor. Not because, as many in the West like to deceive themselves, she followed after things spiritual, but because she did not follow after them sufficiently; she did not seek to make the spirit the master of the whole of life, but instead impoverished the mental and physical so as to give the limited spiritual an easier domination. Even Gandhi succumbed to that dubious quietism when he adjured the English people not to take arms against Hitler, but to use only "spiritual force." "If these gentlemen choose to occupy your homes, you will vacate them. If they do not give you free passage out, you will allow yourself, man, woman and child, to be slaughtered but you will refuse to owe allegiance to them." [12] In the memorable words of Arthur Koestler: "It would have taken a great deal of corpses to keep Bapu in non-violence." [13] Using spiritual force alone is man's highest and ultimate law of conduct; but until it has also become the dominant law of his conduct, immobility and inertia in the face of evil are infinitely more destructive than the principle of strife we are seeking to overcome by not resisting.

The error of Asia has been to declare man's physical existence a peril and a deviation from spiritual living instead of seeking to transform it by the power of the greater truth behind mind and life. The error of the West was to deny this truth and make the intellect the key-power of our existence: and this is the error at the root of our decline. So in the cultural confrontation between East and West, it is no longer a self-confident European civilization that is offering its light to a semi-barbarous Asiatic, with the latter gracefully accepting it. Yet there are still many who regard anyone leaving the great high roads, desolate and outworn, of the Western world to seek out a higher truth, as committing a regrettable error, their search dismissed as an irrelevance or indeed a relapse into barbarism. In fact they are seeking to redress a fatal imbalance, first within themselves, and by extension within their culture. No attempt is as crucial or as fraught with danger as this. Many have already succumbed to the danger: they have rushed wildly after every oriental prophet, guru or maharishi; they have picked the pockets of "Eastern wisdom"; and they have been pushed into the obscurities of archaic faiths and superstitions. It is, in fact, an old danger. Faust, sitting pale and worn among all the vain appliances of his intellectual enquiry, and realizing that all his efforts have been in vain and no answer to his questions can be extorted by intellectual wisdom, gives himself to magic; but it is yet another false path.

The forms the search for the intangible and the yearning for meaning take, are ultimately far less important than what they say about human nature and human needs. Counterfeiters exist only because there is true gold. And by separating the genuine search from the nightmarish world of the exploding, self-expressing ego, we will be able to identify the longing behind the search with the vague longing in our own souls. There is nothing fanciful about spiritual development; it is potentially the most natural development of all, because it is always a question of learning ourselves and never of learning something foreign. What we need is not exotic substitutes for, but vital enrichments of, our culture; not an opium but a deepened self-knowledge. Those who read Buddha's speeches and become Buddhists or discover the Upanishads and turn into Hindus, may have found some comfort for themselves, but they have taken an emergency exit out of a barren existence. They have yielded to the temptation to copy when the need is to derive new meanings from old teachings only as maps and guides on the road to discovering ourselves and making conscious our own truth. As for those who warn against a drowning of the intellectual West by an Eastern deluge, they underestimate both the strength of our Western inheritance and the underlying unity between the spiritual truths that have been at least intellectually recognized in the West and the highest spiritual conceptions of the East. The drive toward universality, toward discovering the profound unity that underlies all spiritual experience, is a vital first step on the way to emancipating ourselves both from transitory religious forms and from the restless world of intellectual appearances. Only then will we be able to move away from a dogmatic Christianity that regards all foreign spiritual wisdom as part of a "heathen" tradition; and, liberated from mortifying half-truths, we will finally recognize the need to activate within ourselves the neglected powers of the soul.

There has never been as great a demand as there is today for new foundations, new attributions of significance, new symbo s and new interpretations. And the hungry sheep look up and expect the changes to be introduced from above. In one sense they are right; but in another they are profoundly wrong. They are wrong if they expect more of yesterday's, and for that matter today's, solutions—solutions that treat human beings as raw material resigned to passive acceptance of centrally imposed reforms. But they are right in the sense that any new principle of existence must first establish itself in the few, and then through radiation in those who are ready, until it is finally realized in all. There is no doubt that by a very wise evolutionary law, our evolution is linked to the totality—and not one soul will be lost because nothing can be saved if all is not saved. This is why all appeals to a small remnant of humanity accompanied by aristocratic aloofness and scorn for the masses are so totally misguided. At the same time it is not democratic, but a dangerous folly, to ignore the inescapable truth that men are unequally developed and that our evolution has always depended on the few pressing forward from stage to stage: "A normal lizard", wrote Hermann Hesse, "never hit upon the idea of trying to fly. A normal ape never thought of abandoning his tree and walking upright on the ground. The one who first did that, who first tried it, who had first dreamt about it, was a visionary and eccentric among apes, a poet, an innovator, and no normal ape. The normal ones, as I saw it, were there to maintain and defend an established way of life, to strengthen a race and species so that there might be support and vital provision for it. The visionaries were there in order to venture their leaps, to dream of the undreamed-of, so that perhaps sometime a land animal might emerge from the fish and an ape man from the ape." [14] Today the need is not for the kind of leaders who will found mass movements and command followers—still less is it for leaders who look at men and nations as ladders to be climbed, prey to be devoured and things to be conquered and dominated. The need is for leaders who, through their own achievements, will raise mankind to new possibilities; because the day a single human being conquers the difficulties of expansion to a higher consiousness, he raises us all to the possibility of a similar transformation.

This is why those political and social conditions which are necessary to our free growth and development are indeed our inalienable rights. And all collectivist ideals, which seek to limit or extinguish these rights by subordinating the individual to the state, are, their rhetoric notwithstanding, deeply reactionary: they seek to subordinate free men because they really aspire to a static condition, and by depriving society of the leadership that only such men can provide, they are also depriving it of progress. For the free individual is the only conscious progressive, and through his leadership alone does a progressive society become possible; the instinct of the collectivity is to stand still in its established order, while the group-man can only follow in the wake of the individual. Progress, growth, realization of wider being, give the greatest sense of fulfillment to the individual; status, uniformity and order to the collectivity. And when the collectivity as enshrined in the state is established as the dominant principle, all attempts at leadership toward change will be treated as an offense of impatient individualism against the peace, routine and security of the established, state-enforced and state police-controlled order.

Yet it is only such "impatient" individualism that can set in motion new ideas and offer the discovery and the chance of a new self-creation to the communal mind. This is the highest function of leadership: not to command and master, but to formulate explicitly what already belongs to us as unconscious knowledge; to crystalize our hesitant, stammering vision; and to help us activate the healing energy within ourselves. The first step will have to be to rip the veils away from the mass of dishonesties and trivialities that are cluttering our inner vision and rotting our soul. Then we may come to realize how deeply the venom of skepticism and pessimism has penetrated both our culture and ourselves, and how inescapably it dooms us to futility and paralysis. But although false ideas may be refuted by argument, by true ideas alone can they be expelled. So the aim of the new leaders will not be to get quick results and scalps from beaten foes, but to awaken within us the knowledge that can lead us out of shadows and images into the truth; and to act out with their lives proof that the goal can be reached. "You must write a tragedy on the death of Caesar," Napoleon urged Goethe. "This could become the principal task of your life. You could show to the world how Caesar would have achieved the happiness of humanity if only they had allowed him the time to execute his vast plans." We smile: but do we really know better? We still look to the professional architects, the political and technocratic builders of society, to produce the systems and universal prescriptions that will save us from disintegration.

But such systems, when accepted as the final expression of the integral truth of things, treat the individual like a cell or an atom lost in the mass, and so confuse humanity with matter where uniformity alone is the hallmark of the group. Moreover, they lead to the greatest falsehood of all: that the state is greater than the individuals in it, and can, with impunity and to the highest hope of humanity, arrogate to itself this oppressive supremacy. But the organized state is neither the sum of the best minds of the nation nor even the sum of the communal energies. It is a collective egoism much inferior to the best of which any country is capable. What that egoism is in its relation to other collective egoisms, we know, and its ugliness should by now have been forced on our vision and our conscience. As for the disease and falsehood of modern political life, it is patent in every country in the world. It is only our hypnotized acquiescence in this organized sham that cloaks and prolongs the malady.

The beginnings of the malady are very old; they predate both the practice of socialism and the theory of historical materialism. From Bodin to Hobbes, from Hobbes to Rousseau, and from Rousseau onward we can trace a growing emphasis on the omnipotence of the state, and a growing antipathy to all intermediate structures and institutions between an all-powerful government and the naked individual. The first sentence of Rousseau's *Social Contract* could appropriately have been chosen as the motto of all those who in our own time have sought to throw off the chains of formalized interdependence and of all traditional forms of community. But "throwing off the chains" has led not to a life of greater and growing meaning, unencumbered by conventions and superficialities, but to a society where men are sinking into the narrow precincts of themselves, connected with others by very little other than self-interest.

"The idea of forming a single class of all the citizens would have pleased Richelieu," wrote Mirabeau secretly to the king a year from the beginning of the Revolution. "This equality of the surface facilitates the exercise of power. Several successive reigns of an absolute monarchy would not have done so much for the royal authority as this one year of revolution." And in the name of equality, the modern, increasingly despotic Western states are absorbing into themselves all the functions of authority and influence that used to be dispersed among a number of intermediary institutions and disseminated throughout society. The attack against the authority of autonomous institutions is carried out not in the name of man but in the name of society. The existence of a unified and harmonious society that, according to the social contract theories, predates the state, and in the name of which anything can be justified is of course a myth—but a myth that has turned out to be very convenient for modern totalitarians. As no political boundaries are designated for society, the interests of which are assumed identical with the interests of the individual, it is quite easy, by some successful nibbling and some imperceptible shifting of terms, to reduce the state to "society in its political aspect," and therefore to a benevolent agency for making effective the wishes of the community. It all hinges on one fundamental assumption: the assumption of a preestablished harmony of society. But the unity of society is not a fact but an aspiration.

There is an inner substance that provides the binding force of society, but it is located neither in society as an all-embracing, descriptive abstraction nor in the people as a multitude of subjects—and still less in an organization as potentially coercive as the state. It is a substance that can be articulated only to the extent that men live in agreement with the highest, the divine, part of themslves. Only then is what Aristotle called *homonoia,* the spiritual agreement between men, possible. But men manifest their spiritual selves with different degrees of intensity and continuity; and as the social bond depends on the spiritual reality that men have in common, it will remain weak while the incidence of man's participation in his spiritual truth remains infrequent and spasmodic.

"Society," said Burke, and he has since been echoed by all traditionalists, "cannot exist, unless a controlling power upon will and appetite be placed somewhere; and the less of it there is within, the more there must be without." [15] This is true, as far as it goes; the problem is that it does not go very far. Internal control of will and internal suppression of appetite are indeed infinitely preferable to external controls and restrictions; but this is hardly the highest state to which men and societies can aspire. It would have been, if man were an ephemeral physical creature, a form of mind and body that aggregates and dissolves. But he is not: he is a living power of the eternal truth, striving to know itself by living its own self-revealing life. Personal ethics and social conventions are only a corrective against the egotistic rule of life; they tone down and hedge the desires for a gross or a subtle domination and exploitation of others, but they do not abrogate them. They mitigate through inward and outward checks and controls the strife, friction and collision of social and political relations. But only through the higher law of our being can we discover an automatic means of reconciliation, free reciprocity and unity. And then the social virtures are practiced not as virtues—that is, not by separate and constrained effort—but as the fulfillment of one's nature: indeed, it would require effort not to practice them. "I give nothing as duties," said Whitman. "What others give as duties I give as living impulses—shall I give the heart's action as a duty?"

The search for unity, for an ultimate principle that underlies all diversity, has been the motivating force of philosophy and scientific thought since the sixth century B.C. From the pre-Platonic philosophers of Miletus and Samos to the Pythagoreans, and from the Pythagorean grand synthesis to the Unified Field Theory on which Einstein worked unsuccessfully throughout the second half of his life, the dominant impulse has been to discover the principle by which the world is knit together—the primordial unity that through variety strives toward the supreme aim of unity-in-variety. The question is of much more than sterile theoretical interest, as is shown by the tragic attempts in our century to bring the "ultimate" realities of the abstract systems of idealist philosophy into existence. At the opening of the nineteenth century, Fichte proclaimed that the ultimate reality is the Ego—which he conveniently interpreted in a manner wide enough to include the idea of German national egoism. At much the same time, Hegel persuaded himself, by verbal logic again, that nothing is real except the whole, the Absolute. By subordinating man's will to this universal principle, he provided an impeccable basis for all totalitarian systems—and, more specifically, for Marxism, which substituted classes for Hegelian nations as the counters both of the logical and of the political game.

Totalitarianism is the inescapable political outcome of postulating "the whole" as the ultimate reality; the process by which an abstraction is reduced to a political entity should by now be sufficiently familiar to preclude either horror or surprise. And those who reject the ego, submit to the Dionysian element in them, and end up hunting in packs and tribes the meaning of their lives, have with equally disastrous consequences for themselves—though less disastrous ones for the collectivity—surrendered their individual ego to an abstraction. But although egotism, even more than many other isms, is wrong, the ego is at the core of consciousness, and the only entity to which the individual can legitimately surrender it is his higher self—except that then it is not a surrender but a glorious fulfillment.

Idealizing the ego as the ultimate entity is just as destructive as idealizing a logical abstraction of the absolute: it can only lead to the conclusion, articulated by Nietzsche just before the doors of his mental prison closed about him, that there is room in the world only for hermits—or, at the most, hermits in pairs. In a less dramatic, though in retrospect no less damaging way, it led to the rootless laissez-faire individualism that weakened social bonds and precipitated the aggrandizement of the ubiquitous state. The vice of nineteenth-century individualism and of all present-day attempts to revive it, is that they are based on the egoism of man's mental and physical being, and so fail to recognize man's spiritual unity with others. Yet only on such a unity can man's complete self-development in an unhazardous and unassailable freedom be founded.

Until this unity is attained, man's freedom can only be protected by a proliferation of institutions, customs and associations that defend his rights against anarchistic individualism and despotic collectivism alike. For civic men are not born but made; and the social instincts, varying widely from individual to individual, may atrophy altogether as long as man's egoism remains uninformed by a feeling of the higher spiritual unity to which we belong, in which we participate and with which we are striving to identify. All the great inspirers of our civilization have helped reconcile our localized selves and our imperfect societies to this cosmic order and perfect harmony, the "circle whose center is everywhere and whose circumference, nowhere," and of which we are an as yet unconscious part. The extent of the reconciliation has been very unequal throughout our history; the more definite and pronounced it is, the easier it becomes to achieve a harmonized common existence that does not depend on the mechanical ordering of life from above. Such a free, organic unity, which is after all our highest social aspiration, is as far removed from the collective unity that depends on the subordination of the individual as the present external unity of mankind, brought about by international broadcasting and the press, is from the ultimate spiritual unity of humanity.

From the particles of an atom, through individual societies, to the planets circling the sun, the disruptive, centrifugal forces are balanced by binding forces which hold the system together as a whole. The centrifugal forces that assert in a society the individual's independence and autonomy are originally balanced by the centripetal forces of customs and traditions; gradually social and political institutions codify custom and tradition, and religion fosters social ethics and morality. But it is an unstable equilibrium. Those social forces do indeed stop the banks of the river from crumbling and keep the stream flowing; but at different periods, the most consciously progressive among individuals have felt the established social principles as inhibitions, and the process of socialization as an imposition making impairing demands on their free development. Not content with preserving the banks of the river they have sought to discover the laws that govern its flow. For social and political institutions and traditions, being the result of man's imperfection, are imperfect in themselves, and must therefore always be imperfect in their course and effect. So there inevitably arrives a point when our social principles are brought up short, fail us, turn into false, or half-true, assertions of the mind, and cover realities that are not merely different but often directly opposed to the conventions. This is why there is nothing more perilous than a mystical attachment to any set of institutions. It was such an attachment that led the Duke of Wellington to announce in 1830 that the human mind would scarcely attain such excellence as England's unreformed Constitution: the existing Constitution, he said, was so perfect that he could never take the responsibility of tampering with it. Within a fortnight his government had fallen and the Whig ministry under Lord Grey, pledged to bring in Reform, had taken its place. Throughout history, statesmen have confused what urges on and perfects a society with what for a time consolidates and preserves it, but ultimately smothers and suffocates it by depriving it of the living force of evolution.

A scornful disbelief in all institutions and a revolt against all conventions has been accompanied in our time by the dangerous conviction that an ideal social order can be invented; indeed, that it can be scientifically constructed and politically imposed. Society came to be seen as a stagnant pond that must be forcibly diverted into another and better channel; and every busy political halfwit is seeking—and many have triumphantly announced that they have found—the laws of social development in the shallow waters of the pond. But the laws of society are inextricably bound with the total order of things, and can neither be known nor applied except through the discovery of the sources of order in the microcosm of man's soul.

The order of human life can only be explored and guided when we accept, first, that there is a highest purpose to which all human actions should lead, and second, that this highest purpose cannot be achieved through the collectivity, and is not, therefore, the province of politics. Freedom is the ultimate and only *political* end; the highest good is the ultimate end of man as man, and only through its manifestation in individual men can it gradually become the established principle of the collectivity. Both authoritarian conservatives, willing to use the authority of the government to promote virtue, and liberal collectivists, determined to use the coercive state to achieve the public good, are oblivious of the unavoidably individualistic nature of our evolution. A government is representative in the constitutional sense alone; it cannot be—and therefore should not claim to be—representative in the existential sense of realizing the highest ideals of humanity. As for the state, it is a mere convenience, and a clumsy convenience at that, for our common development. It is a military, political and economic force, and no amount of fictions, catchwords and state philosophies will turn it into an ethical entity; this is why the call of the state to the individual to immolate himself on its altar, like a victim of ancient sacrifice to a huge and shapeless idol, is the surest bar to progress, and the surest way to uniformity and stagnation.

The altruistic ideal, the discipline of self-sacrifice, the need for a growing solidarity, are not in dispute. But the loss of the self in a huge state machine is not what these ideals mean, nor is it the way to their consummation. The failure to recognize the need for a sense of community and the possibilities of human cooperation has been the fatal weakness of English individualism; the turning of a utility for cooperative action into an excuse for rigid control is the tragic flaw of present-day collectivism. By subordinating the individual, society strikes at the very source of its life and growth.

Our aim is not merely to survive, but to expand and evolve, and what the Darwinians have tried to express by their notion of the struggle for life is in fact a struggle for growth: a continuous attempt to live a life of increasing meaning as the only answer to the problem of creation, and the only way of illuminating the obscurity of the Creator. So far we have sought to achieve this increased meaning through principles and doctrines, formulas and concepts. But no intellectual principle can stand dominant in the web of life, and if we so treat it, it gets falsified in its meaning, loses much of its virtue, and ultimately dooms us to artificiality and sterility.

Yet men are bent on escape. The question is whether the escape will take the form of a collective flight to an illusory state haven, or whether we will realize in time that the only escape from a world beset by meaninglessness is to be found in those aspects of man's spirit that have for so long been denied life. What is certain is that the men who lead us out of our decaying world and into the new, will not be the facile, unthinking "men of action," chin stuck at an optimistic angle, foreheads bulging with legislative remedies, eyes moist with state visions; and just as certainly they will not be those who believe that they can make man perfect by machinery, and straight by tying up his limbs. They will, for a start, be men not afraid to shout that the emperor wears no clothes, even if this makes them profoundly unpopular and the emperor profoundly uncomfortable.

As the emperor today is the ideas dominating our age, in control of politicians and electorates alike, the new leaders will make profoundly uncomfortable all those who have unthinkingly identified themselves with the prevailing ideas, and who take to the hills the moment they are invited to acknowledge a higher truth above the law of the herd, by which they have been living. But then the words of those who rise above circumstance, and seek to give life to timeless truths, have always been hooks to catch man's conscience and daggers to enter his ears; and they have been feared as such.

> . . .Conscience dark
> with its own or another's shame
> will indeed feel thy words to be harsh;
> but none the less put away every falsehood

and make plain all thy vision,
and then let them scratch where is the itch.
For if thy voice is grievous
at first taste, it will afterwards leave
vital nourishment when it is digested. . . .

This was Cacciaguida's charge to Dante in *Paradiso.* And thousands before and since have treated the miracle of great men pointing the way to a higher life as a reproach on themselves and an implicit satire on their age. They praise narrowness as virtue and dismiss all visions based on the potency of things as insubstantial fantasies. "He is a dreamer. Let us leave him. Pass."

Swift said once that you could tell a man of genius by the number of dunces gathered against him. But this would be true only if we regarded anyone who stands against a man of genius as by definition a dunce. Otherwise we have to accept that some of the most intellectually distinguished and impeccably well-informed men have shown a presumptuous lack of understanding toward men of genius. In our century, Bertrand Russell informed us that "there is something smug and unctuous abut Socrates, which reminds one of a bad type of cleric. . . . He was not scientific in his thinking, but was determined to prove the Universe agreeable to his ethical standards. . . . As a philosopher he needs a long residence in a scientific purgatory." [16] And Shaw was even more sweeping: "The superior being, being immeasurable, is unbearable."

The cock in Aesop scratched a pearl into the light of day and declared that to him it was less valuable than a grain of millet seed. And so indeed it was. The pearl is only a pearl to him who knows its value. The first step toward knowing the value of the pearl is the recognition of our present ignorance; we have to recognize what we do not know, and yet long to know, before we can understand. And we have to be not merely sick and tired of our life as it is, but sick and tired of being sick and tired, before we are prepared to disturb our preconceived beliefs and endemic habits to accommodate a transforming truth. More often than not, even those who do not dismiss a disturbing truth outright take from it only what suits their preconceptions, and reject the rest on which the illumination depended.

"I will not destroy it for ten's sake," was God's reply to Abraham's plea that the City of Sodom be spared if ten righteous men could be found therein. When it comes to the truth that sustains the world, our standards of quantitative good have to be revised. And today, when even the memory of the great transforming truth seems to have been lost, the men who first take a step toward recovering it will act through their lives, their beliefs and their teaching, as a kind of magic mirror making visible for all who can see what is invisible in us and in the life of our time.

"Philosophy and common sense," writes Peter Medawar, "though often parted, have long agreed about the uniqueness of individual man. . . . Science now makes it a trio of concordant voices, for the uniqueness of individual mice and men is a proposition which science can demonstrate with equal force, perhaps with deeper cogency, and certainly with a hundred times as much precision. . . . But far from being one of his higher or nobler qualities, his individuality shows man nearer kin to mice and goldfish than to the angels; it is not his individuality but only his awareness of it that sets man apart." [17] And unless man recovers the *awareness* of his individuality, he will indeed be reduced to the state of mice and goldfish—relieved to hand over to the state his freedom in return for his feed.

The meaning of man's awareness of his individuality is not to be found in the biological improbability that makes every single one of the three billion members of our species unique, labeled by specific protein configurations at the surface of cells, and identifiable by whorls of fingertip skin; such an expression of unique individuality is after all basic to all orders of creation in a world where no two giraffes, and for that matter no two grains of sand, are exactly alike. Nor is it to be found—a much more popular misconception this—in the uniqueness of man's mind; indeed, wired together as we are by radio, telephone, satellites, magazines and airplanes, manically exchanging information and "communicating" with each other, it could be said that our brain is the most public organ on the face of the earth. And of course nothing could be further from the meaning of man's awareness of his individuality than the conception of the gentleman who does not wish to be confused with the scum, or the Bohemian indulgence of man freed from the social conventions of morality by a superficial aestheticism: these are travesties of individualism and supercilious grimaces. The "I" in us which is not our opinions, our habits, our profession or our traditions, and which would be "I" even if everything else crumbled away, is the awareness of our godlike individuality which is preparing to emerge in us through our own, and humanity's, evolution.

Man's individuality is not an encumbering weight hindering him from flitting about at ease in the spiritual cosmic spaces. On the contrary; evolution proceeds from the like to the unlike, from the general to the particular, from the homogeneous to the heterogeneous. Only through the expansion and the intensification of the consciousness of his individuality can man achieve the universal consciousness which, far from treating this life as the shadow cast by the glory revealed beyond, draws to it the treasures of the spirit, and transforms it. And this is why the stifling of the individual is the stifling of god in man.

Individual lives cannot run upon free parallels, and men cannot escape from relationship; the individual's effort to discover his innermost truth and live by the highest law of his own being soon leads him to the discovery of the universal law and truth to which he can relate them. The oneness he will achieve then will be the manifestation in reality of the triple principle of liberty, equality and fraternity that man has been striving to achieve by a series of increasingly destructive illusions. And we will realize for the first time that democracy has a deeper meaning than democrats understand. There is no more sterilizing an idea than the belief that the greatest truth that has as yet been discovered only by a few sages and holy men is not ultimately realizable by all. As if our evolution could possibly stop with the emergence of self-realized experimental man; or as if the greatest universal truth of spirit discovered by life could not be the spirit of that life, but could only be realized outside it through an ascetic exodus out of the narrow walls of ordinary existence.

The trouble with our modern democrats is that they are in fact republicans in the literal and Latin sense: they care more for the Public Thing than for any private reality. In the grip of their public passion, they have come to believe that they can best serve the public good by imposing, through politics, total solutions to all human problems. It is therefore hardly surprising that the one-eyed Titans of the gigantic political establishments of our day are disillusioned, nor is it to be marveled at that they have come to despair of the Republic. They have sought the answers and solutions in political action, and now they cannot see how they can prevent all the frustrated human aspirations that have been piling up from cascading down in one overwhelming landslide. In the meantime, the Titans—blind these rather than one-eyed—of the modern scientific establishments continue to assure us that, through all sorts of revolutionary changes in technology, confidently postulated for the future, we can determine our destiny right down to deciding whether two heads might actually not be better than one. Others are looking to the stars and dreaming of space flights to other worlds and of providing a *terra nova* for man on Venus; while still others would rather it were Mars.

But the *terra nova,* the new basis beyond our actual world, that most have been seeking through politics and some through technology or planetary escapades, is in fact in ourselves: almost tangible and certainly within reach of human experience. It is to those who lead the way to its discovery and who refuse to think the battle lost, that, like the ancient

Romans, we shall have to put up statues: "For they did not despair of the Republic." And their hope will be based on the realization that our democracies will be saved only if men turn away from public solutions and return to themselves. If this seems to take us away from action, it will be only to lead us to the secret of action and of changing our world: to the conscious knowledge that all transformation that is radical and lasting proceeds from within outward, the outward being the inevitable consequence of the inner.

CHAPTER NOTES

1. THE UNWITTING ACCOMPLICES

[1] In conversation with Samuel Rosenman (organizer of the Brain Trust and later Special Counsel to the President). Quoted in an essay by Rosenman in *The History Makers,* ed. Lord Longford and Sir John Wheeler-Bennett (London: Sidgwick and Jackson, 1973), p. 254.

[2] Voltaire, *Oeuvres Complètes de l'abbé de Mably,* vol. IV (London, 1783), p. 3.

[3] Ibid., p. 10.

[4] In a speech in the North German Reichstag on April 16, 1869, quoted in G. V. Plekhanov: *The Role of the Individual in History* (London: Lawrence and Wishart, 1940), p. 25.

[5] Thomas Mann, *Doctor Faustus* (London: Penguin Books, 1968), p. 236.

[6] Stephen J. Tonsor, "The Drift to Starboard," *Modern Age*, Summer 1969.

[7] John Chamberlain, "Dean of Conservative Columnists," *National Review*, July 14, 1970.

[8] Alexander Solzhenitsyn, *The Gulag Archipelago* (New York: Harper and Row, 1974), p. 173.

[9] In a speech to the House of Commons, April 28, 1976.

[10] From George Meredith, "Modern Love."

[11] Alexis de Tocqueville, *Ancien Regime* (London: John Murray, 1873), p. 199.

[12] From Alexander Solzhenitsyn, "Nobel Lecture," published by the Ad Hoc Committee for Intellectual Freedom, 1973.

[13] *The Daily Mail*, April 6, 1976.

[14] *The Times* (London), June 22, 1976.

[15] Ludwig von Mises, *Omnipotent Government* (New Haven: Yale University Press, 1944), p. 48.

[16] Tony Benn, Secretary of State for Energy, at a Labour Party meeting in London on November 23, 1975.

[17] J. K. Galbraith, *A Contemporary Guide to Economics, Peace and Laughter* (London: Andre Deutsch, 1972), pp. 224–25.

[18] From "The Ethics of Elfland," in *G. K. Chesterton*, selected by W. H. Auden (London: Faber and Faber, 1970).

[19] F. A. Hayek, *The Constitution of Liberty* (London: Routledge and Keagan Paul, 1960), p. 400.

[20] Gustave Thibon, *Back to Reality* (London: Hollis and Carter, 1955), p. 66.

[21] Sören Kierkegaard, *Journals 1853–55* (London: Collins, 1965), p. 278.

[22] From Solzhenitsyn's introduction to a collection of letters he received after the publication of *One Day in the Life of Ivan Denisovich.* Quoted in "Solzhenitsyn and Samizdat" by Michael Nicholson, in *Aleksandr Solzhenitsyn—Critical Essays and Documentary Materials*, ed. John B. Dunlop, Richard Haugh, and Alexis Klimoff (New York: Collier Books, 1973), p. 91.

[23] Solzhenitsyn to a Slovak interviewer, quoted in "Solzhenitsyn: Art and Foreign Matter" by Donald Fanger in *Aleksandr Solzhenitsyn—Critical Essays and Documentary Materials*, ed. John B. Dunlop, Richard Haugh, and Alexis Klimoff (New York: Collier Books, 1973), p. 160.

[24] From Alfred Jarry's play *Ubu Roi—Ubu Enchainé*, Act I, Scene ii.

[25] G. K. Chesterton, "The Twelve Men," in *Tremendous Trifles* (Beaconsfield: Darwen Finlayson, 1968), p. 55.

2. OLD TRUTHS AND NEW HERESIES

[1] Harold Macmillan, *Tides of Fortune* (London: Macmillan, 1969), p. xiii.

[2] H. L. Mencken, *On Politics* (New York: Vintage Books, 1960), p. 120.

[3] Alexis de Tocqueville, *Ancien Regime* (London: John Murray, 1873), p. 338.

[4] David Cecil, *Melbourne* (London: Constable, 1965), p. 353.

[5] F. A. Hayek, *The Constitution of Liberty* (London: Routledge and Keagan Paul, 1960).

[6] K. R. Popper, *The Logic of Scientific Discovery* (London: Hutchinson, 1959), p. 280.

[7] Louis W. Koenig, *The Chief Executive* (New York: Harcourt, Brace and World, 1964), p. 27.

[8] William F. Buckley, "The Party and the Deep Blue Sea," *Commonweal* 55 (January 25, 1952), p. 391–393.

[9] Koenig, op. cit., p. 4.

[10] Tocqueville, op. cit., pp. 85–6.

[11] "Of Reformation in England" in *The Prose Works of John Milton,* ed. J. A. St. John, (London, 1909–14), Vol. II, p. 364–5.

[12] G. K. Chesterton, *Tremendous Trifles* (Beaconsfield: Darwen Finlayson, 1968), p. 164.

[13] During his testimony to the Senate Watergate Committee, November 14, 1973.

[14] Malcolm Muggeridge, *The Thirties* (London: Hamish Hamilton, 1967), p. 255.

[15] Paramahansa Yogananda, *Autobiography of a Yogi* (Los Angeles: Self-Realization Fellowship, 1973), p. 516.

[16] Ibid.

[17] Popper, ibid.

[18] During her first American tour as Leader of the Opposition in September 1975.

[19] Daniel P. Moynihan, *Maximum Feasible Misunderstanding* (New York: Free Press, 1970), pp. xiii–xiv, 170.

[20] Alexander Solzhenitsyn: "Starting the Day," *Encounter,* March 1965.

[21] William F. Buckley, *Up From Liberalism,* pp. 179–83, quoted in George H. Nash, *The Conservative Intellectual Movement in America since 1945* (New York: Basic Books, 1976).

[22] Address to the Trades Union Congress, September 5, 1966.

[23] Address to the Conservative Party Conference, 1973.

[24] Edward L. Bernays, quoted in Louis W. Koenig, op. cit., p. 206.

[25] Ralph Raico, "Thomas Szasz and the Age of Psychiatrism," *The Alternative: The American Spectator,* May 1976, p. 18.

[26] Ibid., p. 19.

3. THE IMPOSSIBLE STATESMANSHIP

[1] Maurice Edelman, "How the New System of Patronage in Government Scatters the Confetti of Privilege," *The Times* (London), October 14, 1975.

[2] Raymond Fletcher, "Proof That the Impossible Takes a Little Longer," *The Times* (London), March 22, 1976.

[3] From posthumously published drafts of Marx's book *The Holy Family,* quoted in Igor Shafarevich, "Socialism in Our Past and Future," in *From Under the Rubble* (London: Fontana, 1976), p. 30.

[4] C. G. Jung, *Memories, Dreams, Reflections* (London: Fontana, 1967), p. 389.

[5] David Steel, "Throwing Away Our Money and Skill," *The Times* (London), July 26, 1976.

[6] Roland Huntford, *The New Totalitarians* (New York: Stein and Day, 1972), p. 122.

[7] Ibid.

[8] Ibid., p. 124.

[9] Ibid., p. 177.

[10] "Utopia's Dark Side," *Newsweek,* May 3, 1976.

[11] Ibid.

[12] Laurens van der Post: *Jung and the Story of Our Time* (London: The Hogarth Press, 1976), p. 33.

[13] William Shakespeare, *Troilus and Cressida,* Act I, Scene iii.

[14] Peter Jay, "Sincere and Foggy Notions," *The Times* (London), October 9, 1975.

[15] *The Times* (London), August 9, 1976.

[16] Helmut Schoeck,*Envy* (London: Secker and Warburg, 1969), p. 313.

[17] Margaret Mead, *Cooperation and Competition Among Primitive Peoples* (New York: McGraw Hill, 1937), p. 466.

[18] A. and P. Toynbee, *Comparing Notes: A Dialogue Across a Generation* (London: Weidenfeld and Nicholson, 1963), p. 52.

[19] W. G. Runciman, *Relative Deprivation and Social Justice* (London and Berkeley: University of California Press, 1966), p. 270.

[20] Alexander Solzhenitsyn, "Repentance and Self-Limitation," in *From Under the Rubble* (London: Fontana, 1976), p. 127.

[21] Alexander Solzhenitsyn, *August 1914* (London: Penguin Books, 1974), p. 594.

4. THE TOTALITARIAN TEMPTATION

[1] During a talk in 1970 with Admiral Elmo Zumwalt, then Chief of Naval Operations, quoted by Zumwalt in his book *On Watch* (New York: Quadrangle, 1976)

[2] *New York Herald Tribune,* November 10, 1975.

[3] Gore Vidal talking to Philip Oakes, *New York Times,* December 14, 1975.

[4] In a paper circulating in Moscow in the spring of 1976, quoted by Peter Osmos in "When One Dissident Criticizes the Others," *International Herald Tribune,* March 15, 1976.

[5] Alexander Solzhenitsyn, "As Breathing and Consciousness Return," in *From Under the Rubble* (London: Fontana, 1976), p. 24–5.

[6] "The Savagery Turning to Benevolence," *The Times* (London), May 28, 1975.

[7] Robert G. Kaiser, *Russia—The People and the Power* (London: Secker and Warburg, 1976), p. 104.

[8] C. L. Sulzberger, "Does National Marxism Exist?" *International Herald Tribune,* March 10, 1976.

[9] *The Times* (London), September 1, 1975.

[10] Ibid.

[11] *International Herald Tribune,* May 3, 1976.

[12] Professor George Wald, *The Progressive,* December 1975: "Our country suffers from a condition I think of as 'saturation politics' . . . we have ended with a numbed, dazed, punch-drunk public, incapable of further response."

[13] Samuel Rosenman, "Roosevelt," in *The History Makers,* ed. Lord Longford and Sir John Wheeler-Bennett (London: Sidgwick and Jackson, 1973), p. 248.

[14] Benjamin C. Bradlee, *Conversations with Kennedy* (London: Quartet, 1975), p. 101.

[15] Lewis Thomas, *The Lives of a Cell* (New York: The Viking Press, 1974), p. 27.

[16] *The Observer,* July 21, 1963.

[17] From Goethe's essay on the Pentateuch appended to the *West-Oestlicher Divan,* quoted in J. M. Robertson, *A Short History of Freethought* (New York: Russell and Russell, 1957), p. 366.

[18] H. L. Mencken, "The New Deal Mentality," *American Mercury,* May 1936, p. 4.

[19] C. G. Jung, *Memories, Dreams, Reflections* (London: Fontana, 1967), p. 357.

[20] F. A. Hayek, "The Intellectuals and Socialism," in *Studies in*

Philosophy, Politics and Economics (London: Routledge and Keagan Paul, 1967), p. 194.

[21] "Nyerere: Why Critics Call Him St. Julius," *The Observer*, November 23, 1975.

[22] Leon Trotsky, *The History of the Russian Revolution* (London: Gollancz, 1932), Part III, chap. 6.

[23] Elliot Richardson, *The Creative Balance* (New York: Holt, Rinehart & Winston, 1976).

[24] Walt Whitman, *Leaves of Grass* (Philadelphia: David McKay, 1884), p. 10.

[25] In an interview with national wire service correspondents at the beginning of his second year in office, August 8, 1975.

5. LEADERS, IMAGES AND PHANTOMS

[1] George Bernard Shaw, *Everybody's Political What's What?* (London: Constable, 1944), p. 371.

[2] Nigel Fisher, *Iain Macleod* (London: Andre Deutsch, 1973), p. 14.

[3] In an interview with Lord Chalfont on BBC Television, March 11, 1976.

[4] Harold Wilson in an interview with Brian Connell, *The Times* (London), August 2, 1976.

[5] G. K. Chesterton, "On Lying in Bed," in *Tremendous Trifles* (Beaconsfield: Darwen Finlayson, 1968), p. 51.

[6] *The Observer*, October 3, 1976.

[7] Harold Wilson's interview with Brian Connell, ibid.

[8] Sourian's famous saying, quoted in Arthur Koestler, *The Act of Creation* (London: Picador, 1975), p. 145.

[9] *The Daily Mail*, February 3, 1976.

[10] *The Observer*, September 26, 1976.

[11] "From Ramsay MacDonald to Mr. Heath, the Battles for a New Leader," *The Times* (London), March 27, 1976.

[12] *A Crossroads of Freedom: The 1912 Campaign Speeches of Woodrow Wilson*, ed. John W. Davidson (New Haven: Yale University Press, 1956), p. 83.

[13] *Writings*, ed. A. E. Bergh (Washington: Thomas Jefferson Memorial Association, 1907), Vol. VI, p. 257–8.

[14] Herman Hesse, "Books on Trial," in *My Belief* (London: Jonathan Cape, 1976), p. 93.

[15] The description is Malcolm Muggeridge's.

[16] Shaw, op. cit., p. 295.

[17] David Wood, "Coalition or a Bill of Rights?" *The Times* (London), June 4, 1976.

[18] Claire Palley, "Society and the Law: A Little Learning Can Be a Dangerous Thing," *The Times* (London), July 21, 1976.

[19] The description is Doris Kearns', in her *Lyndon Johnson and the American Dream* (London: André Deutsch, 1976).

[20] John Gunther, *Inside Australia* (New York: Harper and Row, 1972), p. 98.

[21] Ibid.

[22] Joe McGinniss, *The Selling of the President* (London: André Deutsch, 1970), p. 236.

6. "THE DAY CINDERELLA NEARLY WASN'T ALLOWED TO MARRY HER PRINCE"

[1] In a Fabian pamphlet, *Religious Education in State Schools,* p. 17.

[2] *International Herald Tribune,* February 6, 1976.

[3] Walter Lippmann, *The Good Society* (London: Allen and Unwin, 1937), p. 254.

[4] *The Times* (London), September 30 and October 1, 1975.

[5] Tolstoy, *My Religion* (London: Walter Scott, 1889), p. 262.

[6] The Samaritans (a group founded in Britain to help those in despair and prevent suicides) reported that a quarter of the 200,000 who approached them in 1975 were under twenty-four.

[7] C. G. Jung, "Psychotherapists or the Clergy," in *Modern Man in Search of a Soul* (London: Routledge and Kegan Paul, 1961), p. 264.

[8] E. M. Forster, "Tolerance," in *Two Cheers for Democracy* (London: Penguin Books, 1965), p. 55.

[9] Louis Schneider and Sanford M. Dourbusch, *Popular Religion: Inspirational Books in America* (Chicago: University of Chicago Press, 1958), pp. 44, 58, 107.

[10] Richard Cobb, *Tour de France* (London: Duckworth, 1976), pp. 3–4.

[11] Edward Luttwak, "Seeing China Plain," *Commentary,* December 1976.

[12] Eric Hoffer, *The True Believer* (London: Secker and Warburg, 1952), p. 179.

[13] In *The Guardian,* March 20, 1975.

[14] Alexander Solzhenitsyn, "Nobel Lecture," published by the Ad Hoc Committee for Intellectual Freedom, 1973.

7. FROM IMAGINATION TO CONSCIOUS KNOWLEDGE

[1] Edmund Leach, *A Runaway World?* (London: BBC, 1968), p. 1.

[2] Laurens van der Post, *Jung and the Story of Our Time* (London: The Hogarth Press, 1976), p. 133.

[3] William F. Buckley, *Rumbles Left and Right: A Book about Troublesome People and Ideas* (New York: Macfadden, 1963), p. 134.

[4] Brian MacArthur, *The Times* (London), December 28, 1967.

[5] Roland Huntford, *The New Totalitarians,* (New York: Stein and Day, 1972), p. 204.

[6] Ibid, p. 214.

[7] Edward de Bono, "It's the Thought That Counts," *The Guardian,* May 4, 1976.

[8] W. M. Rossetti, "Prefatory Memoir of William Blake," in *Poetical Words* (London: G. Bell and Sons, 1874), p. 80.

[9] Johan Huizinga, *Men and Ideas* (London: Eyre and Spottiswoode, 1960), p. 318.

[10] Ernest van den Haag, "An Open Letter to Sidney Hook," *Partisan Review* 17 (July-August 1950), p. 607.

[11] William Henry Chamberlin, "Conservatism in Evolution," *Modern Age,* Summer 1963.

[12] "On Divination," ii, 33, *Treatises of Cicero* (London: Bell and Daldy, 1871).

[13] Franz Funck-Brentano, *Luther* (London: Jonathan Cape, 1939), p. 260.

[14] *The Observer,* September 5, 1976.

[15] "Only Months to Plan For 250,000 Years?" *The Observer,* December 21, 1975.

[16] Van der Post, op. cit., p. 39.

[17] G. H. Lewes, *The Life and Works of Goethe* (London: J. M. Dent, 1864), p. 535.

[18] William Shakespeare, *Hamlet,* Act III, Scene i.

[19] Thomas Mann, "Nietzsche's Philosophy in the Light of Recent History," *Last Essays* (London: Secker and Warburg, 1959), p. 146.

[20] Alexis de Tocqueville, *Ancien Regime* (London: John Murray, 1873), p. 281.

[21] Hermann Hesse, *Narcissus and Goldmund* (New York: Bantam Books, 1971), p. 277.

[22] The Gospel of Thomas: Saying 29.

[23] Lewes, op. cit., p. 535.

[24] Edward Carpenter, *From Adam's Peak to Elephanta* (London: Swan Sonnenschein, 1892), p. 153.

[25] Frederick Pollock, *Spinoza's Life and Philosophy* (London: Duckworth, 1899), p. 86.

[26] George Bernard Shaw, Preface, *Back to Methusaleh.*

[27] Meriol Trevor, *Newman's Journey* (London: Fontana, 1974), p. 233.

[28] Hermann Hesse, *My Belief* (London: Jonathan Cape, 1976), p. 44.

[29] Trevor, ibid.

[30] Edward Gibbon, *Decline and Fall of the Roman Empire* (London: Crosby, Nichols, Lee and Co., 1860), Vol. VI.

[31] James Cameron, "A Celestial Telephone Exchange," *The New York Review of Books,* June 24, 1976.

[32] Bertrand Russell, *Mysticism and Logic* (London: Longmans, Green and Co., 1918), p. 52.

[33] Bertrand Russell, *History of Western Philosophy* (London: Allen and Unwin, 1961), p. 767.

[34] Robert Alfred Vaughan, *Hours with the Mystics* (New York: Charles Scribner's Sons, 1893), Vol I, p. 80.

[35] *The Works of Francis Bacon,* ed. Spedding, Ellis and Heath (New York: Hurd and Houghton, 1878), Vol. II, p. 82.

[36] K. Seelig, *Albert Einstein* (Zurich: Europ & Verlag, 1954), p. 44.

[37] Alfred Tennyson, *A Memoir by His Son* (London: Macmillan, 1897), Vol. II, p. 90.

[38] Plato, *Symposium* (Oxford: Clarendon Press, 1875), Vol II, p. 71.

[39] Charles Darwin, *The Origin of Species* (London: John Murray, 1873), p. 429.

[40] Frederick Pollock, *Spinoza's Life and Philosophy* (London: Duckworth, 1899), p. 85.

[41] G. K. Chesterton, "The Ethics of Elfland," in *G. K. Chesterton,* selected by W. H. Auden (London: Faber and Faber, 1970), p. 181.

8. FOR THEY DID NOT DESPAIR OF THE REPUBLIC

[1] *The Diary of Samuel Pepys,* ed. Robert Latham and William Matthews (London: G. Bell and Sons, 1974), Vol. VIII, p. 602.

[2] *Opus Epistolarum,* IV, 337 (No. 1139).

[3] W. M. Wheeler, *Social Life among the Insects,* (London: Constable, 1923), p. 12.

[4] Leopold Labedz, *Solzhenitsyn: A Documentary Record* (London: Penguin Books, 1972), p. 144.

[5] Johann Müller in a letter to Baron de Salis, August 6, 1879, quoted in Alexis de Tocqueville, *Ancien Regime* (London: John Murray, 1873), p. 276.

[6] The formula is Mussolini's, quoted in Jose Ortega Y Gasset, *The Revolt of the Masses* (London: Allen and Unwin, 1932), p. 134.

[7] Paul Kammerer, *New York Evening Post,* February 23, 1924, quoted in

Arthur Koestler, *The Case of the Midwife Toad* (London: Picador, 1975), p. 132.

[8] Mark Twain, *A Connecticut Yankee at King Arthur's Court* (New York: Pocket Books, 1948), p. 56.

[9] Robert Blake, *Disraeli* (London: Methuen, 1969), p. 765.

[10] Quoted in Koestler, op. cit., p. 140.

[11] Voltaire, op. cit., Vol. XVII, p. 187.

[12] T. A. Raman, *What Does Gandhi Want?* (Oxford: Oxford University Press, 1943), p. 24.

[13] Arthur Koestler, "Mahatma Gandhi—Yogi and Commissar," in *The Heel of Achilles* (London: Picador, 1976), p. 245.

[14] Hermann Hesse, "Fantasies," in *My Belief* (London: Jonathan Cape, 1976), p. 61.

[15] Edmund Burke, "A Letter to a Member of the National Assembly," *The Works of the Right Honorable Edmund Burke* (Boston: Little Brown, 1866), Vol. IV, p. 52.

[16] Bertrand Russell, *History of Western Philosophy* (London: Allen and Unwin, 1961), p. 156.

[17] P. B. Medawar, *The Uniqueness of the Individual* (London: Methuen, 1957), pp. 143, 185.

INDEX